DATE DUE

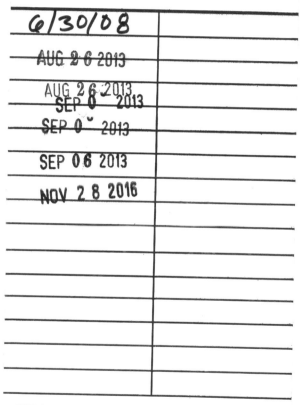
BRODART, CO.   Cat. No. 23-221-003

LAW, PSYCHOLOGY, AND JUSTICE

SUNY series in New Directions in Crime and Justice Studies
Edited by Austin T. Turk

Law, Psychology, and Justice

Chaos Theory and the New (Dis)order

Christopher R. Williams
and
Bruce A. Arrigo

STATE UNIVERSITY OF NEW YORK PRESS

Published by
State University of New York Press, Albany

For information, address State University of New York Press,
90 State Street, Suite 700, Albany, NY 12207

Production by Cathleen Collins
Marketing by Anne M. Valentine

Parts of chapter 2 appeared previously in
Justice Quarterly 12(3) and are reprinted with
permission of the Academy of Criminal Justice Sciences.

Library of Congress Cataloging in Publication Data

Williams, Christopher R., 1972–
    Law, psychology, and justice : chaos theory and the new (dis)order / Christopher R.
Williams and Bruce A. Arrigo.
        p. cm. — (SUNY series in new directions in crime and justice studies)
    Includes bibliographical references and index.
    ISBN 0-7914-5183-6 (alk. paper) — ISBN 0-7914-5184-4 (pbk. : alk. paper)
        1. Criminal law—Psychological aspects.   2. Psychology, Forensic.   3. Insanity—
Jurisprudence.   4. Chaotic behavior in systems.   I. Arrigo, Bruce A.   II. Title.
III. Series.

K5027.W55 2001
345'.001'9—dc21

                                                                                    2001018407

10 9 8 7 6 5 4 3 2 1

For all those mental health consumers who struggle to be heard amidst the clamor of reform enacted by and for clinicolegal decision brokers, thereby manufacturing illness politics.

For Little Buddha and Mr. T.: Always the source of delight and fancy.

Contents

Contents

PART THREE
The Just(ice)

Acknowledgments

Monographs of this sort are never the exclusive product of the author. This is certainly the case with this book. Over the years, both of us, in our own ways, have been troubled by how the legal and psychological systems establish mental health law policies seemingly without critically reflecting upon the assumptions and/or values upon which the reforms are proposed and subsequently enacted. Regrettably, the controversies we explore in this monograph are no exception to this longstanding practice. From Bruce's early years working as a mental health outreach worker in Pittsburgh, Pennsylvania, to Chris's more recent doctoral studies in forensic psychology, law, and public policy, this book is informed by both detailed field observations and a systematic assessment of the pertinent literature. Both were indispensable to our critique.

We are grateful to many individuals who helped refine our ideas, making them more compelling, provocative, and, ultimately, erudite. In particular, we thank Professor Jane Younglove and Dr. Beth Arrigo for their dedication to this project. In addition, we thank the many doctoral students at the Institute of Psychology, Law, and Public Policy in Fresno, California who listened thoughtfully to our ideas, encouraging us to make the prose more accessible, grounding our conceptual insights in the everyday world of psychiatric citizens. Finally, we thank our respective families. Unquestionably, sound scholarship requires sacrifice. Parents, spouses, children, and other loved ones can help foster the caring and supportive space within which one's ideas can be transformed into meaningful action. We are forever indebted to our families for letting us dream, discover, and create.

Introduction

The Theoretical, the Controversial, and the Just(ice)

> . . . whatever is lawful is in some way just; for the provisions of
> legislative science are lawful, and we say that each of them is
> just.
> —Aristotle, *Nichomachean Ethics*

Intellectual history is fraught with synthetic and cross-disciplinary strategies
for comprehending social and human problems. One of the more significant manifestations of this approach is the law-psychology (i.e., the justice
and mental health) interface. Although a relatively recent expression of
integrative and interdisciplinary analysis, the law-psychology connection
provides a new and different set of tools for better understanding theoretical, methodological, and practical concerns, impacting forensic research,
policy, and programming. Indeed, a number of controversies are found at
the crossroads of "clinicolegal" decision making, particularly when the legal
apparatus relies on the psychological community for guidance (e.g., definitions of mental illness, predictions of dangerousness, forensic evaluations,
courtroom testimony), or when the law demarcates the contours of mental
health practice (e.g., the right to refuse psychiatric treatment, executing
the mentally disordered, civil commitment) (Arrigo, 2000a).

On a more theoretical and speculative level, psychology has advanced
a new and provocative line of criticism which fundamentally questions
the purported benevolence of legal power, policies, and practices (e.g., Fox
& Prilleltensky, 1997; Fox, 1997). As a radical assessment of psycholegal
thought and decision making, observers note that not only does law,
informed by the psychological sciences, fail to render humane and empow-
ering judgments, it is substantially responsible for denying justice and
impeding social change (Fox, 1993, 1997, 1999). The broad implications

1

are that neither the mental health nor the legal system can assert that they embody mutually exclusive aims with self-prescribed and self-regulated methods for accomplishing their objectives. Indeed, psychology regards itself as a formidable voice in matters of legal consequence, and the law maintains its authority in matters of individual and social welfare (Fox, 1993; Haney, 1993).

While psychology often avows to "humanize" the legal discipline (Melton, 1990), offering guidance as to the most effective and therapeutic means of achieving juridical aims, public and professional challenges to various mental health abuses have prompted the law to consider the unique interests of the psychiatrically disordered, especially as users of mental health services. For example, can the law, through psychology, be therapeutically practiced (e.g., Wexler & Winick, 1996; Winick, 1997a)? Can psychology, through the law, maintain the essential dignity and human rights of psychiatric citizens (Arrigo, 1996)? To date, the results have been questionable at best (Fox, 1999; Ogloff, 1999). While psychology undoubtedly has something to offer the law, and while the law arguably has some interest in the activities of mental health professionals, these associations are often more complex and misguided than one might assume. In short, the evolving relationship the mental health and legal systems (uncomfortably) share has spawned some of the more contentious and heated controversies within contemporary social science circles (e.g., Arrigo & Williams, 1999a, 1999b), dramatically impacting our regard for crime and justice (Arrigo, 2000a).

Accordingly, this book intends to establish a more informed understanding of several notable and perplexing issues situated at the crossroads of law and psychology. Our use of the word "informed" is deliberate. We mean to provide both a legal *and* a psychological appraisal of selected, though targeted, mental health law controversies, and to examine the limits of the psycholegal prism, particularly in light of several theoretical developments found in the natural sciences that ostensibly contribute to our overall grasp of law, psychology, and justice. Thus, this book ultimately proposes to offer greater conceptual clarity on several puzzling and enduring clinicolegal matters. In what follows we briefly describe the conceptual lens through which our investigation will unfold.

THE THEORETICAL

The conceptual lens through which our inquiry into mental health law will be conducted is known as *chaos theory* or *nonlinear dynamical systems theory*.

In order to understand the philosophical contours of chaology in relation to law and psychology, it is first necessary to describe, at least provisionally, our general position on this science (for an overview see Smith, 1995).

Chaos theory represents a relatively new scientific model for understanding or seeing the complex behavior of systems (i.e., natural or social) that move or change over time (referred to as "dynamical" systems). The problematic nature of these systems is related to their characteristic tendency to display disorderly or seemingly chaotic behavior. For example, the pattern of waves washing up against a coastal shoreline appears to occur randomly, unpredictably. The apparent disorder represents a fascinating domain of inquiry, and students of chaology study how various systems behave nonlinearly (i.e., irregularly and indiscriminately). In addition, they examine the order that lurks *behind* or *within* apparent randomness.

As one might imagine, attempts to understand the (dis)order looming in and around the cosmos can be traced back many centuries. Unfortunately, however, much of what we know about chaos theory is still in its infancy, with its core principles coming mostly from the physical sciences, especially theoretical and applied investigations in quantum physics and advanced mathematics. Indeed, as a scientific domain of inquiry, nonlinear dynamics did not receive widespread publicity until the publication of Gleick's (1987) text, *Chaos: Making a New Science*. His work was the first to cogently and provocatively present, in consolidated fashion, a series of discoveries, theorems, and explanations of similar phenomena investigated by researchers in several disciplines (e.g., physics, chemistry, biology, mathematics), based on the insights of chaology.

In the wake of Gleick's work, researchers in both the natural and social sciences have seized upon his findings, applying principles of chaos to the investigation of various phenomena. For example, nonlinear dynamics are increasingly noted in psychological and sociological literature as a means of describing (or discussing) events thought to be unexplainable (e.g., Butz, 1997; Milovanovic, 1997). As Young (1991, p. 290) observes, chaology has been instrumental in altering the mission of science: instead of exclusively pursuing universal laws, generating predictable, certain, and stable truths, the knowledge equation is now compelled to consider elements of variation, change, and randomness . Indeed, chaos theory directs our attention to those previously disregarded factors of human social interaction, defined as anomalies, inconsistencies, or "noise" in a system.

As a complex theory, chaology is perhaps best regarded as a collection of interrelated principles or ideas. Briefly stated, they include, but are not limited to, the following: (a) iteration, (b) bifurcation, (c) sensitivity to initial conditions, (d) attractors, (e) fractal space, (f) self-organization, and (g) dissipative structures. Each notion tells us something about the methods by which systems begin to change, adjust to change, or appear after change. These principles are the "building blocks" of chaos theory. We note that each principle can function as an independent mechanism for understanding the behavior of complex systems, or can operate in conjunction with one or more of the other postulates. For purposes of our investigation of law and psychology, we will provide descriptive information on each chaos theory principle, and subsequently link these notions to a series of mental health law controversies.

Additionally, we note that our overall analysis assumes a decidedly critical tone. This is deliberate. We are largely persuaded by the contributions of critical theoretical inquiry as applied to social problems and the drama of civic life. Unlike many other perspectives, the aim of critical theory is to expose the institutional and conventional forms of knowledge that define (and regulate) contemporary society (Kellner, 1989; Young & Arrigo, 1999). Thus, by challenging the status quo, the inconsistencies and injustices that often accompany prevailing sociopolitical beliefs and practices are made manifest (e.g., Bottomore, 1984; Held, 1980). In this regard, then, critical inquiry is the bearer of "dangerous" knowledge (Kincheleo & McLaren, 1998, p. 260).

Relatedly, we embrace the tradition of critical criminology. Where critical theory raises macrological questions about freedom, epistemology, science, and the like, critical criminology examines the lived oppression, exploitation, and/or alienation to which certain groups are summarily subjected, displacing prospects for citizen justice (Arrigo, 1999a; Groves & Sampson, 1986). We submit that the integrative and cross-disciplinary arena of law and psychology has yet to be exposed fully to either orientation (cf. Arrigo, 1996); however, given the discipline's power structures, ideological influences, and epistemological frames of reference, a critique along these lines is certainly warranted.

THE CONTROVERSIAL

Evidence of the law's involvement in matters psychiatric and persons mentally disabled is found throughout much of Western civilization (Lindman & McIntyre, 1961; quoted in Perlin, 1999, p. 3). Thus, the sundry issues the psycholegal arena confronts today are not recent manifestations of perplexing human social behavior. Instead, they are enduring and evolving matters necessitating critical attention. The care with which these enduring issues have been addressed has been subject to changes in the juridical sphere and in the behavior of society. On the legal side, these changes are, perhaps, best characterized as increases in the amount of law under which society functions or fails to function. The trend in contemporary criminal and civil justice has been to implement new laws to account for transforming problems which arise over the course of time (e.g., Arrigo & Williams, 1999a). Moreover, as the law responds to meet societal conditions giving rise to developing psychosocial concerns, problems at the crossroads of law and psychology increase as well. Inevitably, then, much of what we know about mental health law remains largely untold, if not altogether unseen. Accordingly, the controversies themselves are vast and uncharted.

Notwithstanding these dynamics in law and psychology, we have selected four distinct but interrelated controversies to explore. These issues and our treatment of them are not exhaustive. The purpose of the present project is to examine conceptually and speculatively the potential contribution a chaos theory analysis may provide for better comprehending targeted and relevant controversies in mental health law. In this way, we hope to shed some new and much needed light on the important relationship found within the law, psychology, and justice divide.

We have intentionally limited our critique to pressing issues in the *civil* mental health law arena. In other words, we concern ourselves with judicial proceedings that are of a noncriminal nature. While these proceedings potentially involve a loss of liberty and, in this sense, may be best understood as "quasi-criminal" (Melton et al., 1997, p. 38), they arise from circumstances not directly involving the criminal adjudication process. We recognize that the latter would include equally worthwhile mental health law controversies (e.g., incompetency-to-stand-trial [IST], not guilty by reason of insanity [NGRI], sentencing of mentally ill offenders, treatment in correctional settings, and execution of the psychiatrically disordered). In addition, we acknowledge that there is, at times, considerable overlap between the criminal and civil side of mental health law and policy (Reisner & Slobogin, 1997). We are, however, concerned exclusively with significant and perplexing issues affecting individuals who are not introduced to the legal system by way of arrest. For our purposes, therefore, we note that four such controversies appear prominently in the civil mental health law literature.

The Meaning of Mental Illness

Contemporary psychology is rooted in the idea that some human beings are not only different from others but, in some meaningful ways, less "healthy" than others. This position gives rise to the concept of mental illness (Scheff, 2000). Mental illness critically informs legal proceedings where questions about one's psychological status are of concern. Understanding this concept, however, is not without controversy. Indeed, as a psychological and sociological construct, it must be defined accurately for purposes of the law, otherwise a citizen may suffer a wrongful and/or unwarranted abridgment of his or her civil liberties. This necessary precision is conspicuously absent from many state and federal statutes (Perlin, 1999). Thus, the legal system typically bases its psychological status determinations on ambiguous and debatable interpretations for what constitutes illness and health (Winick, 1995). As a practical matter, it remains unclear whether mental illness can be defined and, if so, according to what standard and whose rules (Arrigo, 1996). The profound uncertainty surrounding this fundamental matter necessarily invites philosophical discussion into the nature of meaning itself. We submit that only when the more general and fuzzy question of meaning is addressed, is it possible to appreciate the particular problems posed by defining mental illness in the psycholegal field.

Defining and Predicting Dangerousness

While many of us may freely refer to some things or some people as "dangerous," rarely do we critically assess what we *mean* by such a characterization. Moreover, it is unlikely that we systematically reflect upon those reasons justifying our use of this descriptor. These matters are the domain of the law informed by the psychological sciences. Indeed, the law relies on prevailing clinical interpretations of dangerousness to justify abrogating the rights of individuals (e.g., the involuntary civil confinement of persons thought to represent a danger to themselves or others). Under these circumstances, the law defers to psychology, soliciting an informed opinion (i.e., prediction) as to whether a given individual will act violently in the future. We note, however, that such clinical predictions are routinely inaccurate (e.g., Monahan, 1996), incapacitating persons who are no more violent than their nonpsychiatrically disordered counterparts (Arrigo & Williams, 1999a). Thus, similar to the psycholegal problems posed by defining mental illness, the construct of dangerousness is fraught with uncertainty and ambiguity.

Involuntary Civil Confinement

A finding of mental illness and dangerousness produces civil commitment. Confinement is recognized as a necessary and legitimate state-sanctioned response under two distinct situations: (a) The disordered person must be involuntarily hospitalized in order to protect society and its citizens from harm; and (b) the disordered person must be involuntarily hospitalized in order to protect the mentally ill person from harming him or herself (Arrigo, 1993a; Reisner & Slobogin, 1997). Unlike criminal confinement where retributive aims are pursued, civil commitment is a paternalistic expression of social control (Arrigo, 1993b), limiting the rights of individuals to think and act as they choose. We question the decision-making process that gives rise to such judgments. Both the legal and psychological communities play a pivotal role in such determinations. Further, as we previously suggested, definitions of mental illness and dangerousness are themselves inherently suspect. Accordingly, we question the values that underscore a civil commitment finding and the methods by which it is enacted.

The Right to Refuse Mental Health Treatment

In part, the justification for involuntarily subjecting individuals to civil confinement is to provide psychotherapeutic "treatment." Theoretically, treatment is designed to arrest the symptoms that give rise to dangerous thoughts, feelings, impulses, or behaviors, and, under these conditions, it legitimizes the state's suspension of the disordered citizen's civil liberties. The right to refuse treatment is the law's challenge to the administration of unwanted medical intervention. Historically, persons experiencing psychiatric illness have had limited protection against the absolute and unbridled power of mental health professionals to assess, diagnose, and treat (e.g., LaFond & Durham, 1992; Myers, 1993; Szasz, 1987). Consequently, persons with these disorders have suffered the debilitating effects of imposed or coerced treatment (e.g., Arrigo, 1996; Rothman, 1971, 1980). These effects are particularly devastating when psychotropic drugs (e.g., antipsychotic medications) are the preferred method of therapeutic intervention (Durham

& LaFond, 1988). Thus, one's right to refuse treatment is the legal response to unnecessary, intrusive, and excessive medical care and attention. However, to what extent should this right be availed to psychiatric citizens? This, too, is a question warranting critical analysis as the answer impacts the mental health law system and those exposed to its decision-making practices.

The four controversies we have outlined above will be the subject of our critique. Our interest in these topics, while certainly directed toward an assessment of how the legal and psychological communities understand these controversies, lies beyond this worthwhile level of analysis. Indeed, we are uniquely concerned with how these four issues in mental health civil law promote, or fail to promote, citizen justice. To this end, we submit that the principles of chaos theory, as a consolidated template for critical inquiry, may tell us something more or something other about the prospects for justice in the psycholegal arena. We recognize that chaology does not speak of justice per se; however, by appropriating its considerable theoretical insights we endeavor to show how justice does or does not matter at the law-psychology divide.

THE JUST(ICE)

To best appreciate this book's focus on justice, it may be helpful to recall what its role is in law-psychology scholarship. If one were to canvass the recent psycholegal literature, one would find a breadth of scholarship reporting findings of interest for psychologists, lawyers, judges, and the like; however, little explicit reference to the concept of justice or the impact of the research for justice would be provided (Arrigo, 2000b). Interestingly, however, the genesis for the law-psychology movement was to foster justice (e.g., Fox, 1993, 1997). Initial attempts to establish a workable and meaningful relationship between the often competing legal and mental health communities were motivated by the assumption that "the union of social science and law promotes justice" (Tapp & Levine, 1977, p. xi). These early efforts produced a collection of scholars and practitioners that sought to bring justice to the subdisciplinary field of law and psychology (Haney, 1993).

On balance, however, we note that psycholegal scholarship has produced little in the way of critically inspired commentary, failing to address substantially questions of fairness, humanity, dignity, autonomy, self-determination, empowerment, proprietorship, etc., as central themes in the overall analysis (Arrigo, 2000b). Instead, the standard fare of mental health law research provides interesting but technical direction on such matters as jury behavior, eyewitness testimony, sex offender treatment, and the like, absent a detailed assessment of the social and political landscape that considerably informs such matters. In short, where these endeavors woefully miss the mark is in strategically exploring the broader implications that psycholegal scholarship could have for large-scale change and citizen justice (Arrigo & Williams, 1999a; Fox, 1993, 1997). Accordingly, we maintain that a critical, chaos theory investigation of the four, previously identified, civil controversies in mental health law, may offer a useful approach by which to access where and how justice has been diverted and where and how it may be retrieved in the psycholegal arena.

ORGANIZATION OF THE BOOK

This book is divided into three broad parts and each part is made up of several chapters. Part I represents a more detailed assessment of the important theoretical components of our overall thesis. In chapter 1 we provide a historical overview of chaos and chaos theory. This overview addresses the development of nonlinear dynamics as a philosophical position and as a scientific endeavor. The intent with this historical commentary is to demonstrate the contemporary utility of chaos theory for addressing complex problems in the physical and social sciences. Chapter 1 also discusses a number of important definitions. The expressions "chaos," "chaos theory," "nonlinear dynamical systems," and related words and phrases will be systematically addressed.

Chapter 2 situates our interest in chaology within a larger conceptual prism. This prism is postmodernism. In particular, we explain how (contemporary) theory building in law and criminology occurs within either the modernist or postmodernist intellectual tradition. We describe several overarching themes generally informing theoretical analysis, and suggest how each theme is understood from these two perspectives. Along the way, we suggestively indicate where and how chaos theory contributes to the postmodern enterprise. Chapter 2 builds upon the historical insights of chapter 1, focusing chiefly on sociological and epistemological dynamics relevant to the development of chaology.

Chapter 3 explains in detail the essential principles of chaos theory. Working knowledge of these concepts is necessary for the application chapters that follow. In this explication, we are guided by the wisdom of Barton (1994). He notes that "the level of technical understanding required to [comprehend] chaos, nonlinear dynamics, and self-organization from the perspective of mathematics or physics is generally not necessary for [social scientists]" (p. 5). However, we also recognize that a rudimentary grasp of basic chaos theory principles is required for our critical investigation of law and psychology. Thus, chapter 3 intends to accomplish this objective by describing, with some specificity, the seven concepts that constitute this field of inquiry. As stated previously, these include the following: (a) iteration, (b) bifurcation, (c) sensitivity to initial conditions, (d) attractors, (e) fractal space, (f) self-organization, and (g) dissipative structures.

Part II moves away from the theoretical into the realm of the controversial. This portion of the book constitutes the application segment or, in effect, the actual analysis of law and psychology. It is further arranged, in some meaningful way, into the four, previously identified mental health law controversies. Each of these topics represents a distinct chapter in the book; however, it is more accurate to consider them as overlapping concerns rather than independent controversies. Indeed, the decisions in one area of mental disability law (e.g., the right to refuse treatment) most often rely on other areas of mental disability law (e.g., "dangerousness") for guidance. Thus, to some extent, the chapters in Part II build upon one another and can be read that way. Then, too, we realize that each application chapter is sufficiently different from the next such that each can stand on its own.

Accordingly, chapter 4 examines the issue of mental illness and its definition. Chapter 5 addresses the matter of dangerousness and its meaning/prediction. Chapter 6 explores the topic of civil commitment and the process by which it unfolds. Chapter 7 investigates the right to refuse treatment and the conditions under which this occurs. Within each of these chapters, we describe how both law and psychology uniquely interpret these phenomena. In addition, we spell out the limits of conventional psycholegal inquiry for each controversy. Finally, within each of the respective chapters, we offer an interpretation of the four mental health law topics, informed by chaos theory and its principles. This analysis suggests where and how justice is or is not promoted in the context of clinicolegal decision making.

Part III critically assesses the implications of our application work (i.e., chapters 4–7) for the future of law, psychology, and justice. Chapter 8 considers this matter based on a detailed investigation of a single, precedent-setting mental health law decision. This is the case of *In the Matter of Billie Boggs* (1987). As a single case study, the appellate ruling includes all of the psycholegal controversies examined in Part II. Thus, our intent in chapter 8 is to document carefully the pivotal implications of a chaos theory analysis in relation to "real world" dilemmas. Along the way, we describe the critical and interpretive studies that have thus far substantially assessed notable civil controversies in mental health law, including the *Boggs* decision. This commentary situates the subsequent chaos theory critique within an appropriate body of law-psychology scholarship. In addition, we suggestively describe how related appellate decisions can be subjected to the principles of nonlinear dynamics, demonstrating chaos theory's overall utility as a conceptual (and practical) approach by which to investigate psycholegal problems.

Similar to our assessment in chapter 8, the final chapter is mindful of how, if at all, justice is rendered through the law in matters psychiatric. Specifically, chapter 9 systematically reviews the key points raised throughout the body of the book, focusing on the contributions of chaos theory to the psycholegal field. Chapter 9 suggests that while principles found in nonlinear dynamics dramatically reveal important limits to citizen justice and social change, the future of mental health law must necessarily include the implementation of decision-making practices that more intimately promote the dignity and humanity of psychiatric consumers. Several provocative observations along these lines are tentatively enumerated.

PART ONE

The Theoretical

CHAPTER ONE

Delineating (Dis)order, Defining Chaos

Nature and Nature's Laws lay hid in Night:
God said, Let Newton be! And all was Light!
——Berlin, *The Age of Enlightenment*

What you cant calculate, you think, cannot be true;
What you cant weigh, that has no weight for you.
——Goethe, *Faust*

OVERVIEW. *In the following chapter, we describe what chaos theory is. We do this by situating the field within a larger context of historical developments generated in both philosophy and science. Along these lines, we are mindful of the "modern" worldview, quantum physics and the "postmodern" perspective. Our commentary here is integral to the analysis contained in chapter 2. Where chapter 1 describes important shifts in science and philosophy, impacting the evolution of chaos theory, chapter 2 locates these shifts within a larger sociological and epistemological frame of reference relevant to theoretical studies in law and criminology. In addition, chapter 1 provides a working definition for chaos theory and for several of its related concepts. These observations will prepare the reader for our subsequent discussion on the principles of nonlinear dynamics or disorder found in chapter 3.*

THE DISCOURSE OF MODERNITY AND THE ROOTS OF ORDER

The development of Western civilization is characterized by a number of important historical epochs. The seventeenth to the mid-twentieth century is generally acknowledged as the "modern" period of transformation (Young & Arrigo, 1999). This time frame, extending from the mercantile era of post-feudalism to the advanced industrial phase of capitalism, is rooted principally in the Enlightenment philosophy of reason and science as the path to knowledge, truth, prediction, and control (Borgmann, 1992). In addition,

15

however, the modern paradigm evolved from pioneering and innovative efforts in physics and mathematics in which mastery over the universe was no longer thought to be impossible (Best & Kellner, 1997). The fusion of these philosophical and scientific revolutions spawned a dramatic break with the past and, consequently, gave birth to a new direction for the future. Indeed, as Berlin (1984) observes when commenting on the intellectual climate of seventeenth century Western Europe, "[it] stands like a barrier between us and the ages which preceded it, and makes the [ideas of previous ages] seem remote, fanciful and, at times, almost unintelligible (pp. 14–15; 1956). Thus, when we speak of the modern epoch, we speak of "a battle, a bit of arrogance, a cry of rebellion, a gesture of rejection (even destruction) of what is past" (Solomon & Higgins, 1996, p. 175). In short, this "barrier," this "battle," is one of law and order assailing and renouncing the disorder, ignorance, superstition, and blind faith that distinguished much of the pre-modern dawning of the world (Benson, 1989; Harvey, 1989).

The Scientific Revolution

The genesis of modern science, and the birth of the scientific revolution, reside in the Renaissance with Copernicus (1473–1543) who hypothesized a heliocentric universe. Following Copernicus, the cosmos were no longer regarded as geocentric. Indeed, astronomers increasingly recognized that the earth was, in fact, planetary in the sun-centered heavens. Sometime thereafter, Kepler's (1571–1630) laws of planetary motion proposed the first mathematical and, thus, scientific understanding of astronomy. What had been, for over two thousand years, a universe deemed incomprehensible by even the wisest of scholars, was suddenly understood to be a simple collection of parts amenable to the laws of mathematics and physics. Kepler's findings offered empirical support for a Copernican universe. More profoundly for the modernist project, however, was the conviction that the behavior of the world and the people in it could be similarly explained by universal laws awaiting human discovery.

The telescopic breakthroughs of Galileo (1564–1642) contributed significantly to the modernist project. His astrological findings gave the scientific community the first observational support for Copernicus's hypothesis and Kepler's laws. More importantly for the history of science, however, were his methodological theorems. Although the source of considerable debate since his death, his formulations continue to have a profound impact on most present-day scientific inquiries. In contrast to centuries of philosophical speculation which assumed the mantle of authority in all epistemological matters, Galileo argued that the only legitimate basis of knowledge about the world was to be found in observation. Thus, for Galileo and his followers, natural and experimental observation alone led to indisputable, axiomatic truths. We note that this logic pervades much of what we take as "fact" or knowledge in the physical and social sciences today.

In addition to Galileo's work in astronomy and his celebrated position concerning observational techniques, are the insights of Sir Isaac Newton (1642–1727). At the core of modernity's paradigmatic shift, he provided the final theoretical and empirical building blocks for a new era. As Berlin (1984) notes, Newton

> performed the unprecedented task of explaining the material world . . . of making it possible, by means of relatively few fundamental laws of immense scope and power, to determine . . . the properties and behavior of every particle and every material body in the universe, and that with a degree of precision and simplicity undreamt of before. Order and clarity now reigned in the realm of the physical science. (15)

Indeed, Newton's (1687) *Mathematical Principles of Natural Philosophy* assigned innovative meaning to the theoretical speculations of Bacon and Descartes. In discovering universal laws of gravity and motion, and the applicability of mathematical principles to describe these laws, he single-handedly created a new epoch in the history of Western civilization. After Newton, what once had constituted the eternal mysteries of life, were but orderly mechanisms of a great machine—a "cosmic clock." The universe was "law-abiding, orderly, universal, and fully predictable. All events—past, present, and future—were determined by the same laws; chance and indeterminacy played no role in the smoothly running gears of nature" (Best & Kellner, 1997, p. 200). Accordingly, Newton is acknowledged as one of the chief architects of modern science and the modern world.

Determinism, Reductionism, and the Cosmic Clock:
Understanding and Explaining the World

Laplace's (1749–1827) "demon" in Newton's universe is an inviting metaphor for understanding the profound impact of the scientific revolution in modern thought and its approach to all of society. In short, modern science promised an orderly and controllable world and, consequently, the possibility of human omniscience. Indeed, the conviction was that the patterned regularities governing civilization were discernable through the senses, and explicable by way of scientific reason. Properties could be measured, mathematical techniques could be applied to such measurements, and the world and its processes could be translated into the language of simple laws.

In explicating a world governed by law and order, modern science appointed itself epistemological and metaphysical avatar over matters previously subject to unquestioned obedience and conformity, given dogmatic superstitions and prejudices. This paradigm of law and order reinvented the foundations of human knowledge, depicting parts (i.e., laws) of the world as mechanical components of a greater cosmic machine that functioned with the regularity and precision of a well-wound clock—a position that continues to exert tremendous influence on our thought and decision-making processes even today. Consider, for example, the manner in which the "machine" metaphor routinely informs scientific efforts. Researchers attempt to understand the human brain by envisioning it as a sort of calculating computer (Dupre, 1993, pp. 2–3), and, relatedly, computer engineers ponder how their technology systems can function more like human brains.

Modern science's steadfast reliance on mechanical precision is best understood in the context of philosophical determinism. In its most condensed form, determinism proposes a theory of universal causation. In other words, every event has a cause or a *necessary* antecedent without which the event would not have taken place. Thus, every occurrence in nature occurs of necessity. In psychology, for example, the behavioral-based thesis of Skinner (e.g., 1971) and the biologically based assertions of Freud (e.g., 1914), represent varying degrees of deterministic worldviews. In the context of science and philosophy, the most notable figure advancing deterministic views at this time was Pierre-Simon Laplace. He suggested that, given the knowledge of both the laws of nature and the state of the universe at a particular moment, he could predict all future events. Laplace's (1814/1951) "demon," born of Newtonian physics, cast a vast shadow over the world of the unpredictable.

Thus, returning to the metaphor of the machine or "cosmic clock," we understand how, given the assumptions of determinism, a precision instrument with its component parts will, once set in motion, behave in a regular, lawful manner consistent with cause-effect logic for all eternity (Dupre, 1993, p. 3). Comprehending the functioning of this instrument and its discrete parts gives rise to laws and they, in turn, give rise to human knowledge of the universe:

> [For modern science] the cosmos is a vast machine governed by universal and invariable laws that function in an orderly way that can be comprehended and controlled by the rational mind. (Best & Kellner, 1997, p. 197)

The mechanistic paradigm, however, is limited unless one adequately grasps the relationship of the parts to the whole. To understand the laws that govern the functioning of parts, an additional methodological step is required. One of the most powerful tools scientists have at their disposal when searching for knowledge about the intricate workings of a machine (e.g., society, organizations, people) is reductionism. As employed by Western science (as opposed to philosophical reductionism which often assumes a different meaning) (e.g., Husserl, 1983), reductionism "imagines nature as equally capable of being assembled and disassembled" (Briggs & Peat, 1989, p. 22). The process of disassembling the object would reveal the underlying components of the machine that could consequently be reduced, for theoretical purposes, into the effects that those components had on other system components.

Although this perspective originally dominated science's approach to physical systems, it was not long before reductionism was extended to all aspects of the world, including human behavior and the meaning of life. Reduction of systems to their component parts could reveal the intricate interrelations existing within that organization or structure. Reductionism, then, facilitated modern science's insatiable quest for knowledge; that is, explanatory and predictive understandings of the universe and its inhabitants. We note that the explanation for this voracious pursuit of true knowledge was linked to the philosophical revolution occurring around the same time. Indeed, the reinvention of philosophy was, in part, a product of Descartes' (1596–1650) search for absolute certainty, methodological rigor, and mathematical demonstrations of the same. For purposes of our historical analysis, we will not explore these particular associations as they move us away from the focus on chaos theory and its development. The changing attitude toward the world, however, was most apparent in the empiricism of Francis Bacon.

"Knowledge Is Power":
Predicting and Controlling the World

Determinism describes a world governed by a lawful order with the (conceptualized) predictability that laws often bring. The discovery of universal theorems or postulates, then, represented breakthroughs that explained previously imperceptible, unknowable, and incomprehensible processes and phenomena. When Francis Bacon (1561–1626) made his infamous claim that "knowledge is power," he was, in effect, referring to the promise of modern science; namely, that genuine knowledge of the universe was not only possible, but was now probable. It was not merely knowledge for its own sake that was desirable; a contemplative pastime of many premodern philosophers, rather, it was *applied* knowledge that was enticing and intoxicating. Indeed, the function of applied knowledge was mastery and control of nature and the world: "to extend more widely the limits of power and greatness of man, [to command natural forces for] the relief of man's estate" (Best & Kellner, 1997, p. 198).

The kind of knowledge advocated by Bacon is best understood as *instrumental knowledge,* or erudition for purposes of domination and control. The value of knowledge, then, was that it was meaningful only to the extent that it served some other, greater end. For Bacon and modernity, this end was the prediction and control of nature. The means by which nature would be harnessed included mathematical techniques, employed in the service of constructing laws of data collection as a scientific method, involving "careful observation and controlled, methodical experiment[ation]" (Solomon & Higgins, 1996, p. 165).

For Bacon, then, nature was something to be understood, mastered, and shaped for human purposes. This vision is consistent with the modern conceptualization of the world as subject to mathematical and physical explanation, producing knowledge of practical utility whose value was defined by its service to this end. By this very process, modern science "presided over the 'death of nature' and transformed the living natural world into a dead machine" (Best & Kellner, 1997, p. 197). The "death of nature," however, had other consequences—some of which were described by Bacon himself in his *Novum Organum* (1620/1960). The progressive mastery and control of nature *for* human ends, resulted in both increased knowledge of nature, and increased estrangement *from* nature. While the latter had existential significance, the former had social significance as well. Not only did modern science provide the keys that unlocked the mysteries and, consequently, ensured the mastery of nature, it invented the working tools for explaining the mysteries of the human being. Indeed, modern science made possible a power over things and over people that had, to that point, escaped the wisdom of the premodern era. During this period of prediction and precision, to know was the power to control natural processes; it was the power to possess control over human and social processes (Horkheimer & Adorno, 1972).

The transition from the premodern to modern era unmistakably produced widespread, revolutionary change. Indeed, the collective efforts of philosophy and science, beginning with Copernicus in the early 1500s and ending with Bacon in the early 1600s, accomplished a task that altered the course of Western history. The task was the reinvention of knowledge itself; that is, what we know, how we know it, and what we do with this newly acquired acumen once we discover it (Tarnas, 1991). The first of these speaks to the logic of determinism; the second to the scientific method; and the third to the association between human beings and nature and, consequently, between human beings and other people. However incalculable the influences of modernity, the history of this period makes abundantly clear that the order of the world rested on certain theorems, impartially ascertainable through reason and scientific inquiry. Indeed, science was to be avatar of reason and objectivity: its methods were empirical, its laws were deterministic, its results were universal.

THE "DISORDER OF THINGS" AND THE REJECTION OF THE MODERN WORLDVIEW

Though the modern worldview would (and continues to) exert a powerful influence on contemporary science and society, it has, nonetheless, received its share of criticism. This refutation is both scientific and philosophic in nature. The latter comprises notable figures and trends in the history of social thought. Thus, any limited coverage of these criticisms would be, in effect, an extensive chronicling of post-Enlightenment philosophy. This undertaking, while worthwhile in its own right, deviates somewhat from the chapter's overall intent. The former, in turn, is not so much ensconced in epistemological and metaphysical dilemmas as it is mired in the problematic nature of modern theoretical physics. This scientific criticism, however, rests on a number of complex mathematical revelations. Describing specific formulas and detailing intricate equations is well beyond the scope of this project. Given both concerns, we instead limit our investigation to a general accounting of the notable luminaries and the major movements challenging the logic of modernity, with some allusion to their particular historical significance.

Philosophical Refutation: From Kant to Postmodernism

The philosophical criticism of which we speak has been (and is) concerned chiefly with the existential and social consequences of the modern paradigmatic shift. Some of the early condemnation came from within modernity itself. Kant's (1724–1804) defense of free will and Rousseau's (1712–1778) appreciation of nature in place of civilization (i.e. the domination of nature for human purposes) are poignant examples. In addition, some of the more influential assaults were launched by the German Romantics in the late eighteenth and early nineteenth centuries, including Johann Schiller (1759–1805) and Gotthold Lessing (1729–1781), especially the latter's preference for aesthetics over the dispassion of science. Other notables included Johann Herder (1744–1803), Friedrich Schelling (1775– 1854), and, in a similar but more literary vein, Johann Wolfgang von Goethe (1749–1832). Romanticism generally is respected for its critique of Enlightenment rationality and its elevation of the passionate, the creative, and the subjective. As a bonafide movement, it marked, perhaps, the first humanistic reaction to the emerging objective and scientific world of which it was a part.

Under the considerable influence of philosophers such as Søren Kierkegaard (1813–1855), existentialism, as well, critically responded to the conceptualization of the world as a coherent, law-governed, rational, and predictable system. Existentialism was an uneasy reaction to the unintelligibility, sense of meaningless, and (undirected) freedom that accompanied the disorder of the world. Later existentialist thought would attempt to confront the troubling question of what we should do as misdirected subjects, in a world without a universal and rational sense of purpose (Sartre, 1956). The primary contribution of early existentialism to the critique of modernity, however, was its focus on the subjectivity of the individual and its emphasis on the absence of ultimate order in the universe.

With roots in both romanticism and existentialism, a more direct assault on modernity came in the twentieth century in the form of postmodern criticism. For example, Nietzsche's (1844–1900) notion of perspectivism holds that objective knowledge is a futile endeavor. We note that perspectivism has been suggested as a replacement term for Einstein's (see below) notion of "relativity" (Best & Kellner, 1997, p. 211). In addition, as we subsequently describe, perspectivism assumes an important role in our critique of law and psychology.

As postmodernism and its theoretical variants will receive detailed attention in chapter 2, we will not catalog its considerable contours here. For now, however, we recognize that postmodernism represents the very antithesis of the modern worldview, critically questioning and resisting reductionistic methods, the pursuit of totalizing knowledge, universal truths, and globalizing values, and the absolute commitment to an ordered, pre-dictable, and controlled society. As we will disclose, these postmodern observations are compatible with many ideas found in chaos theory and the principles of nonlinear dynamics. Indeed, as chapter 2 will make evident, several contemporary postmodernists draw upon the insights of chaos theory (as opposed to modern science) to make sense of the world.

The persons and movements we have briefly discussed, provocatively disclose the type of philosophical challenges that have been leveled against modernity. These criticisms are less important for explaining the historical developments related to disorder and chaos; however, they are significant in that they represent something of a deracinating tradition. Indeed, they embody a critical response to the modernist project and all that it signifies for society, culture, and human interaction. What is more noteworthy in the context of nonlinear dynamics, though, are the particular scientific refutations of modernity. It is to these matters that we now turn.

Scientific Refutation: Poincaré and the Limits of Modern Science

Despite the widespread popularity and practical value of the modern para-digm, there remained inconsistencies that were, at times, extremely prob-lematic. These inconsistencies are best understood as behavioral anomalies or, better still, *normal* behavior which failed to conform to modern laws of physics and mathematics. Newton's mathematical principles, for example, seemed to explain the movement of the planets, especially in comparison to earlier explanations. Consequently, it was generally believed that, using motion equations, systems (of many sorts) could be predicted pre-cisely (Goerner, 1994, p. 29). This assertion relied on the effective use of calculus to approach systems whose behavior was amenable to existing mathematical laws. These laws and their subsequent explanations were widely accepted, employed, and celebrated.

Sometime later, however, Jules Henri Poincaré (1854–1912) would challenge the notion that calculus could "unravel the world" (Goerner, 1994, p. 30). As the "grandfather" or elder statesman of chaos theory (Butz, 1997), Poincaré understood what might be regarded as the "illusion" of reductionism (Briggs & Peat, 1989, p. 26). Poincaré's theoretical assertion and Newton's mathematical shortcomings, are best exemplified in the context of the "mechanics of closed systems" (ibid., p. 27). A closed system is a structure or organism that behaves from within itself. That is to say, it is closed to contamination from outside influences and, thus, lends itself well to order and prediction (ibid.). The equations that classical (Newtonian) physics employed to understand the behavior of such systems were, in short, incomplete.

What Poincaré established was that, while Newtonian solutions to planetary motion were reliable when addressing a two-body model of motion (e.g., sun-planet), they were less effective (in fact, not at all effective) when a third body was involved. An accurate mathematical model fully capable of predicting the behavior of planets necessitated the inclusion of a third entity (e.g., the sun, the moon, and a planet). Three-body equations, however, could not be worked out precisely. With the inclusion of a third body, planetary motion could only be *approximated*, not accurately predicted. Approximation, though employed as the device-of-choice in the face of such problems (and still employed today), could not accurately explain the influence of the third variable. Thus, the infamous "three-body problem" (or, "many-body problem") was born.

This "problem" can de defined as follows: the addition of a third term increases the *complexity* of systemic behavior. The problem is one of nonlinearity—a dilemma that classical linear equations were not equipped to solve. While linear equations could accurately predict the reciprocal influence of two bodies on one another, adding (the behavior of) a third body produced additional effects that were not always as conducive to forecasting. Poincaré found that even slight perturbations could encourage a planet "to wobble drunkenly in its orbit and even fly out of the solar system altogether" (Briggs & Peat, 1989, p. 28).

The principles of nonlinear dynamics that explain such possibilities will be described in chapter three (see, e.g., iteration, sensitive dependence, and bifurcations). For now, however, we note the profound implications of the three-body problem, particularly in relation to modern science.

Indeed, seemingly simple systems (including the motion of three planets), could be so complex in behavioral dynamics, that they could not be predicted with any significant degree of success (Butz, 1997, p. 6). Accordingly, the Newtonian model that had dominated Western thought for over two hundred years now seemed as if it was on the threshold of inevitable collapse. Following Poincaré, physics was less preoccupied with working from *within* a Newtonian model, and became more immersed in the revolutionary approaches that came to be known as relativity and quantum mechanics.

Altering Newton's "Perspective": Relativity in Motion

Albert Einstein (1879–1955) is best noted for introducing *relativity* into the world of science. In a sense, subject and object became less diametrically opposed and more interactive and mutually dependent. This, of course, would be a frontal assault on the "detached observer" phenomenon that modern science promised and practiced, the detached observer being one who was capable of knowing the world objectively and absolutely. Einstein's insights regarding science and society are both compelling and evocative; however, at their most rudimentary level they can be summarized. According to Einstein, descriptions of the physical world and, hence, observations of it, remain in a continual state of flux due to the varying position of the observer. In other words, the movement of the observer must effect the nature of that which is observed. The physical world, including its movement, behavior, and change, is relative to the position of the one observing that world at any given instance (Einstein, 1956, 1961). In more simplified terms, Einstein's first contribution was in recognizing that objectivity is defiant, if not altogether illusory. It should be noted, however, that Einstein did not abandon objective measurement as a goal of science. Rather, his genius consisted of simply introducing the notions of subjectivity and relativity as problematic for this scientific pursuit.

For Einstein, the universe encompassed nothing absolute or constant. Rather, everything within it was continuously moving relative to everything else within the cosmos. This notion would have important consequences for the classical cause-effect logic that is central to the modernist agenda. Indeed, if everything was relative to everything else, then causal relations (i.e., what is past, what is present, and what is future) must also be relative to the position and speed of the one who perceived these relations. In more simplified form, Einstein proposed that it was extremely difficult to ascertain precise cause-effect sequences and, consequently, to apply cause-effect logic to the world, given the (omni)presence of relativity. Additionally, we note Einstein's significant role in the development and criticism of quantum physics/mechanics. Although our treatment of this theoretical physicist is decidedly brief, we now turn to the influence of quantum theory.

Quantum Revolution: The Discontinuity and
Uncertainty of the Physical World

In 1900, Max Planck (1858–1947) presented a hypothesis that would later result in his being called the "father of quantum physics." Planck's hypothesis was in direct contrast to Newtonian physics, which had held that the movement of matter was smooth and continuous. Planck, however, suggested that the emission and absorption of energy by atoms comes, in fact, by way of discrete bundles called "quanta." Furthermore, these "quanta" behave as abrupt bursts and are discontinuous. The impact of this notion on the world of science was considerable. In short, it contradicted the modern conception of physical systems as "constituted by a continuous chain of causally related events" (Matson, 1966, p. 122). On a broader or more fundamental level, what this meant was that the "most basic elements of reality . . . c[ould] not be isolated, precisely identified or predicted," or "grasped 'as they really [we]re'" (Best & Kellner, 1997, p. 214). When coupled with the understanding that the observer always influences that which is observed (hence eliminating the necessary condition of neutrality required for objectivity), the realization that the physical world was itself subject to "bursts" that disrupted its continuity rendered the prediction of behavior unattainable (ibid.).

    With these very limitations in mind, Werner Heisenberg (1901–1976) described what has come to be known as the "uncertainty principle." The nature of the physical world is such that it is impossible to ascertain accurately both position and momentum of subatomic particles. The degree of uncertainty that ensues cannot be eliminated and, consequently, its role in quantum theory must be acknowledged rather than dismissed. Given the presence of indeterminacy, Heisenberg maintained that the laws of physics needed to be restated; no longer described as absolutes, but instead as *relative* certainties. Heisenberg's thesis constituted a fundamental break from Newtonian physics. To be sure, both were interested in predicting the behavior of matter; however, quantum theory understood that "the element of uncertainty in the subatomic world prevent[ed] exact understanding and that the predictions it ma[d]e involve[d] only probabilities, statistical regularities, and not certainties" (Best & Kellner, 1997, p. 214). Where Newtonian logic promised precision and exactness, quantum mechanics promised the *un*-representability of the basic core of our physical reality. In the wake of these discoveries, Niels Bohr (1885–1962) and other investigators argued that science must come to terms with the indeterminacy that defines the physical world. Chaos theory would be the impetus for this necessary reconciliation.

WHAT CHAOS IS

We have endeavored to show how the rejection of the Newtonian "modern" paradigm, represents the maturation of an evolving *leitmotif* of scientific and philosophical criticism. Recently, these admonitions have been reconceptualized as elements of a more holistic understanding of the role of disorder in systemic behavior. Collectively, they represent a point of departure for fashioning a portrait of a world determined by the laws of chaos, rather than those of order. We submit that the best way to appreciate what this means is to become acquainted with the principles of chaos theory. In the sections that remain in this chapter, we offer a provisional definition of what chaos is, and what the theory explores.

At the outset, we note that the terms "chaos" and "chaos theory" have been increasingly employed in reference to a vast array of physical and social behaviors, relevant to a broad array of investigative domains. For our purposes, however, it is not necessary to understand the precise ways in which chaos theory is utilized among these fields of inquiry. Rather, one must have a fundamental grasp of that which is common across the disciplinary terrain. In other words, we are interested in the basic features of disorder, as employed by proponents of the theory in the academic community. The best way to describe what chaos theory studies, is to explain what it is.

DEFINING CHAOS

The "chaos" that is described in the study of nonlinear dynamical systems theory is not analogous to, nor does it have the same connotations as, what we generally assume is its meaning, namely, a state of complete disarray or that which inspires utter confusion (Stewart, 1989, p. 16). Chaos, in the latter sense, represents total disorder, disorganization, turmoil, and distress. The chaos of nonlinear dynamics, however, "is not the logical antithesis of order" (Best & Kellner, 1997, p. 220). Rather, the disorder we have in mind is characterized by an *underlying order* within a seemingly disorderly system. This is often referred to as "order within chaos." Additionally, chaos theory describes the emergence of *order out of chaos*. This notion is often linked to "complexity theory" rather than chaos theory. The degree of overlap between the two doctrines, however, is such that they are often catalogued as components of a single line of inquiry. Therefore, for our purposes, we will collapse both theories into one and simply refer to them as chaos theory (see, e.g., Horgan, 1996 on the variations of chaos and complexity theories).

The characteristics we have just mentioned (order within chaos and order from chaos) will be more thoroughly recounted in chapter 3 when presenting the principles of chaos theory. For now, however, our intent is to describe that to which chaos theory itself applies, or that which is characterized by chaos theory principles. The most sophisticated, yet complete, definition of chaos theory comes by way of Kellert (1994). As he defines it, chaos theory is "the qualitative study of unstable aperiodic behavior in deterministic nonlinear dynamical systems" (p. 2). In the interest of explicating his meaning for chaos and chaos theory, we explore Kellert's proposal in more detail.

Systems

In the context of chaos theory, the term *system* refers to a collection of elements that are identifiable as having an interdependent relationship with other elements that collectively function toward some greater purpose or organization. In other words, chaos theory reserves no special meaning for the word "system" itself. For theoretical purposes, it refers to an assemblage of interrelated objects or processes within a particular realm of investigation (Kellert, 1994). Thus, for example, a law student who undertakes the study of the legal system may draw a figurative frame around its objects and/or processes (e.g., courts, judges, attorneys, written laws, rules, and regulations), labeling the contents of that frame a "system" (ibid.), and subjecting it to analysis. Similarly, a psychologist interested in the *human* system may understand the client as a collection of interrelationships, encompassing one's thoughts, affective states, physiological functioning, and even external dynamics (e.g., sociological, environmental) that contribute to individual behavior (e.g., a psychosocial system) (Butz, 1997). Of course, the same logic applies to the system of politics, religion, economics, ecology, and the like. For purposes of our critique, the systems we consider include those of the individual and society, psychology and the law.

The relationship between coexisting elements or variables of a system at one point in time determines the "state" of that system. Thus, identifying (the position of) each element of a system at a given time would reveal a portrait of the system as a whole of interacting elements. If the relative values for the variables of a system are identifiable, the state of the system is more easily identifiable. Ascertaining the state of the system, in turn, is often necessary for understanding the coordination of systemic components, the system's relationship to other systems, and the changes in state that the system has undergone or will undergo. The state of a system, however, will often change with time.

Dynamical Systems

A system that moves, or changes over time, is referred to as *dynamical*. Dynamics "explore the effect of various forces on the behavior of systems over time and the manner in which these systems seek optimal stable states" (Barton, 1994, p. 5). In other words, the study of dynamical systems is interested in ascertaining the component elements of a system, the "state" of that system, the variables that influence that state, and the ways in which the system changes as a result of, or in response to, those influences. Ideally, once a figurative frame has been drawn around the system's components, the "state" of a system is ascertained by *quantifying* the value of those component variables at a given time. This process allows, based on mathematical processes, the prediction of future or past states of the system. The assumption is that, knowing the "initial conditions" of a system and the appropriate mathematical rules or procedures, we can accurately predict the future conditions of the system. This is the "law and order" approach to assessing systemic behavior that is attributable to "modern" science and the Newtonian paradigm.

As we have seen, however, this paradigm can be problematic, particularly when applied to certain types of systems; namely, nonlinear systems.

First, the calculations needed to ascertain the future state may be too difficult (Cohen & Stewart, 1994, p. 189). Second, knowing the *exact* state of a
system is effectively impossible given that "real measurements always
involve small errors" (ibid., p. 190). In part, this stems from the fact the
most precise measurements available to contemporary physics are not sufficiently exacting to allow for a necessary degree of accuracy. This is where
the *dynamic* nature of a system is significant. Small errors in measurement
will, if the system does not change, remain small errors. If, however, the
system changes, what were initially small errors may become large errors
that falsify predictions. This logic will be more apparent in chapter 3 when
we discuss the principles of chaos theory.

The systems implicated in our present critique are dynamical systems.
The legal system, for example, is dynamic in that its components (e.g.,
laws, judges, defendants, witnesses) change with time. Statutory revisions
and emendations, the emergence of new case law, and changes in court personnel are several relevant and significant examples. Individual systems
(i.e., people) are dynamic in much the same way. In addition to changes in
social relations, environment, and the like, the psychological "state" of an
individual is one of continual flux. Thus, a "depressive" episode may
appear, disappear, and reappear. In addition, these changes may be related
to modifications in other components of the individual system such as
interpersonal associations, change of residence, and many other factors.
Thus, it follows, that the systems of psychology and law (individual and
society) may be thought of as dynamical, subject to the same general characteristics of other dynamical systems.

Nonlinear Dynamical Systems

Nonlinearity is a descriptive term applicable to the behavior of certain types
of dynamical systems. Other dynamical systems, however, are linear. Linear
dynamics is premised upon the assumption that systemic variables change
in a smooth or continuous fashion (Kellert, 1994, p. 2) and, thus, can be
modeled using equations that account for this continuity. In practice, the
results of two or more equations are combined to obtain another solution.
Thus, linear dynamics is somewhat successful in describing the behavior of
systems in which "small changes produce small effects and large effects are
obtained by summing up many small changes" (Briggs & Peat, 1989, p. 23).
In scientific research, for example, linear equations are the "cornerstone of

statistics" (Barton, 1994, p. 6). In performing an ANOVA or entering data into a multiple regression equation, for example, linear equations are used to describe the relationships that exist between variables (ibid.).

Thus, linearity is a product of differential equations (i.e., equations involving rates of change), where the sum of two solutions is again a solution (Stewart, 1989, p. 81). The mapping of linear differential equations would reveal a straight line (Hayles, 1990, p. 11). As noted, these equations work well with most dynamical systems, as they change in a continuous (i.e., smooth) manner. With a differential equation, the "state" of a system at one point in time can determine the state of the system at a later (or even earlier) time, by incrementally changing the variables and adding smaller solutions to obtain a larger solution (Kellert, 1994, p. 3). In this way, linear differential equations may be thought of as *additive*.

These additive equations do not, however, work well when addressing natural systems in which behavioral change may be sudden or occur in quick "jumps" (Barton, 1994). These sudden changes or behavioral "jumps" are what define nonlinear dynamical systems. They change in ways that, while sometimes smooth or continuous, are, at other times, not smooth or continuous. Thus, they cannot be modeled well using linear equations whose mapping reveals a straight line: their behavior is *not* a straight line but, rather, a straight line with occasional jumps. A distinguishing characteristic of dynamical systems pursued by chaos theory, then, is the *nonlinearity* of a given system.

In addressing nonlinear dynamics, a different class of equations must be employed. Nonlinear equations are applicable to phenomena which are *dis*continuous, such as explosions or high winds (Briggs & Peat, 1989, p. 23). In contrast to the proportional (i.e., small cause equals small effect, and large cause equals large effect) nature of linear functions, in nonlinear equations, small changes in one variable can have a *dis*proportionate impact on other variables (ibid., p. 24). In addition, solutions to nonlinear equations do not generally have explicit solutions (Hayles, 1990, p. 11) and are not additive. Thus, they are difficult, if not impossible, to solve and are not generalizable to other solutions (Barton, 1994, p. 6). Indeed, individual solutions are highly particular. Consequently, the system's future behavior, as a result of nonlinear jumps, cannot be accurately predicted. Given that specific (closed-form) solutions are unattainable, the behavior of nonlinear dynamical systems must principally be measured *qualitatively*.

As a qualitative measure, chaos theory "investigates a system by asking about the *general* character of its long-term behavior, rather than seeking to arrive at numerical predictions about its *exact* future state" [italics added] (Kellert, 1994, pp. 3–4). Rather than concerning itself with the prediction of a precise future state, qualitative analysis envisioned by chaos theory determines what circumstances will lead to one future state as opposed to another (ibid., p. 4). Qualitative questions may be asked about any dynamical system.

Chaos theory, however, focuses on those systems that display *unstable* and *aperiodic* behavior (ibid., p. 4). Instability can be briefly described as the system "never settling into a form of behavior that resists small disturbances" (Kellert, 1994, p. 4). In other words, the system is not sufficiently robust so as to never be significantly disrupted by small changes in its variables. A stable system, on the other hand, can be considered robust, or able to "shrug off" a small disturbance and continue without major disruption.

The *aperiodicity* of system behavior refers to "no variable describing the system [undergoing] a regular repetition of values" (Kellert, 1994, p. 4). The effects of small disturbances continue to manifest in the overt behavior of the system, and behavior is never repeated. Thus, behavior appears random and precise prediction is impossible. An example of aperiodic behavior is that of history. While some events throughout history may appear to be similar to previous events, they are never exactly the same. History never repeats itself exactly. Further, small disturbances throughout history have precipitated significant and long-lasting changes in all spheres of human concern (ibid., pp. 4–5).

In the context of the present critique on mental health law, nonlinearity can be thought of as characterizing all human systems (i.e., the individual), and those organized and managed by individuals and/or groups of individuals (e.g., law, psychology). The future behavior of the law, for example, cannot be predicted with any degree of accuracy because of its nonlinear nature. Notwithstanding the role of precedent which encourages the juridical sphere to perform in a linear manner, sudden jumps or fluctuations in behavior are identifiable throughout the history of law. The jumps can be regarded as breaks with precedent, encouraged by societal, cultural, political, economic, moral, legal, etc., changes. Similarly, on an individual level, sudden breaks play a significant role in the lives of all persons. While one's life may be characterized by stability and predictability for a certain length of time, this period of time is indeterminate. Any number of factors (e.g., the death of a loved one, a new job or interpersonal relationship, or even spiritual "awakening") can foster a loss of previously existing continuity. Accordingly, we assert that human beings, society, the law, and psychology are nonlinear dynamical systems that are characterized by instability, aperiodicity and, consequently, are better suited to qualitative analysis.

Deterministic Nonlinear Dynamical Systems

The final element of Kellert's proposed definition of chaos theory is the *deterministic* nature of nonlinear dynamical systems. We have addressed the meaning of determinism in the context of modern science. The determinism of nonlinear dynamical systems, however, is different in a very significant way. As we previously stated, the future behavior of deterministic systems is rigidly ascertained by the initial state of the system. This is Laplace's (1814/1951) "demon" of universal causation, linked to Newtonian physics. In other words, once having identified the initial conditions or initial state of the system, one can predict its future state based on absolute mathematical principles. If the exact initial conditions of the system are known, the *linear* nature of its change (i.e., smooth or continuous) allows the future state to be accurately measured before it even appears.

Linear dynamical systems are deterministic because "they are composed of only a few differential equations, and because the equations make no explicit reference to chance mechanisms" (Kellert, 1994, p. 5). In other words, they are not affected by the "jumps" that characterize nonlinear dynamical systems and, consequently, are both determined and predictable. Systems displaying nonlinear behavior, however, are *deterministic but unpredictable*. Though characterized as deterministic, they are, nonetheless, unpredictable because of their inherent tendencies (e.g., instability, aperiodicity). As previously mentioned, the deterministic nature of nonlinear dynamical systems is complicated by an inability to know the exact state of a system at any given time, and the difficulties with calculating future states using mathematical equations. Thus, chaos theory endeavors to understand systems which are both deterministic and unpredictable.

The ways in which nonlinear dynamical systems are deterministic will be examined in chapter 3 when exploring the principles of chaos theory. For now, however, we note that while systems governed by chaos display behavior that is unpredictable and that jumps into different patterns, they are, nonetheless, patterned. Within this pattern, the system has infinite possibility for movements, thus allowing it to stir and oscillate essentially all over the place. It does not, however, jump outside of its global pattern.

Thus, it may be thought of as determined in that its range for movement is limited to that allowed by its particular pattern. For this reason, chaos theory examines systems that are said to be *globally but not locally predictable*.

The ways in which the systems of law and psychology, society and the individual, are characterized by this element of nonlinear dynamics will be explored in Part II of this book, specifically within our various applications (chapters 4–7). What remains to be seen, however, is how this science of disorder comports with the more postmodern (rather than modern) intellectual tradition into which we argue chaos theory is more appropriately linked. We direct our attention to this matter in the next chapter.

CHAPTER TWO

Postmodern Law, Crime, and (Dis)order

On the Limits of Modern Theory and Knowledge

OVERVIEW. *This chapter situates the theory of chaos into a larger, though hetero-dox, intellectual tradition known as postmodernism. This tradition remains in its infancy on the North American continent and is virtually unknown among crime and justice scholars. We begin our investigation by identifying what postmodernism is in relationship to law and criminology. Several terms fundamental to an appreciation of postmodernism's potential contribution to justice-based research and practice are intro-duced. We then examine more closely and systematically several sociological and epis-temological assumptions underscoring modern approaches to crime and justice and juxtapose them against their postmodern counterparts. These assumptions are not exhaustive; however, they do represent important building blocks for understanding how law and criminology currently operate and how they could be reconfigured. These precepts include: (a) the social structure of society, (b) role formation, (c) human agency, (d) discourse, (e) knowledge, and (f) social change. We conclude by suggest-ing how the postmodern framework in law (and criminology) functions as a blueprint for advancing the chaos theory agenda.*

WHAT POSTMODERNISM IS

The postmodern perspective, prominent in law and criminology during the late 1980s, signaled an epistemological break from traditional cause-effect relationships, linear processes in thought, reason, and logic, and absolutistic strategies for empirical, knowable, investigation (e.g., Minda, 1995). Some have suggested that the postmodern perspective assumes its position within the more radical fringe of critical criminology (Schwartz & Friedrichs

35

1994, p. 221–222). Others question if it isn't critical criminology which is itself an expression, an extension, of the postmodern condition. As Cohen (1990, p. 22) ponders when reviewing critical criminology's evolution: "[It is] part of the wider postmodern skepticism about the faith that with good will, scientific knowledge and rationality, human problems [can] be solved."

Efforts to define the appropriate role of the postmodern critique as linked to contemporary issues in law and criminology continue to receive growing attention in the academy (e.g., Arrigo, 1993a, 1996; Cornell, 1993, 1991; Manning, 1992; Milovanovic, 1997a; Smart, 1989). This flourishing of critical analysis continues to sustain itself, despite significant challenges to some of the ideological underpinnings informing this emerging, albeit heterodox, "sense of theory" or school of thought (Hunt, 1990, p. 539). With respect to these challenges, there are many types of disagreement leveled against postmodernism and it is a bit of an oversimplification to reduce them to their more conspicuous and vehement forms. Notwithstanding, sociolegal and criminological opponents assessing the value of postmodernity's logic are generally divided along two, major camps.

Some critics dismiss the theory altogether, charging that it is nothing more than subjectivism, relativism, fatalism, nihilism (Hunt, 1990, 1991, 1993; Teubner, 1992). As these scholars point out, if defining such notions as truth, knowledge, progress, order, and the like is ultimately impossible, what, if anything, can be said about society, events in it, the human condition, or our encounters with the social order? Other less virulent commentators are quick to point out the limitations of postmodernism. Rather than casting the theory as an anarchical and antithetical form of knowledge, these investigators caution that postmodernism, in seeking to expose the inherent contradictions, inconsistencies and other so-called irregularities in the construction of phenomena, offers no recipe for improvement, tenders no forward-thinking advice, identifies no alternative script or text (Cohen, 1990, 1991, 1993; Handler, 1992; Rosenau, 1992) Put simply, these skeptics are concerned with the perceived pessimism of a theory built around deconstructing or "trashing" other approaches without offering something of substance in their place.

Despite these (and other) collective criticisms, a more deliberately focused investigation of the postmodern in (criminal) justice is conceptually (and methodologically) wanting. Accordingly, this chapter explores how the postmodern agenda can provide some different ways of understanding law and criminology. Further, this chapter considers how studies situated in the postmodern can tell us something more or something other about what view jurisprudes, criminologists, and criminal justicians have of themselves in relationship to their respective research and/or practice roles. Both of these matters are potentially significant because they offer alternative vistas by and through which to engage in reflective social criticism. As we will demonstrate, the foregoing investigation is especially useful because the postmodern enterprise alerts us to what we do not know, and subverts the fundamentally comfortable structures of thought, images of reality, and certainty of thinking that underlie conventional (criminal justice) science. It is in this critical context, then, that we can begin to outline the limits of modernist criminology and identify some of the key parameters for chaos theory's relevance to law and justice.

Our investigation will emphasize a provisional assessment of several core sociological (and epistemological) forces underpinning both conventional (i.e., modernist) and nonconventional (i.e., postmodernist) theory construction in law and criminology. These themes of import include: the social structure of society; role formation; human agency; discourse construction; knowledge or sense-making; and social change. We take the position that this conceptual approach offers greater potential for appreciating postmodernism and its likely contributions to criminal and legal thought. Along the way, various justice-based illustrations will be used to help ground the otherwise dense and philosophical material.

Understanding the Postmodern Perspective

Before examining the six themes of significance noted above, a comment or two is warranted about the frame of reference the reader is asked to adopt when faced with any research situating itself within the postmodern perspective. Although several statements along these lines were tentatively introduced in the introduction and chapter 1, several, more specific observations are warranted at this juncture. This assessment is predicated upon what we take to be the theoretical constituents and/or antecedents of this nontraditional orientation. We rely heavily upon the philosophy of poststructuralism, the science of semiotics, and the logic of deconstructionism (Arrigo, 1993a, pp. 27–75; see also Einstadter & Henry, 1994, chap. 12; Benson, 1989, p. 158–161).

1. *Post-structuralism*. Post-structuralism is primarily a French and German orientation to the sociology of knowledge in

which the unveiling of "deep" structures in language systems (such as in law and criminology) is never understood to be entirely possible. Post-structuralists maintain that the meaning of "texts"—whether spoken or written, or whether visual images such as film or nonverbal images such as communication by gesture—always explode and scatter, defying the certainty of any one particular truth or any ultimate Truths.

2. *Semiotics.* Semiotics is the study of language understood as a collection of *signs* (Kevelson, 1988). There are many languages (e.g., sports, medicine, computers, engineering, law), therefore, there are many sign systems. Semioticians maintain that all words, phrases, gestures, etc., within a language system, represent something more or something other than the things themselves. Accordingly, semioticians examine the multiple and evolving meaning(s) communicated in and through discourse.

3. *Deconstructionism.* Deconstructionism is a literary and discursive method of analysis which shows how all human affairs, all social phenomena, are assembled, can be disassembled and, eventually, reassembled to incorporate excluded "voices" or multiple and, at times, contradictory images of reality. Deconstructionism, as the preferred form of postmodern inquiry, accomplishes this goal by teasing out the warring factions of significance (i.e., implicit and explicit messages representing values) communicated in the discourse of any text.

In addition to an appreciation of the postmodern perspective's theoretical origins, is this critique's particular view on language and communication. As social scientists, we learn to "accent" or encode reality from within a particular speech mode. Indeed, as members of various social networks we tend to communicate our intent and meaning by invoking a specialized grammar, representing that collective. For example, when trying to explain the subtleties of a sport (e.g., baseball and the "infield fly rule") to someone who knows little to nothing about the game, we quickly experience the problem of speaking about that sport without relying upon its distinctive grammar: we situate ourselves and are inserted within the "language of the game" (Lyotard, 1984, p. 10; see also Wittgenstein, 1953). To amplify the matter further, to do "good law," the litigator must embrace system-supporting declarations, advancing current knowledge or understanding of the legal sphere. The expressions *legalese* or *law speak* are invoked to convey this point. The discourse itself, then, is a specialized language system (Milovanovic, 1986, pp. 281–296) most appropriately known to practitioners or others uniquely informed. Those of us who have deliberated over the interpretive details of a copyright contract, a lease agreement, a will, an appellate transcript, and the like can appreciate how conveying legal intent occurs from within a particular communicative market.

The postmodern perspective presents the same invitation to discourse as does any language system. The listener or reader must enter and be situated within the specialized coordinates of postmodernism. Thus, customary thought processes are challenged—if not altogether repudiated—as reflected in the form and content of many postmodern critiques. As Milovanovic (1993a, p. 314) suggests when considering the application of Lacanian psychoanalytic semiotics to law:

> To read Lacan one must undo the conventional ties and psychological commitments to discourse and develop more intuitive ideas generated by a new vocabulary that attempts to provide the unconscious . . . with a somewhat recognizable voice.

There is, however, one additional matter relevant to *postmodern talk* not at issue for any other distinctive code. The writing style within this body of work is typically abstruse, suffering from a somewhat solipsistic and self-aggrandizing edge of discontent (Palmer, 1990; Ritzer, 1990). Schwartz & Friedrichs (1994, p. 228), commenting on the dense and cryptic dimension of the writing, warn that postmodern analyses can be viewed as "gratuitously obscure, incoherent, and undisciplined." Alternatively, they suggest that there may be more of a political agenda, necessitating some serious consideration. As they ponder:

> Is the obstacle the fact that the rest of us are unable to liberate ourselves from the constraints of interpreting the world in the familiar idiom of rational, contemporary social science? If we reoriented ourselves, would we find modes and styles of understanding that are ultimately more valid and more revealing in a changing, endlessly complex world? (Schwartz & Friedrichs, ibid.)

Following this latter reading of the postmodern perspective, we take the position that a theoretical project as outlined (i.e., vis-à-vis the foregoing themes) is not an arrival at truth but, rather, is a *departure* from it

(Barthes, 1988, pp. 263–265). In other words, the explication which follows is more in the way of sensitization: raising provisional questions about the "peripheral core" of law and criminology leads to subsequent provisional questions, and so on and so forth. Thus, the text presented must be seen as layered or tissued; that is, it merely identifies "ruptures" or digressions in conventional meaning and invites the reader to assume greater responsibility for discovering (interpreting) the identified themes in their ubiquitous unfolding.

(POST)MODERN THEORY-BUILDING IN LAW AND CRIMINOLOGY

At the outset, we admit there is something deliciously ironic about presenting a postmodernist version of law, crime, and justice while relying upon a more traditional and shared (i.e., logocentric) system of communication. In other words, if postmodernism signifies a perspective outside of or apart from standard methods of knowing, experiencing, living, how can one invoke that discourse which is itself anathema to the postmodern enterprise in law and criminology to, nevertheless, explain that enterprise? Although philosophically we concede the contradiction, methodologically the aim is to provisionally make a case for the conceptual project which, for now, can only be accomplished from within the conventional reader's frame of reference. Accordingly, we utilize traditional categories of logic (e.g., consistency in thought, syllogistic reasoning, principles of coherence), to interpret the meaning of postmodern theory for purposes of criminology and law. This approach does not detract from our argumentation; rather, it simply acknowledges one area where further analysis beyond the scope of this chapter is required. In sum, then, the objective here is to introduce the reader to and teach the reader about the relevance of postmodern criminological and legal theory construction by writing (i.e., discoursing) in its unique grammar and system of communication. To amplify our position, we now turn to the six dimensions under consideration.

The Social Structure of Society

Currently in vogue are conceptions of law and criminology which borrow heavily from structural-functional ideology. The legacy of Durkheim, Weber,

Parsons, and Merton find expression in Luhmann's (1985, 1992; see also Teubner, 1988, 1993) systems theory of autopoeisis, Dworkin's (1986) coherence principle of juridical reasoning, Posner's (1986, 1992) economic efficiency rationale privileging social accord, Hirschi's (1969; see also Gottfredson & Hirschi, 1990; Nettler ,1984) control theory assessing crime and deviance. Underlying these and other consensus-oriented approaches are notions of order, stasis, predictability, normativity, positivity, homogeneity. These forces are understood to be at the center of our existence. Society is said to be governed by global organizing principles which seek discovery and articulation. Causal explanations of law and crime begin by invoking linear, predictable (stimulus-response) forces or heretofore concealed but anchored realities which the deviant repeatedly and certifiably transgresses.

Admittedly, various strains of *conflict* criminology have endeavored to expose several of the structural conditions in society which promote status quo practices in law, crime, and deviance (e.g., Black, 1976; Collins, 1975; Quinney, 1970). However, they have mostly failed to address the commodity of discourse which privileges certain modes of linguistic production while invalidating others (Arrigo & Bernard, 1997; Rossi-Landi, 1977; and for Marxist-based applications in law and criminology, see Arrigo, 1993c, pp. 16–20; Milovanovic, 1986, pp. 294–296). In this regard, then, typical modernist conceptions of conflict ideology unwittingly adopt the consensus position that language is neutral.

The postmodern agenda, however, situates itself within an altogether different logic. The centerpiece for its enterprise is a resistance to linear foundations; that is, a debunking of predictability and permanence—not simply as a gesture of political opposition but more particularly as an acknowledgment of the indeterminate structuration of the life-world (Giddens, 1984, 1990). Predictable unpredictability (chaos theory or orderly disorder) is said to condition interaction in the social sphere. Indeed, postmodernists, relying upon the advances of quantum physics/mechanics (Bohm, 1951, 1981; Wolf, 1981, 1984); catastrophe theory; Heisenberg's (1958) *uncertainty principle* (i.e., reality is observer-created even at the level of subatomic events); and Godel's theorem (1962) on the impossibility of formal closure (i.e., the absence of finiteness or bounded realities), identify and embrace a perceived paradigmatic rupture within the origins of social formations.

The natural scientific community, informed by the works of Feigenbaum (1980), Briggs and Peat (1989), Stewart (1989), Prigogine and

Stengers (1984), Porter and Gleick (1990), Gleick (1987), and Mandelbrot (1983) initiated this foray into the realm of essential structural instabilities. Here, the challenge was to Aristotelian logic, Euclidian geometry, Newtonian physics and to all overarching principles of order contained in the positivistic, deterministic, naturalistic sciences. This theory has it that order lurks within apparent randomness. This randomness itself represents a set range of results, an underlying, but not predictable, order; that is, chaos. To illustrate: A few years ago a group of researchers at Harvard Medical School created a stir when demonstrating how the human heart operates as a *chaotic system*. Contrary to conventional medicine, these scientists pointed out how an erratic heart is healthier than one showing a perfect EKG. As they suggested: "Counterintuitively, increasingly regular behavior sometimes accompanies aging and disease. Irregularity and unpredictability, then, are important features of health" (Marino, 1994, p. 11). Following this line of inquiry, a similar analysis could help account for the figuration of other natural phenomena thought to be accidental and anomalous, for example: the pattern of waves washing up against a coastal shoreline; the sundry designs of windblown snowscapes; the symmetry of brain wave activity during bouts of dissociation.

This logic of natural instabilities or *far-from-equilibrium conditions* as structuring the social order has found some legitimacy in the social scientific community as well. In particular, diverse application studies in criminology (e.g., Arrigo, 1995b; Arrigo & Young, 1997, 1998; Pepinsky, 1991; Young, 1991) law (e.g., Arrigo, 1995, 1996, 1994; Brion, 1991, 1995; Milovanovic, 1993a, 1993b, 1996), and social justice (e.g., Arrigo, 1996b, 1997a; Arrigo & Schehr, 1998; Milovanovic, 1997; Williams & Arrigo, 2000) are now just beginning to explore the significance of orderly disorder practices in justice-related research. To date, however, the insights of chaology have more routinely been reserved for developments in literature (Hayles, 1990, 1991; Serres, 1982a, 1982b) and psychoanalysis or psychology, respectively (Abraham, Abraham, & Shaw, 1990; Butz, 1991, 1992; Deleuze & Guattari, 1987; Milovanovic, 1992; Wolinsky, 1993, 1991).

As we have already suggested, the importance of this new science, must not be too quickly discarded when challenging mainstream (modernist) understandings of law and criminology. Chaos theory proposes that the *initial* (foundational) circumstances under which events occur are indeterminable because no permanent fixed structural mapping is knowable or, indeed, even possible. Thus, at best, the existence of perpetual fragmentation explains the homologous relationship or "coupling" between structure and milieu (Hunt, 1993; Jessop, 1990; Luhmann, 1992). Theory construction in law and criminology often begins with global assumptions (situational crime rationales notwithstanding). However, these totalizing assumptions about individual actors, specific events in the social order, precise definitions of a deviant's behavior, etc., are positioned within a normatively contrived and homeostatically articulated arrangement of reality. *The nature of law and crime is such that it is retrievable, reducible and, therefore, essentially knowable and controllable.* It is this equilibrium model which is itself illusory and, ultimately, rejected. In other words, chaologists regard such absolutistic characterizations as devoid of the subtleties, the contradictions, and the incompletenesses symbolizing the more organically based dynamics of the life-world (e.g., its serendipity, irony, incommensurability, spontaneity).

Nonlinear conditions of flux are more appropriately viewed as ordering the universe, according to chaos theorists. Thus, a butterfly flaps its wings in Southeast Asia and a hurricane is caused in Florida; a chance encounter in a grocery store and one's future selection of a career, a spouse, and a place to call home is determined; a President attends a summit with other world leaders and a "crash" in the Wall Street market is triggered; a jury renders a verdict in a criminal trial and several major metropolitan cities are besieged by riots, bloodshed, and violence; a little boy (Ryan White) contracts AIDS and an entire nation ensconced in denial instantly realizes the devastation of a disease which discriminates neither on the basis of age, race, class, or sexual orientation. In each of these cases what we have is structuration (predictability) stemming from initial conditions of flux (indeterminability). In other words, order emerges out of chaos (apparent randomness).

Role Formation

The postmodern regard for position or status significantly departs from the modernist approach. The latter schema celebrates the socially prescribed responsibilities and privileges coordinating the role. The effect is a reduction; that is, a closure to possibilities of greater being or becoming. Thus, individuals assume and live out stable and predictable characterizations which tend to promote "either or" identifications. People are interpreted as deviants or conformists; law violators or law abiders; villains or heroes;

liberals or conservatives; straights or gays. As one virulent commentator admonishing the positivist approach asserts:

> Modern science . . . has separated subject and object, mind and body, self and other, human and animal, man and woman and earth. All objects in the modern world, even the human subject and human body, are treated as lifeless, as cadavers. (Malhorta Bentz, 1993, p. 122)

In the postmodern sciences, roles are open-ended and effusive. Following the contributions of chaology, identity is a constant source of negotiation. The example in law of the "hard case" is instructive here. The judge is presented with at least two possible resolutions. It is in that instance when a jurist deliberates and ponders the decision that polarized tension, in the form of validating legal heritage versus endorsing legal heresy, fosters a situation of resolute undecidability (Brion, 1991, p. 64–75). However, after several rulings regarding difficult cases, a decision-making pattern (a juridical identity) is recognizable.

Moreover, the issue of negotiating identity is not without verification. Here negotiation stands for the proposition that the constitution of one's self has meaning *only* in relation to one's projects over time. Existential-phenomenological thought first developed this theme in connection with intuiting, through a *directed glance of attention* (i.e., the eidetic reduction via intentionality), one's *transcendental ego* (essential identity formation) (Husserl, 1983, pp. 199–201), or intersubjectively experiencing one's bodily and perspectival *being-in-the-world* (Heidegger, 1962; Merleau-Ponty, 1962). Ethnomethodologists further refined this notion in their critique of the social construction of reality as constituting the *stock of knowledge* (Berger & Luckman, 1966; Garfinkle, 1956, 1967; Schutz, 1964). Interactionists contributed in their dramaturgically informed regard for the *presentation of the self* (Goffman, 1959, 1966, 1967). Constructivists participated in their investigation of social problems as typifications (Best, 1989; Spector & Kitsuse, 1987).

Postmodern or "second wave" feminist commentators add to the question of role formation in their critique of the gendered subject in discourse. The psycholinguistics of Luce Irigaray (1985, 1990), the literary criticism of Julia Kristeva (1984, 1980, 1977) and the educational psychology of Carol Gilligan (1982; see also Brown & Gilligan, 1993; Gilligan et al., 1990) have each been, in their own way, significant to the postmodern feminist movement. More recently, the application of these insights have found their way into studies on law (Arrigo, 1992; Cornell, 1991, 1993; MacKinnon, 1987, 1989; Smart, 1989, 1992) and criminology (Arrigo, 1993d; Gelsthorpe & Morris, 1990; Smart, 1990). Standpoint epistemology identifies where and how the differential statuses of women and minorities in society continue to experience exclusion in criminal and legal practices (e.g., Cain, 1992; Currie, 1993, pp. 15–19; Daly & Chesney-Lind, 1988). Postmodern feminism, however, makes sense of these differences, validates these multiplicities (i.e., gender, race, and class) *within the discourse of theory-building.*

The essential challenge of second wave feminism is to articulate a grammar (an *écriture féminine*) freed from the misogynous trappings of the phallocentric culture and language (Arrigo, 1992, pp. 21–24). It is this privileged malestream code which possesses the capacity to define women and minorities (i.e., role-appropriate formations) only in masculine terms. Under these terms *phallogocentric* interests (i.e., gender-based conventional logic) (Arrigo, 1992, p. 19; Irigaray, 1985, pp. 70–72; Lahey, 1985, p. 538; Smart, 1989) are advanced and esteemed. Thus, by extension, embedded in such notions as law, crime, victimization, and control is uni-accentuated power; that is, power anchored by a specialized discourse where individual identity is always and already a reduction enveloped in masculine meanings.

Human Agency

The modernist regard for the subject's pivotal role in communicating meaning, being, identity, freedom, discourse, embodiment, and the like was most celebrated during the Renaissance era. The prominent intellectual movement was Enlightenment philosophy and its preeminent spokesperson was René Descartes. Cartesian epistemology presupposed the *a priori* existence of a knowing, acting, unified subject. The thinking being was understood to be rational, stable, purposive. This centered and ubiquitous subject (or "I") was at the core of all human affairs. The modernist's appreciation for subjectivity was best exemplified in Descartes' renowned maxim: *Cogito, ergo sum.*

Unlike the rationalistic, mechanistic, and individualistic prescription of Cartesian logic, postmodernity offers an alternative reading of role formation. Several proponents of the latter perspective are persuaded by the contributions of Jacques Lacan (1975, 1977, 1985, 1991) and his psychoanalytic semiotics on intra-psychic (internal) and intersubjective (interpersonal) communication (see, e.g., Arrigo, 2000d for diverse law and justice applications). This emphasis on Lacan (and his epigones) is not surprising, given that many well-known and highly regarded postmodern observers (e.g., Julia Kristeva, Michel Foucault, Roland Barthes, Luce Irigaray, Jacques Derrida, and Jean Baudrillard) were known to have attended Lacan's famous Parisian lectures, delivered during the 1950s through the 1970s (Arrigo, Milovanovic, & Schehr, 2000).

The Lacanian version of subjectivity presents a vastly different understanding of the self- actualizing and self-governing individual. For Lacan the unconscious is structured much like a language where the speaking being (*l'être parlant*) is more determined than determining; that is, more regulated by unconscious workings which are themselves situated in competitive grammars (discourses) communicating multiple and, at times, contradictory meanings. Ultimately, however, the mellifluous voices of the primary process region (i.e., the unconscious or *Autre*) are harnessed and brought under (anchored by) one language system, consistent with materialistically based and system-maintaining discourse (Arrigo, 1994, 1995b, 1996c). In other words, our unconscious thoughts are *already accented* (i.e., systemically encoded) with desire, representing the logic of capital and saturated in a phallocratic economy (Althusser, 1971; Lacan, 1977, p. 193, 303–316. For a feminist critique of Lacanian *phallic desire* see Irigaray, 1985; Ragland-Sullivan, 1986; Sellers, 1991. For an application to law and criminology, see Arrigo, 1993d, 1995a). Thus, the subject in speech is not centered, unified, self-actualized; rather, the individual is more appropriately *de-centered*, divided, determined. Descartes' famous aphorism is recast as: "I think where I am not, therefore I am where I do not think" (Lacan, 1977, p. 166). Put another way, rather than the plenary, unified "I", Lacan proposes a version of the subject determined by *both* conscious states and the effects of unconscious processes (Arrigo, 1996c).

Intimately linked to the idea of human agency is the place of desire. Modernity's understanding and regard for it is expressed perhaps most vividly in some of the works of Freud (1927, 1949). Desire symbolizes that which must be regulated, held in check, or placed in abeyance. It is a conservative force which must be reckoned with if order and predictability are to prevail. One's unconscious longing(s), if left unattended to, will result in psychic disorganization and social dis-equilibrium.

In the postmodern conception of human agency, the desiring subject also figures prominently. Once again we must turn to Lacan for guidance. In the Lacanian conception, desire represents that excess or that which is beyond existential fulfillment, awaiting articulation. This desire is what Lacan was to term *jouissance* or *jouis-sense*. The subject finds his/her need to convey personalized meaning (and being) in the act of speech denied (silenced) precisely because ideologically repressive state apparatuses (Althusser, 1971, p. 143) (e.g., faith communities, the corporate sector, the educational sphere, the criminal justice apparatus) superimpose the coordinates of their discursive communicative structures (their linguistically accented reality) upon the discourse of others. Thus the desiring subject, endeavoring to communicate his/her interiorized longing, seeking to articulate his/her intrinsic meaning and being, is imprisoned (determined) within the prevailing language system in use.

Lacan (1991) has described this process in greater detail, demonstrating how the de-centered subject functions as the unwitting participant in the *discourse of the Master* (see also Arrigo, 1994, 1996, 1998, 2000c; Bracher, 1988). The *discourse of the Master* is one of four specialized discourses developed by Lacan along with the discourse of the *University, Hysteric, and Analyst*. The relationship and complexity of these communication modalities have been examined by others (e.g., Arrigo, 1994, 1995b, 1996, 1997a; Bracher, 1993; Lee, 1990; Milovanovic, 1992). Accordingly, they will not be explicated here. For our purposes, following the *discourse of the Master*, subjects constitute and are constituted by that unique grammar advancing only system-supporting declarations (i.e., the logic of capital as phallocratically conceived). Lost in the discourse is the possibility for establishing genuine, more authentic, forms of interaction and intersubjective communication.

Both law and criminology provide fertile ground wherein the (juridic) subject is exposed to the state's practices of linguistic hegemony. Elsewhere, we have examined Lacan's four discourses in the context of law, mental illness, and criminal insanity (e.g., Arrigo, 1996). In particular, a Lacanian-inspired critique of the "what happens" (the storytelling) in the psychiatric courtroom is illustrative of what form desire takes by way of this justice-rendering tribunal. Seeking to be released from involuntary civil confinement, the "committee" (i.e., the subject-in-law) must appear before an administrative tribunal. During this "adversarial" hearing, testimony is presented designed to assess the mental stability of the petitioner (i.e., Is the committee no longer a danger to self and/or to others?). In order to demonstrate one's emotional stability, the petitioner must linguistically comport him/herself in such a way that one's desire, expressed to the court, is consistent with that language signifying psychological wellness. However, desire anchored by speech consistent with psychological wellness (i.e., system-maintaining discourse) may deny the disordered defendant's linguistic and concomitant social reality. Hence, the committee is subjected to a forced choice. On the one hand, the petitioner could engage in a self-imposed semiotic cleansing, sacrificing personal being and existential longing for that desire, that meaning, representing the values of the psychiatric court-room (i.e., the language of clinicolegal science). On the other hand, the committee could announce that subjectivity, could embrace that suffering, breathing meaning into the emotional soul and body (Goodrich, 1990, p. 268) of the disordered citizen's linguistic reality, and, hence, precipitate one's return to institutional confinement. The manifestation of this prob-lematic in the psychiatric courtroom is the essence of linguistic oppression.

Although hegemony—manifested in the presence of uni-accentuated desire—may sustain itself, the postmodern critique offers transformative pos-sibilities for the articulation of one's heretofore repressed desires. In addition to such de-centering activities as Lecercle's (1985) insistence on the disrup-tive language of the body (*délire*), Deleuze and Guattari's (1986, 1987) sug-gestion of *minor literatures*, and Serres (1982a, pp. 65–70) notion of *noise*, is Lacan's (1985, p. 145) excursion into alternative forms of *jouissance* (e.g., an *écriture féminine* or a supplementary discourse grounded in an uncultivated and nonmisogynized feminine sexuality). Moreover, Lacan provides us with his description of the *discourses of the Hysteric and Analyst*. The latter two concepts will be briefly explored in the next section where "desire in lan-guage" is more closely examined. Instructive here, however, is the recogni-tion that for postmodernity desire symbolizes a liberating, freeing and positive presence (Dews, 1987, p. 132). Where modernity seeks the *territorialization of desire* (Deleuze & Guattari, 1987), postmodernity endeavors to emancipate it. The latter perspective accomplishes its objective by legitimating previously excluded voices and by revalidating those language systems which communi-cate the marginalized citizen's unencumbered meaning and essential being (Lacan, 1977, p. 275; Lee, 1990, pp. 95–99, 168–170).

Discourse

Unlike the modern sciences, the postmodern perspective views language as value-laden, nonneutral, and politically charged. Discourse represents the interests and goals of oppressive power elites or other collectives. This understanding in criminological and legal theory construction has roots in

Legal Realism and includes such notables as Holmes (1897), Pound (1908), Frank (1930/1963), Llewellyn (1930, 1931), Llewellyn and Hoebel (1941), and Rumble (1968). Today, the Realist tradition has resurfaced in the form of the Critical Legal Studies (CLS) Movement. It is infused with the more acerbic dynamics of postmodern discontent. CLS writers endeavor to unmask the layered dimensions of subjectivity and indeterminacy inherent in traditional understandings of law and crime, victimization and control, justice and punishment (Arrigo, 1993a, pp. 51–55; Benson, 1989, pp. 161–165; Kelman, 1987; Peller, 1985). As one commentator has remarked when exploring the junctures and disjunctures between Legal Realism and Critical Legal Studies:

> . . . [W]hile the realists too believed law was politics, right down to the partisan politics of individual judges, the politics CLS has in mind is the deeper political ideology of liberal individualism, which privileges the individual over community, hierarchy over equality, the private sphere over the public, free will over social cause explanations. These privileged norms—and the classist, racist, sexist, and domineering arrangements which result from them—are systematically cemented into our culture by legal discourse; *departures from the norms are repressed, treated as exceptions.* (Benson 1989, p. 164; emphasis added)

More recently, however, the CLS agenda and its emphasis on discourse construction has been supplanted by criminological and legal ideology embracing Michel Foucault's work on *disciplinary institutions* and Jurgen Habermas's treatment of *steering mechanisms* (Arrigo, 1993a, 1993b, 1992; see also Lecercle, 1985 on the *violence of language*). In brief, these investigations point out how certain forms of technology or discoveries in science promote new modes of surveillance, (e.g., advances in forensics, criminology, and epidemiology inform our response to crime control), such that certain discourses are privileged as knowledge/truth discursive formations. These normalizing practices are linked to power and affirm only those knowledge assertions advancing the prevailing truth regime. Any resistance such as the invocation of alternative grammars (e.g., oppositional speech patterns or codes)—despite challenging the legitimacy of the prevailing language system—is thwarted through sociolinguistic hegemony and reification. Through these disciplinary mechanisms (i.e., hegemony and reification) a certain discourse, a specialized grammar, maintains its privileged status. This esteemed discourse, as a system of communication (i.e., a system of meaning), embodies desire invalidating that difference constitutive of resistant or oppositional citizens.

The rich psychoanalytics of Lacan is instructive here as well, particularly when signaling how much semiotic activity occurs prior to the coupling of the spoken word (paradigm) with the actual speech chain(s) (syntagm). Desire in language begins at a more nonreflexive, unconscious level. What we say and how we say it (Lacan's paradigm-syntagm semiotic axis) depends on the effects of other pre-uttered forces, including the condensation-displacement axis and the metaphor-metonymic axis. For Lacan, these three tropes are constitutive of a semiotic grid (Milovanovic, 1992; see also Arrigo, 1997, 1998 for criminological and legal applications). Their combinatory impact is what is meant by intra-psychic and intersubjective communication. Exploring these overlapping axes—although the source of rich theoretical insight pertinent to law and criminology—is beyond the scope of the present chapter. For our purposes, however, we wish to point out that the interactive effects of the grid produce the spoken word and *represent* the first level of semiotic production. The first sphere is the structural axis (i.e., the unconscious, systemic encoding of desire) previously discussed in relationship to subjectivity.

In addition to the systemic level of semiotic production and the internal and interpersonal level of semiotic activity, Lacan introduces the joint effects of the *discourse of the Hysteric and Analyst*. These are two other communication modalities developed by Lacan. The potential for overcoming the dictatorial hold of language experienced by the oppositional citizen (e.g., the disenfranchised masses who make up the bulk of persons channeled through the criminal justice system) reside in these discursive formations. In these Lacanian depictions, different forms of *jouissance* would find embodiment in the structure of alternative, nonauthoritarian grammars. For example, in the context of the clinicolegal apparatus where defendants are in search of psychiatric justice, replacement speech patterns embodying the jargon of inconsistency, absurdity, indeterminacy, incompleteness, flux, and the like, would need to be valorized (Arrigo, 1996). Of course, this newly embraced language system would need to be affirmed to the extent that it, too, did not function as a privileged and therefore oppressive code (Arrigo, 1996a). We maintain that such a system of communication would offer transformative possibilities for denoting alternative, more complete, expressions of *jouissance*.

Related to these Lacanian notions is constitutive theory. As developed in criminology (Henry & Milovanovic, 1996, 2000) and law (Hunt,

1993), constitutive thought examines the dialectics of linguistic control. Proponents of this ideology maintain that the complicity of the subject (e.g., judges, defense advocates, police agents, victims, lay professionals, the media) in acquiescing to language and its dictatorial constraints needs to be investigated. In brief, constitutive theorists argue that crime reduction and justice-rendering are coterminous and will only come about when subjects abandon their co-constitutive investment in the established doctrine (the ossified language) of criminal justice.

Knowledge

Much of the preceding discussion points to the question of knowledge and the conditions under which it is constituted. For the modernist, knowledge as truth embodies an attainable, certifiable object, awaiting discovery. The epistemology of Enlightenment science endeavored to quantify and posit the world and social phenomena, embracing a tension-reduction dynamic always in search of *ultimate truths* or *totalizing realities*. With the modern episteme, there is a commitment to certainty, closure, finiteness, determinacy, completeness. Much of this period's legacy lives on today in many empirical works, exploring topical issues related to law and criminology.

The postmodern sciences interpret sense-making differently. Lacan's formalizations on both the *discourses of the Master and University* are particularly relevant. As others have suggested, the *discourse of the University* is the more hidden form of the *discourse of the Master* (e.g., Milovanovic, 1993a, pp. 322–323). Lacan's schematizations on both of these formations explain the unconscious processes at work in which unique forms of desire are embodied, deterministically producing only certain legitimated (dominant) forms of knowledge. Unlike "scientific" knowledge which is privileged as the dominant discourse in modernist thinking, postmodern analysis seeks the discovery of "narrative" knowledge (Sarup, 1989, pp. 120–121; see also Arrigo, 1992, pp. 24–27, 1993d, pp. 33–37 on *imaginative discourse*; Lacan, 1985, pp. 143–147 on *mythic knowledge*; Cornell, 1991, pp. 168–196 on the *imagination and utopian possibility*). Truth, justice, reason, progress and other similar abstractions are based on myths, symbols, and metaphors, representing the historicity of a given culture as an incomplete and unfolding life story. Postmodern thought seeks the discovery, articulation, and affirmation of repressed voices (excluded stories), and the codes of speech which constitute their logos. In this regard, then, knowledge is provisional and relational; that is, logic is local not global (Dews, 1987), meaning is contingent not certain (Sarup, 1989), understanding is fragmented not complete (Lyotard, 1984), truth is a departure not an arrival (Barthes, 1988).

In further support of the postmodern agenda are contributions from feminist ideology. In part, the maxim: "the personal is empirical" (McDermott, 1992, pp. 237–245) signals how liberal feminists interpret knowledge. However, that which is personal may also be the site of power and, therefore, may also advance the subordination of those who experience differently. Accordingly, postmodern feminist thought is equipped with the insights of Foucault, Irigaray, Marx, Kristeva, Habermas, and Lacan. Selected works in law and criminology have been especially careful to point out that any systematic constitution as a doctrinal approach possesses the capacity to function as an oppressive methodology (Arrigo, 1993a, pp. 45–51, 1993d, pp. 32, 38–43, 1995a). Thus, there must be a flexible debunking to that which is offered as knowledge: "What is posited must also be reversed, only to loop around again as a supplement to the reversal" (Arrigo, 1992, pp. 20–21). The application of postmodern principles of sense-making to law and criminology challenges and disrupts the sedimented icons of modernist justice. Embedded in the language of such expressions as "burdens of *proof*," "a demand for *factual evidence*," "*actual* legal intent," "*expert* testimony," "*causes* of crime," "the *reasonable* wo/man standard," are notions of power, conveying only certain truths, representing the ideology of the (male-centered) *master discourse*. A blending of Lacan's *discourses of the Hysteric and Analyst*, postmodern feminist ideology, and constitutive theory point to a more liberating process in which alternative or new knowledge claims can find embodiment in intersubjective communication.

Social Change

The modern sciences embrace a linear understanding of historical change. Evidence of this is found in Darwin's (1859/1968) biosocial *theory of evolution*, Weber's (1978) critique of *formal rationality* (see also, Habermas, 1984 on *purposive rational action*), Hegel's (1807/1977) phenomenology of the *Absolute Spirit*. In short, the lingering suspicion in the modernist tradition is that "a backstage mechanism, an outside reality [exists], affecting the human drama" (Benson, 1989, p. 159). Thus, the search for objective mechanisms (e.g., basic structural mechanisms which anchor the law and criminology) not only meaningfully contributes to our understanding of human affairs but also provides reassurance that there is underlying (permanent) stability to the social order.

Change in the modernist framework is therefore a matter of reducing the undifferentiated possibilities to discernible (linear) outcomes through institutional responses. In other words, social transformation begins when ossified systems functionally react to differentiation in the environment. In law, for example, we see this linear regard for social change in Hart's (1961) assessment of the penumbra of uncertainty structuring legal rules. Situated at the "core" of this uncertainty are essential or "settled" meanings. More recently, Dworkin's (1986, p. 216) analysis on legal reasoning shows how judges search for the single best answer to a legal issue by "'finding the interpretation which brings all the relevant legal materials together into the most coherent scheme'" (as quoted in Benson, 1989, p. 164; see also Luhmann, 1985, p. 237 on the surplus of possibilities and law). The result is a tension-reduction dynamic, yielding predictability in social planning.

The postmodern perspective on social change is more attune to the nonlinear features of the lifeworld. The pivotal thinker is Nietzsche (1980) and his notion of "transpraxis" (see also Deleuze, 1983; Henry & Milovanovic, 1991, pp. 305–309). Unlike Hegel's (1807/1977) reaction-negation dynamics regarding the master-slave relationship, Nietzsche points to a more active change phenomenon which includes deconstructionism and reconstructionism. Following Hegel, when one reacts to perceived hierarchical power relations and seeks to repudiate them, the act of negating creates new forms of domination (i.e., the reproductions of relations to productions) which also wield their marginalizing effects on human subjects. Conversely, with Nietzschean transpraxis, critical attention is directed toward the reconstitutive effects, inherent in any attempt to neutralize or challenge that which is negated.

Mindful of our Lacanian analysis on subjectivity, discourse, and desire, postmodernists endeavor to transcend the imposed parameters and imagery of conventional *truth* claims. In other words, they embrace that version of historical change in which flux, chance, indeterminacy, and irony prevail. Social planning requires a *double negation* or *negative dialectics* (Adorno, 1973). Thus, the marginalized subject (e.g., the disempowered citizen in law) must break free from the constraining linguistic categories of traditional reason and rationality imposed by the *discourse of the Master*. Moreover, the subject in discourse must become a divided self embodying that difference which constitutes his/her logos (see Pecheux, 1982 on dis-identification, and Cixous, 1990 on *le dépense*).

In justice-related pursuits some movement in this direction of change can be traced to the peacemaking agenda (e.g., Pepinsky & Quinney, 1991; Pepinsky, 1993). Accordingly, postmodernists recognize the harm, suffering, and pain caused by acts of violence and "seek to examine [what legal and criminological pursuits] might reduce [them] through transforming the totality of relations of which [the harm, suffering, and pain] [are] a part" (Henry & Milovanovic, 1991, p. 309). Much of this transformation relates to our embracing alternative conceptions of society's social structure, role formation, human agency, discourse construction, knowledge or sense-making, along with other themes of import not examined here. Therefore, social change and (social) justice require a responsible and active debunking (i.e., deconstruction) by criminal justice scholars and practitioners addressing the politically constructed, ideologically articulated, and media-driven dimensions of social problems (Barak 1988, p. 585). The task here is not to construct "new and different" versions of truth, justice, law, crime, etc., in ways that typify systematic reconstitutions. This exercise would foster nothing more than the reaction-negation problematic implicit in Hegelian thought. Rather, the peacemaking agenda envisioned here considers the *duality* (or mutuality) implicit in our understanding of victimization, control, punishment, law, and order. Further, this agenda endeavors to change our *linguistic* (and therefore social) relationship to such phenomena in ways that foster a replacement (more liberating) experience of human subjects, the social order, and their interconnectedness.

Summary

The postmodern perspective is not concerned with the scope and magnitude by which it accounts for *the* conditions or *the* causes of social problems. It does, however, seek to understand the manifold and ever-changing ways disparate groups communicate and give meaning to local sites of crime, justice, law, and community. Thus, the idea of postmodernism refers to its relational, positional, and provisional function to interpret, reinterpret, validate, and repudiate multiple discourses and their expressions of reality construction in divergent social arrangements. In this regard, we can speak of *standpoint espistemologies* (i.e., knowledge embedded in divergent ideological frameworks) where each shapes its own circumscribed method, images, and discourse. Therefore, postmodern theory does not presume to understand *the* conditions or *the* causes of criminal or legal controversies by offering either a homeostatically based integrative model or a rigidly specialized theory. Not only would such absolutistic truth claims be illusory but such approaches would themselves oppress different ways of knowing, different ways of communicating meaning.

In justice-related pursuits the questions to be asked must therefore go beyond the normative and positivistic (e.g., What is crime?, Who makes the law?, What are the conditions under which crime and law are created?). Instead, we must question *the conditions under which we come to say what conditions the constitution of law and crime and how does our communication differ from that of others.?* This more reflective activity calls into repute not only the values embedded in one's selection of language in relation to the values embedded in the languaged standpoints of others, but examines how these collective ways of knowing—despite their plurality—are often reduced to only certain patterns of speech, certain expressions of logic in justice. Further, it invites others (scholars, practitioners, students, the public, the media) to do the same. This self-interrogating process challenges all of us to be unremittingly in tune with the desperation of marginalized or excluded voices. Further, it asks us to consider how we may be contributing, knowingly or not, to that very marginalization we seek to renounce. Finally, the postmodern agenda reminds us of the importance of provisional and relational understanding when interpreting social problems. Thus, that version of legitimated reality and the discourse used to encode it with one's meaning and being must not be seen as an ultimate "Truth" or even the final word on a particular truth.

CONCLUSIONS

This chapter explored several sociological and epistemological themes of import embedded in (post)modern thought and related them to law and criminology. We explained how such conceptualizing fostered new and different possibilities for understanding agents and actors in (criminal) justice as well as the overall system itself. This analysis was significant insofar as it identified the limits of knowledge construction in modernist law and criminology, and pointed out new vistas of meaning within the study of crime, law, and justice as advanced through postmodernist thought. Generally speaking, therefore, this chapter helps to situate the place of chaos theory as a worthwhile conceptual orientation to the knowledge process, and as an important theoretical backdrop from which to investigate social issues, including notable controversies in mental health law.

The significance of postmodernism for the future of (criminal) justice enterprises centers upon the ethical dimension of the conceptual project in its alternative vision of and relationship to law and criminology. Here, put simply, we are confronted with an understanding of the life drama and the social order which returns dignity to passion and legitimacy to the inexplicable. Freed from the illusions of grand theory, false consciousness, unrealistic aspirations, unattainable ends, the call is not merely to celebrate the "de-centering" of traditional explanatory rationales through celebrating individual and collective differences, but rather, to face up to ethical accountability and capacity in foundational yet deracinated ways.

Instead of substituting the ethical dimension of our existences with an aesthetics of daily living, the postmodern agenda endeavors to make us all a bit more moral (honest) in relationship to others and our communities. Accordingly, the legacy of postmodern justice, through its integrative sociological and ontological themes, is an invitation to experience the incommensurable fullness of all human actors (e.g., victims, criminals, police agents, correctional officials, courtroom administrators, judges, attorneys) in their contradictory being and becoming, especially as they participate in the irony and the serendipity of the social order. In short, the contribution of postmodernism to law and criminology presents a morality without an ethical code, an awareness absent the familiar, an antifoundational perspective from which we may proceed and begin once again.

CHAPTER THREE

The Principles of Chaos Theory

OVERVIEW.   *In this chapter, we survey the basic principles of chaos theory. These principles, though not mutually exclusive, may be thought of as the defining features of nonlinear dynamical systems. In chapter 1, we described the general attributes of chaos and chaos theory, mindful of major shifts in the philosophy of science. In the previous chapter, we located nonlinear dynamics within a larger sociological and epistemological framework called postmodernism, suggesting how orderly disorder practices are relevant to theory-building in law and criminology. The foregoing chapter, however, should be read as a more detailed description of what it means for a system to be dynamical, nonlinear, deterministic, unstable, and aperiodic. We have identified seven principles with which to work. These seven concepts are presented in such a way that they inform the reader how systems (might) progress from an orderly state, to one of chaos, and back to one of order.*

Accordingly, we first explain those set of principles that describe the movement from order to disorder to chaos, and comment on the scientific insights that have allowed us to see how this order-to-chaos transformation begins and progresses. Additionally, we expound upon those set of principles that demonstrate the presence of order within chaos. Once a system has become destabilized, it tends to attain a certain order within that apparent disorder. This is best understood as a system characterized by local disarray, yet governed by global organization. These particular chaos theory principles function to ensure a certain stability within a system that may have been perturbed by external and/or internal factors. They depict certain orderly dynamics that most often occur well beyond that which is immediately observable. Thus, they represent the positive nature of disorder, that is, the continued orderly functioning of a system even within what appear as disorderly dynamics.

Finally, we examine the process of order arising out of chaos. The chaos theory principles of self-organization and dissipative structures are instructive for this purpose. They are descriptive elements of nonlinear dynamical systems that detail the manner in which a disorderly system will regain a certain stability. This "new" stability, however, is regarded as a better, more complex (and more natural) order than that which previously defined the system. It is in this context, then, that we can discern the potential positive effects of nonlinear dynamical systems analysis. Indeed, as we demonstrate, the principles of self-organization and dissipative structures represent the movement back toward order once the system has progressed from a state of stability to increasing levels of disorder and, possibly, chaos.

ORDER TO CHAOS

The progression of a nonlinear dynamical system from a stable state into a disorderly or chaotic state is made possible by characteristics inherent to those systems. The principles of *iteration, sensitive dependence on initial conditions*, and *bifurcation* provide us with some sense of how and why this progression occurs. Each is intimately related to the others, and equally necessary for chaos. Iteration describes the propensity of nonlinear dynamical systems to behave as a feedback loop, engaged in a self-reinforcing cycle where disorder can increase exponentially. Sensitive dependence on initial conditions tells us that a system's future behavior is very much dependent on the precise state of the system at a given time, and very much sensitive to the effects of external variables at any given moment. Bifurcations describe a route to chaos whereby systems undergo qualitative changes upon reaching certain levels of disorder. These qualitative changes are made possible by the system's sensitivity to its external environment and its iterative nature.

Iteration

In its ordinary language usage, "iteration" refers to something that is repeated; that is, a process of repetition or a repetitious phenomenon. The iteration that characterizes nonlinear dynamical systems is not significantly different. Iteration might best be described as "feedback involving the continual reabsorption or enfolding of what has come before" (Briggs & Peat, 1989, p. 66). Systems prone to chaos tend to "stretch and fold back upon themselves in self- reinforcing loops" (Van Eenwyk, 1991, p. 3). Mathematically, this "stretching and folding" process is modeled using equations that "work on themselves" such that the result is fed back into the equation as the basis for the next computation (ibid.).

For purposes of analogy, this iterative process might be likened to the feedback encountered when a live microphone is placed too close to an amplifier. In such a system, sound enters the microphone, is transmitted through the amplifier, and the amplified sound, in turn, reenters the microphone. The original sound builds upon itself through a process of feedback or self-reinforcement, and will continue to do so endlessly—at least until the microphone is moved away from the amplifier or the volume is reduced. In addition to the increase in volume, however, the *rate of increase* in the volume also accelerates (Van Eenwyk, 1991, p. 3). Thus, the value of the original sound has become subject to self-reinforcement through its continual interaction with the amplifier. The "system" is iterative.

Unlike linear dynamical systems which are, to some extent, predictable, iterative systems are highly unpredictable; that is, they "determine their own destiny . . . for where they have been often seems to have little effect on where they continue to go" (ibid.). This phenomenon is largely attributable to a certain interaction: the inordinate and unrestrained growth that is inherent in the process of iteration and the system's sensitivity to exact present conditions. Vast differences in future states are often observable when two or more systems differ only slightly with regard to beginning state. This effect is known as "sensitive dependence on initial conditions."

Sensitive Dependence on Initial Conditions

In nonlinear dynamical systems, seemingly minute variables can have a significant impact on a system's behavior over time. This is often referred to as the "butterfly effect," because something as small as a butterfly flapping its wings can, theoretically, alter the behavior of an entire weather system (Butz, 1992). Effects such as these have traditionally been dismissed as irrelevant or too small to be of significance for a large system. What nonlinear dynamics has found, however, is that the "state" of a system is extremely sensitive to such perturbations. The future state of a system is largely affected by the *exact* conditions of that system at the time of observation (i.e., its initial state). Thus, a relatively minor variable that alters the initial conditions of a system—even in ways imperceptible—may encourage the system to become something very different than it would otherwise be. This scientific finding is profound: It suggests that even slight variations at one time might produce enormous differences at a later time.

This phenomenon is called sensitive dependence on initial conditions. It was inadvertently discovered in 1961 by meteorologist Edward Lorenz while attempting to predict weather patterns using a classical linear model.

As we have seen, traditional models of prediction were (are) premised on the assumption that identifying the precise state of a system at a given time would make possible the forecasting of that system's state at any future time. Lorenz identified the initial state of his system with the decimal code .506127, and allowed his computer to generate patterns based upon these numerically represented conditions. Lorenz, however, would one day round off the decimal code to .506 assuming, of course, that this would not affect the generated pattern. What he found, however, was something quite unexpected. The pattern based on the three-digit code looked very different from the original pattern created with the six-digit code. A difference in initial conditions of only 0.0001 (one part in a *thousand*) eventually led to widely divergent trajectories (see e.g., Briggs & Peat, 1989; Butz, 1997; Gleick, 1987; Stewart, 1989).

Lorenz's discovery continues to have profound implications for the study of nonlinear dynamical systems. In short, his finding points out the tendency of these systems to be extremely sensitive to initial conditions, inputs, or variables and, therefore, to be extremely unpredictable in the long run. Butz (1997, p. 6) describes Lorenz's studies in meteorology as the "gateway back to Poincaré's work" as it demonstrates mathematically the unpredictability of the world. This sensitivity and, thus, uncertainty is worthy of serious consideration in light of the dominant methods of social science research. Consider the neglect or disregard for minute variables that most often accompany statistical analyses. For example, in grade school we are encouraged to "round" up or down our mathematical formulations. In graduate school, we are taught to "throw out" outliers or anomalies that threaten to disrupt our linear mathematical computations. Often, this "rounding" or dismissal of small pieces of data would, in reality, have little *immediate* impact. For this reason, it continues to be a common practice. The influence becomes quite pronounced, however, when observing long-term behavior. Time, of course, provides an iterative system with an opportunity to iterate; that is, to propel itself from stability, to instability, and finally toward chaos.

Iteration and Sensitive Dependence

Iterative systems, then, have a sensitivity to initial conditions. This is precisely how small differences can lead to striking differences over time—with increasing repetitions (iterations) of the equation. Mathematically, this is captured by the notion of exponential growth. A number or quantity that doubles after a time, and then doubles again after the same amount of time, ad infinitum, is referred to as having *exponential* growth (Ruelle, 1991, p. 39). A good example of exponential growth might be the interest one earns on a savings account. If one were to invest money at five percent interest, after a given amount of time the initial investment will have grown by five percent. After another cycle, the money will again grow by five percent, and so on. While the *rate* of interest does not change, the *amount* of savings gaining interest does. The initial savings has increased over a given amount of time, and continues to increase, yet with each new growth continually *reinvested*. Thus, five percent interest on a ten-thousand-dollar savings account would not merely grow by five hundred dollars a year. Rather, one would earn five hundred dollars of interest the *first* year, and progressively more each additional year because the account is self-reinforcing. At five percent interest, the original investment would double in about fourteen years, rather than twenty years if the interest were not reinvested. Thus, the amount of the initial investment, along with the interest rate, determines the "future state" of the investment. Because the investment grows by way of feeding into itself, it displays exponential growth; that is, it gains momentum, growing more and faster as time passes.

Exponential growth exemplifies the potential effects of sensitive dependence on initial conditions. A small change in the "state" at one time, can produce a future change that grows exponentially. While the savings account example may be predictable or calculable, *nonlinear* dynamical systems do not necessarily or always display growth at a constant and definable rate (i.e., 5%). Thus, the future state of the system becomes unpredictable— we cannot ascertain the *rate* at which the system will grow, given the effects of external variables on that system's behavior. A more realistic example may be an investment in the stock market where the rate of growth is not set at five percent, but can change unpredictably in light of any number of influential factors (e.g., international relations, political developments).

A more visual illustration of the combinatory effects of iteration and sensitive dependence would be a game of billiards. Assume that there are two cue balls on the table. If one is even slightly, even immeasurably (e.g., one thousandth of a millimeter), different in starting place than the other, the two will end up in entirely different places after deflections off of other balls or off the table's sides, and the distance between the balls will grow exponentially with time. Thus, the future state (i.e., position of the cue ball) is sensitive to the initial state (i.e., precise starting position) of the ball (Ruelle, 1998, pp. 41–42). If one ball has only a slightly different trajectory than the other, the longer they are allowed to continue their respective paths (i.e., the more they iterate), the farther apart they will be.

Sensitive dependence on initial conditions, then, is a product of non-linear dynamical systems that complicates predictability. The lack of determinate predictability is a result of the system's future state or behavior being dependent upon its precise initial conditions—coupled with the effects of iteration (i.e., encouraging these differences to be more pronounced with time). Thus, if two otherwise identical systems differ in initial conditions by even the smallest amount, their long-range behavior will deviate dramatically from one another (Barton, 1994, p. 6). These "tiny differences in input" can quickly become "overwhelming differences in output" (Bütz, 1992, p. 1051). By the same token, a system's eventuality is critically contingent upon its state of origin. The less stable a system is, the more likely it is to experience the effects of sensitive dependence on initial conditions. A system that is in a "far-from-equilibrium" state, as indicated by the presence of disorder, is more prone to the effects of sensitive dependence on initial conditions. Given minor variations in the initial conditions of two systems, or subsystems within a system, their eventual relationship cannot be known, controlled, or predicted.

Bifurcations and Period-Doubling Points

Nonlinear dynamical systems may, at any given time, be characterized by any number of states. The progression toward chaos carries a system from a stable state, through different degrees of disorder (representing different "states" of disorder), and, potentially, to chaos. Each significant change in the qualitative state of a system (i.e., to a higher state of disorder) is marked by something called a "bifurcation" (Goerner, 1994). Bifurcations, then, mark *qualitative* changes in the behavior of a system that accompany the system's evolution into disorder and chaos. They are "critical points of destabilization" (Butz, 1997, p. 11) wherein systems are forced into a new "mode" of behavior in reaction to some internal or external stimuli that causes a buildup of stress. Thus, when a system reaches a certain level of stress; that is, a level at which it is no longer capable of sustaining its stability, it reaches a critical point and, consequently, undergoes a qualitative behavioral transformation.

We may think of a bifurcation metaphorically as a "choice" in the evolution of a system. Coveney and Highfield (1990, p. 360) define bifurcations as such a choice following the system's arrival at a crucial point ". . . at which there are two distinct [options] open to a system; similar to a fork at which a path divides in two. Beyond this critical point, the properties of a system can change abruptly." Bifurcations occur when a system is in a certain state (stability, for example) and then something (i.e., an internal or external stressful influence) perturbs the system or knocks it off balance (Butz, 1994, p. 694). In other words, when a system that is naturally unstable and, thus, sensitive to internal and external influence, comes under the influence of a given stimulus, it is destabilized. Given the iterative properties of nonlinear dynamical systems, this stress builds upon itself and off of itself. Upon reaching a certain critical point, the system is forced into a qualitatively different state or mode of being. The bifurcation is the point at which this choice or transformation occurs. While a system may regain stability following bifurcations, it can never regain the *same* stability. Nonlinear dynamical systems exemplify the "irreversibility of time."

Bifurcations in systems, then, arise from "vital instant[s] when something as small as a photon of energy . . . is swelled by iteration to a size so great that a fork is created and the system takes off in a new direction" (Briggs & Peat, 1989, p. 143). When the system increasingly loses stability, reaching more and more critical points at an increasing rate, it becomes trapped in what is called a "bifurcation cascade" (Butz, 1994). Bifurcation cascades can, with time, cause a system to "fragment itself" toward chaos (ibid.). These successive bifurcations can be charted by what are referred to as "period-doubling charts;" that is, with each bifurcation, the amount of time that it takes a system to return to a stable state *doubles*.

When a system reaches the first critical point (i.e., period-doubling point)—mathematically valued at 3.0—it becomes demonstrably less stable and bifurcates. The system oscillates between two separate modes of behavior. If the level of disorder continues to grow, the system will approach another bifurcation—this time at the critical value of 3.45. At this point, the system branches again to produce four possible behavioral outcomes around which it oscillates. At the third critical value of 3.56, the system again bifurcates and has eight possible outcomes. Another bifurcation appears at the critical value of 3.5696, splitting the system into sixteen possible outcomes. Finally, at the critical value of 5.56999, the system branches into infinity. This is the point of *chaos*. Beyond this point, known as the "point of accumulation" (Gleick, 1987, p. 73), periodicity (or periodically revisiting prior values through oscillation) has succumbed to fluctuations that never settle into an identifiable pattern. As we will see a bit later, however, there is a subtle pattern emerging; that is, an *order within the disorder* or chaos.

The internal and external stressors that propel a system toward bifurcation are called "control parameters." Control parameters for a social system might include population, poverty, unemployment, education, etc. Changes in a system's parameters, if substantial enough to "push" the system to a critical value, will encourage the system to bifurcate and come increasingly under the influence of disorder. Thus, the stability of a society is largely dependent on that society's mechanisms for controlling its parameters. If poverty is kept "under control," for example, that society is less likely to evolve toward chaos because of poverty levels. If, however, the system is unable to "check" such economic influences, it may reach critical points at which it bifurcates and, consequentially, undergoes qualitative transformations from which it will be permanently affected.

Iteration, Sensitivity, and Bifurcation

We have thus far identified three principles associated with a system's transformation from an orderly state to one marked by disorder. In sum, the system's sensitivity is responsible for its vulnerability. Vulnerability, of course, is what allows internal and external factors or "stressors" to influence the stability of the system. Once destabilized in this way, the system's iterative nature encourages the disorder—resulting from the loss of stability—to build off of and upon itself. Thus, the amount of disorder present in the system may increase exponentially. At certain "critical points," the disorder is sufficient to force the system into a qualitative transformation. These transformations occur at what are called "period-doubling points" or bifurcations. If such bifurcations continue, the system becomes trapped in a cascade of bifurcations which propel it increasingly toward chaos. At some point, the system's behavior becomes apparently random and unpredictable, yet chaos theory identifies this disorder as indicative of a different sort of order; namely, order *within* chaos.

ORDER WITHIN CHAOS

Order within chaos describes a characteristic underlying the order within the disorder of nonlinear dynamical systems. The principles that explicate this characteristic are those largely responsible for postmodern understandings of chaos, not as extreme disorder, but as *orderly disorder* (see chapter 2 for more). Within the apparent randomness of behavior that systems in chaos display lies a governing attractor that maintains global, systemic order. The principles most identified with this phenomenon are those of the (strange) *attractor* and the *fractal*. The former describes precisely this process of governance; that is, the "attraction" of systemic behavior to certain patterns of movement. The latter, in turn, presents a "picture" of this pattern and describes the implications of unpredictable movement within a deterministic system.

Attractors

Attractors are patterns of stability that a system settles into over time (Goerner, 1994, p. 39). The term stability, while prima facie contradictory in light of our description of disorderly or chaotic systems, is in fact a defining characteristic of nonlinear dynamical systems in states of disorder. The counterintuitiveness of this statement is twofold: First, inherent instability is largely responsible for progression to and through states of disorder; and second, the descriptor "stable" is probably the last term we would think to use to describe a system which, upon initial examination, shows no signs of orderly conduct. Thus, we have seen only the ways in which stability is either not present or has been lost within a given system. The principle of attraction, however, shows us a different side of stability; namely, one that reveals itself in each of the evolutionary states of the system. Most importantly, the stability present in the *most* disorderly states of a system is, perhaps, the most significant and beneficial to any given system.

Briggs and Peat (1989, p. 36) refer to an attractor as "a region . . . which exerts a 'magnetic' appeal for a system, seemingly pulling the system toward it." Thus, attractors function exactly as one would expect: to *attract* the behavior of a system, thus producing order and stability. The quality of order, however, may be extremely complex. Attractors range from the very simple and stable, to those describing amazingly complex behavior that never repeats itself (chaos), yet, is marked by an underlying order. Nonlinear dynamical systems typically display one of four *patterns* of attraction. In other words, they "settle" into, or converge on, one of four identifiable behavioral configurations (Abraham et al., 1990). One should note that these patterns correspond to the various "stages" of order and disorder that are marked by the process of bifurcation. Each critical point brings upon a system a new pattern of order and a new quality of stability.

Behavioral trajectories of nonlinear dynamical systems tend to converge (from simple to complex) on one of four common attractors identified as: (a) discrete point, (b) simple oscillating cycle, (c) quasiperiodic cycle, or (d) chaotic cycle (Barton, 1994, p. 6). Those attractors "pulling" a system upon a discrete point are referred to as *single-point* or *fixed-point* attractors. The most common example of a point attractor is a pendulum. A pendulum that is in motion and not propelled further by some external force, will eventually come to rest. The point directly underneath the pendulum when it stops is such an attractor. It is a point which attracts the motion of the pendulum on each successive swing, bringing the pendulum to rest over that single point (Van Eenwyk, 1991, p. 6). The single point attractor governs the behavior of the pendulum (i.e., system) by "magnetically" pulling the pendulum toward itself. Thus, all movement (i.e., behavior) is attracted to a "single" point.

Attractors which pull a system into a simple oscillating cycle are referred to as *limit-cycle* attractors. Revisiting our pendulum illustration, then, if an external force (e.g., quartz crystal) were to keep the pendulum in motion such that it would never come to rest, it would continuously trace the same pattern of motion (Van Eenwyk, 1991, p. 7). Another example may be an attractor (magnet) at the bottom of a bowl which pulls a marble back and forth across the bowl (as opposed to a rest at the bottom of the bowl) (Butz, 1997, p. 12). A limit-cycle attractor reaches a steady, stable state, yet the state is marked by a repetition of motion—not a fixation of motion; thus, it encourages a "cycle" or cyclic path of movement.

The quasiperiodic attractor is called a *torus* attractor. A torus is a doughnut-shaped figure representing the movement of two limit-cycles interacting with one another (Briggs & Peat, 1989, p. 39). Returning once again to the pendulum example, we may visualize two pendulums interacting with one another, but driven by the same force (i.e., motor, quartz crystal). Either of the pendulum's movements alone will form a limit-cycle attractor. Together, however, the independent limit-cycles will become "fastened together" to create a torus (ibid.). We may also imagine a torus attractor as a pendulum which has been loosened in such a way that it can swing side to side as well as back and forth. Now, rather than a simple limit-cycle (i.e., back and forth) movement, we have a torus (i.e., back and forth as well as side to side movement). Together, the movement is governed by a pair of oscillators.

The final type of attractor, and perhaps the most important for chaos theory, is the *strange* attractor or the Lorenz attractor. This is the chaotic-cycle attractor. The dynamics of a chaotic system, unlike those that are discrete, oscillating, or quasiperiodic, are aperiodic; that is, they never trace the same path twice. Consequently, fixed, cyclic, and torus mapping does not capture the behavior of a chaotic system. When plotted, the behavior displays attraction to a different form; namely, the strange or "butterfly" attractor. Though it may be difficult to grasp the notion that *any* attraction occurs in a system which *never* repeats itself, the strange attractor, nonetheless, captures such a pattern: *it is an order within seemingly random disorder.* Van Eenwyk (1991, p. 7) refers to strange attractors as "the epitome of contradiction, never repeating, yet always resembling, itself: infinitely recognizable, never predictable."

Returning to the example of a marble in a bowl is useful. While the fixed-point attractor would attract the marble to a fixed point at the bottom of the bowl, the limit cycle would attract the marble back and forth across the bowl, and the torus would attract the marble around the bowl (all of which repeat specific patterns of movement), the strange attractor would "pull the marble all over the bowl in a complicated, apparently random, pattern" (Butz, 1997, p. 13). Nonetheless, there would be a pattern to the movement—but a *strange* one at that. The importance of the strange attractor is that its magnetic effect is nonlinear (ibid.). This is what separates it from the other three attractors. While nonlinear, and apparently random, the movement of the system is confined to certain parameters or global boundaries. For example, the marble cannot "leap" out of the bowl. Thus, even though unpredictable and (locally) disorderly, the behavior or movement still occurs *within* the (global) confines that the (strange) attractor places upon the system. Put another way, though seemingly random, unpredictable, irregular, and out-of-control (chaotic), with increasing repetition, the system reveals its boundaries; that is, its pattern emerges.

Attractors provide us with important descriptive illustrations of a system's behavior over time. As Butz (1997, p. 13) notes, "they indicate where a system is in its evolution across time and with regard to stability." Attractors allow us to conceptualize mentally and physically see the movement of a system in a stable, semi-stable, or chaotic state. Thus, attractors provide insight into system behavior by suggesting that systems are indeed attracted to a definable shape (i.e., quality of order); and that the shape to which they are attracted is indicative of the state of the system with regard to stability. The concept of attractors and their relation to one another becomes much more clear when considered in conjunction with bifurcations and the period-doubling route to chaos. Different states, marked by consecutive bifurcations, are governed by different attractors.

Bifurcation and Attraction

When a system is in a steady state (i.e., critical value of less than 3.0), it is governed by a single-point attractor. Thus, the attractor is pulling the behavior of the system to a single point or point of stasis. This is represented as a straight line. Following the first bifurcation (i.e., beyond a critical value of 3.0), the system moves into a cyclic (limit-cycle) attractor. The system is oscillating back and forth between two points. At the second critical point (3.45), the system again bifurcates and is governed by a quasi-periodic (torus) attractor. It is now oscillating between four states, as opposed to two observable states in the limit-cycle phase. Finally, when the system reaches the point of chaos (critical value of approximately 3.6), a strange attractor emerges. The system is now unpredictably "bouncing" between an endless variety of points, but always within the governance of an underlying order.

Thus, we can see how the system, over time and with increasing destabilization, continues to bifurcate upon reaching critical points. In each of these "phases" (i.e., the state characterizing the system between bifurcations), an attractor appears. The steady system is orderly, stabilized by the single-point attractor. The semi-stable system oscillates between two points (the limit-cycle phase). The system oscillating between four states is governed by the torus attractor. And, finally, the chaotic system is represented by the strange attractor. Attractors allow us to see how the system progresses through states of order to increasing disorder and eventually chaos. Within the context of orderly disorder, the most important is that of the strange attractor, which is indicative of chaotic, unpredictable, but entirely determined and globally orderly, states. As we subsequently explain, the strange attractor is also a fractal.

Fractals

Fractals "refer to a particular type of structure created by an iterative, self-referential process" (Goerner, 1994, p. 40). For our purposes, what is important in fractal geometry is dimensionality. Mathematically, fractals are composed of fractal space. Rather than simply having one-, two- or three-dimensionality, a fractal form can have a dimension of 1.2, 2.3 or some other non-integer value (i.e. they have a *fractional* dimension) (ibid.). This fractional dimensionality has two implications: (a) a fractal is indicative of *infinite complexity*; and (b) its measurement depends on *scale*. The former is a product of the iterative generation of its form and its related self-similarity, the latter naturally follows from the complexity emanating from the fractal.

The infinite complexity of the fractal is best described by way of examples from nature. In fact, fractals are representative of most naturally occurring forms. Mountains, snowflakes, clouds, and trees all exemplify the fractal form. What each has in common is a scaled self-similar layering. In other words, "finer and finer magnification of the fractal reveals smaller and smaller versions of the same structure at all levels" (Goerner, 1994, p. 41). Thus, the form of any layer of the fractal is a microcosm of the whole and, thus, of equal complexity (ibid.). The reason for this "layering" and "self-similarity" refers us back to the concepts of iteration and bifurcation.

In short, because iteration builds, not only *on* itself, but also *off of* itself, its new growth is representative of that which existed before. The bifurcation is important because it forces the system to "branch." The branching that occurs at bifurcation (i.e., when disorder brings the system to a critical point), creates a new region which is a smaller version of the whole. When a tree branches, for example, it creates a smaller version of its whole. This process is *adaptive* in that it generates a new stability; that is, prior to branching, the tree had that much less room to grow. With increased room to move, the tree once again becomes stable yet in a more complex way. Thus, the self-similar development of the fractal that occurs at bifurcation and following the system's inability to adapt under its previous state of order, generates even greater complexity. This complexity is most obvious—and most inhibiting for observers—when factored into the measuring process needed to *define* the form under observation.

It is within the context or possibility of measurement that we find the importance of *scaling*. Because fractals are infinitely complex in light of self-similar development, precisely measuring a fractal's form is infinitely complex. The measurement of a fractal depends on scale. Similar to Einstein's objection to Newtonian assumptions about objective observation, scale-dependent measurement tells us that "the world will not only look different to two observers at different scales, it will also measure differently"

(Goerner, 1994, p. 41). In other words, "the measurement you get depends on the size of your ruler . . ." (ibid.). This is perhaps best understood through the classic example of measuring a coastline as a fractal:

> A surveyor takes a set of dividers, opens them to a length of one yard, and walks them along the coastline. The resulting number of yards is just an approximation of the true length, because the dividers skip over twists and turns smaller than one yard, but the surveyor writes the number down anyway. Then he sets the dividers to a smaller length—say, one foot—and repeats the process. He arrives at a somewhat greater length because the dividers will capture more of the detail and it will take more than three one-foot steps to cover the distance previously covered by a one-yard step.

Each successive measurement using a smaller ruler will increase the length of the coastline, ad infinitum. Thus, mathematically, since numbers (i.e., units of measurement) can be infinitely small, the length of the coastline is infinitely long.

Fractals, then, are characterized by infinite detail as a result of their iterative process of generation and the resulting self-similarity of the structure on successively smaller scales of observation. Consequently, the scale-dependency of measurement provides the fractal with an infinite length. Though seemingly confined by a finite area, the fractal provides infinite space for movement within that area. Though a tree may never grow more than ten feet in height, three feet in width, and five feet in depth, it can "twist and turn" endlessly within that finite area. It is limited by a global order, but unlimited in local freedom.

Fractals and Strange Attractors

We have said that the strange attractor is a fractal. Systems in a state of chaos, governed by a strange attractor, are also fractal and, thus, self-similar. The strange attractor, then, might be thought of as nature's way of allowing the endless movement within a fractal space to always stay within some global pattern of behavior. Though somewhat counterintuitive, the infinite complexity and endless possibility engendered by the fractal is, nonetheless, governed by some "higher power." We have said that this higher power is the strange attractor. To illustrate, when "stretching" taffy on a confection machine, we are assured that any two "spots" of taffy that began in close proximity to one another will eventually stray quite far apart; that is, their precise relationship will be unpredictable. By "folding" the taffy back onto itself, however, the machine assures us that no "spot" of taffy will stray too far. The "stretching and folding" process is that of iteration and, while contributing to the disorder within the system, it is also responsible for the global order of the system. This folding back upon itself effects a self-similar, fractal structure whose local behavior (i.e., any one "taffy spot") will be unpredictable, but whose global behavior is determined by its "attraction" to the machine itself. Had the machine more closely governed the extent to which the taffy could move, it would exemplify a different variety of attractor and, consequently, would not facilitate the emergence of fractal space.

The antithesis of the fractal space that emerges from the strange attractor is, perhaps, embedded in the orderly system governed by the point attractor. By contrasting movement within a fractal to that within a nonfractal form, we see the (positive) significance that chaos theory ascribes to *disorder* in the dynamics of systems. If a system is bound by a nonfractal form (e.g., point attractor), it is wholly governed by imposed laws or rules of movement. The potential behavior of that system is extendable only so far as the structured, defined form allows. Consequently, there is no room for movement outside and/or beyond that which the laws allow. If, however, the system was in a state of sufficient disorder, governed by the strange attractor and behaving within a fractal space, it would enjoy a certain freedom not present under other attractors and within nonfractal forms. The contours of the system provide it the opportunity to move beyond that which would be permissible in the nonfractal form. Its behavior is able to be more complex without being completely random and uncontrollable. It demonstrates *order within disorder,* or *orderly disorder.* More importantly, however, it allows the system to adapt and a new "strange" order to emerge with time.

ORDER OUT OF CHAOS

We have thus far described the principles responsible for the transition of a system from an orderly state to a disorderly state, and further depicted the underlying order which lurks beneath the perceptible disorder of such systemic states. Our final theme in this chapter is to describe the emergence of a new global order following periods of disorder and chaos. This process is attributable to the chaos theory principles termed self-organization and dissipation. Each contributes to the notion of order out of chaos, and order within chaos. Thus, the final two principles should not be read as mutually exclusive processes. Self-organization generally describes a new, more adaptive order that issues from periods of temporary disorder. Dissipation similarly informs us that systems tend to seek a certain balance by adapting to the buildup of disorder at far-from-equilibrium conditions.

Self-organization

A characteristic of nonlinear dynamical systems that encourages order rather than disorder is self-organization. Pioneered by Ilya Prigogine in the late 1960s and fully developed in his collaborative text, *Order Out of Chaos* (Prigogine & Stengers, 1984), the approach (i.e., theory) focuses on the order that in fact emerges out of chaos. Barton (1994, p. 7) describes self-organization as "a process by which a structure or pattern emerges in an open system without specifications from the outside environment." In other words, a system which is open (i.e., in constant interaction with its environment) may display an order which is *generated from within,* independent of influences from without. Davies (1989, p. 501) describes it as a "spontaneous emergence of order, arising when certain parameters built in a system reach critical values." Thus, when a system reaches a state or level of disorder, it may "spontaneously" self-organize into a new, more complex order (Butz, 1992, p. 1052).

The concept is similar to what Kauffman (1991) refers to as *antichaos.* Kauffman describes a necessary *transitory* stage between periods of order, a stage that is marked by disorder. In this sense, disorder performs a *necessary* and *beneficial* function in pushing a system from an obsolete adaptive state of order, to a "more flexible contemporary adaptive state" (Butz, 1992, p. 1052). This process is referred to as *order-chaos-order.* Thus, disorder executes the necessary role of forcing an orderly but stagnant system (i.e., an antiquated form of order) into a new, more adaptive order necessary to meet the changing demands of the evolving system in relation to its external and internal environment.

Prigogine recognized the process of self-organization when studying systems at *far-from-equilibrium* conditions, or, conditions created when a system is subjected to "great deal[s] of energy input from the outside" (Briggs & Peat, 1989, p. 136). What Prigogine found was that at far-from-equilibrium conditions, systems do not only break down, but new systems emerge (ibid.). This is the (re)organization of the system upon reaching critical levels of disorder. One of the most commonly cited examples of self-organization at work is the "chemical clock" described by Prigogine and Stengers (1984, pp. 147–148):

> Suppose we have two kinds of molecules, "red" and "blue." Because of the chaotic motion of the molecules, we would expect that at a given moment we would have more red molecules, say, in the left part of the vessel. Then a bit later more blue molecules would appear, and so on. The vessel would appear to us as "violet," with occasional irregular flashes of red and blue. However, this is *not* what happens with a chemical clock; here the system is all blue, then it abruptly changes its color to red, then again to blue. Because all these changes occur at *regular* time intervals, we have a coherent process.

This degree of order stemming from the activity of billions of molecules seems incredible and, indeed, if phenomena such as chemical clocks had not provided visual evidence, we might justifiably remain skeptics. To change color all at once, molecules must have a way to "communicate." The system has to act as a whole. The idea that systems in chaos may communicate or "interact" from within is radical and profound for nonlinear dynamics. In times of chaos, the elements of a system interact—without help from the outside—to form a new order. The concept is not so foreign to those of us who have driven on interstates. Consider the following:

> Driving between rush hours on the thruway, we're only minimally affected by other vehicles. But toward 4 o'clock, traffic becomes heavier and we begin to react and interact with the other drivers. At a certain critical point we begin to be "driven" by the total traffic pattern. The traffic has become a self-organizing system. (Briggs and Peat, 1989, p. 138)

Again, the implication is that "*out of chaos a new stability forms*" (Butz, 1997, p. 14). Further, as we have previously noted, it appears that periods of chaos are *necessary* for new adaptive, stable states to be reached. The necessity of chaos makes sense if you consider that the system was so disturbed by external forces that instability and chaos ensued. Given this understanding, we can assume that the system was not sufficiently adaptive to "handle" the forces. Thus, the process of stability to chaos to self-organization is necessary.

The interrelation of all the principles of chaos theory thus far enumerated may begin to appear evident at this point. Indeed, natural instability creates a vulnerability to disruptive stimuli which, having perturbed the system, encourage stress or disorder to "build up" within the system. The iterative nature of nonlinear dynamical systems assists this disorder in continuing to build off of and on itself. Upon reaching a critical point of disorder, the system bifurcates—its behavior becoming increasingly unpredictable and falling under the governance of one of four attractors. The strange attractor, operative once the system has reached a state of sufficient disorder, dictates the global behavior of the system while allowing local disorder to continue. The system becomes redefined in terms of fractal dimensionality, wherein it enjoys an endless degree of movement within a finite space. In part, the benefit of this freedom is that it allows the system room to grow, adapt, and reorganize into a more complex system capable of sustaining a greater degree of stress from within and without. In short, the system self-organizes into a "stronger" system.

Dissipative Structures

Dissipation refers to a dispersion of energy. For conceptual purposes, energy and disorder are analogous. The amount of disorder in a system is understood as the amount of energy in the system. To understand the concept of dissipation, we need to diverge momentarily and discuss energy and thermodynamics.

The second law of thermodynamics states that disorder always increases. The amount of energy in a system is always increasing because of the process of *autocatalysis*, that is, the participation of energy in reactions in which they are necessary for further production of their own kind (see, e.g., Jantsch, 1980). Conceptually, this process is analogous to iteration. Autocatalysis, along with cross-catalysis and autoinhibition, involve processes in which the "products of some steps feed back into their own production or inhibition" (Briggs & Peat, 1989, p. 140). In terms of chaos theory, the disorder in a system produces more disorder because of the iterative nature of the system—it builds off of and on itself.

Because the disorder is feeding off of itself, and consequently always increasing, the system must be able to order itself or dispel some of the energy so that autocatalytic self-reproduction does not blow it into pieces (Jantsch, 1980). This is the process of dissipation. Dissipative structures are open systems in constant and continual interaction with their environment. Thus, they continually take in energy from the outside and produce energy which they dissipate back into the environment. This energy produced from within is called *entropy*. Entropy is essentially waste, or excess energy in a system. Thus, iteration produces a continual increase in energy, an unnecessary quantity or an excess of entropy. Dissipative structures, then, must continuously dissipate the entropy into the environment while taking in energy from the environment.

Dissipative systems occur at far-from-equilibrium conditions for order to emerge beyond instability thresholds (Jantsch, 1980). If they occur at near-equilibrium condition, order is destroyed and so is the system. Far-from-equilibrium conditions are what bring the order out of chaos; that is, the *new, more adaptive order*. This brings us to one, final point regarding chaos systems, worthy of some brief mention. This is the notion of *irreversibility*. This concept logically follows the preceding discussion. In essence, it refers to the fact that systems can never return to a previous (i.e., the same) state of order. Living organisms and open, evolving systems must adapt to the structural changes that occur with time (Butz, 1997, p. 15). "Despite one's wishes, a 50-year-old man cannot turn back into a 20-year-old man . . ." (ibid.). As Butz (1997, p. 15) accurately sums:

> The reason for this is time, and the changes that occur across time at far-from-equilibrium conditions. As adaptations occur, the structure of the organism changes to accommodate these adaptations, and as such these changes cannot be reversed or undone . . . [T]ime is irreversible and so are developmental processes.

Thus, the system has progressed from order, to chaos, and has self-organized, generating a new, more complex, and adaptive order. There is never a return to the original order. This new organization is not a negative consequence of chaos. The new order that emerges with time is theoretically better that what preceded it; that is, it leaves the system more prepared to manage the forces (also new and changing with time) that will inevitably attempt to disrupt it.

SUMMARY

This chapter described the principles that constitute chaos theory. We have attempted to address them in such a way as to show the progression of a system from order, to chaos, and back to order. We have discussed the concepts of: (a) *iteration*—a self-reinforcing characteristic of nonlinear dynamical systems; (b) *bifurcations and period-doubling points*—"forks" in the route to chaos; (c) *sensitive dependence on initial conditions*—the idea that small differences in input can quickly produce enormous differences in output; (d) *attractors* (point, cyclic, quasiperiodic, and strange)—a point or set of points that draws a system's behavior to it; (e) *fractals*—self-similar geometric structures that are infinitely complex; (f) *self-organization*—the idea that systems in a state of chaos can spontaneously organize themselves to a new, more complex and adaptive order; and (g) *dissipation*—the dispersion of energy in an open relationship with the environment.

Each principle or characteristic assumes a role in either propelling a system toward chaos, generating order within chaos, or establishing an emerging order out of chaos. In reality, many of these principles apply equally to systems at all stages throughout the process. This will become clearer over the course of our investigation of mental health law. However elementary, the overview undertaken in this chapter clearly discloses how chaos theory and its principles dramatically affect natural (and social) systems. It remains to be seen, however, how these principles can be seamlessly applied to those controversies posed by psychology and law, self and society. We now turn to these matters.

PART TWO

The Controversial

CHAPTER FOUR

The Meaning of Mental Illness

OVERVIEW. *In this chapter we critically explore the meaning of mental illness. We do this in several ways. First, we examine the legal definition of mental illness and its role in shaping juridical decision making. Although we are fundamentally concerned with how the legal meaning of psychiatric illness impacts civil commitment determinations, we also briefly compare how this understanding relates to legal findings of the same in criminal adjudication matters. Next, we consider how psychology examines or defines the concept of mental illness. We then explore the limits of legal and psychological approaches to this phenomenon. Given this necessary background, we then apply selected principles of chaos theory to an assessment of mental illness. In other words, we intend to explore the existence (or nonexistence) of mental illness in the psycholegal sphere, informed by nonlinear dynamics, and to consider what this particular understanding of psychiatric illness tells us about prospects for justice in society.*

LEGAL DEFINITIONS OF MENTAL ILLNESS

The concept of mental illness in the legal system varies slightly, depending on the purpose for which it is employed. Two of the most common situations in which a determination of mental illness is necessary are insanity defenses and civil commitment proceedings. The definition of mental illness is somewhat different in each context (i.e., the former is a criminal matter, and the latter is a civil concern). Given that civil commitment will be a recurring theme throughout Part II (e.g., chapter 5 on dangerousness; chapter 7 on treatment refusal), we will be emphasizing the noncriminal dimensions of psychiatric illness. We note, however, that in order to examine appropriately the different approaches the legal system takes toward a determination of mental disease or defect, a brief review of its role in the criminal sphere (i.e., insanity defenses) is warranted.

All tests of insanity or MSO (mental state at the time of the offense) evaluations require a finding of "mental disease or defect" (Perlin, 1994). Each of the standards for determining whether a defendant is "insane" (i.e., McNaughtan, Durham, Substantial Capacity, and Federal standards) has as a prerequisite that the individual be suffering from a mental disorder. Additionally, the mental disease or defect must have assumed a causal role in the commission of the offense (Melton et al., 1997, p. 195). Generally speaking, the term "mental disease" is synonymous with "mental illness" and "mental defect" with mental retardation (ibid.). In determining the presence of a mental illness, the law has historically relied on the medical model for guidance (Arrigo, 1996; Scull, 1989). In other words, psychiatric disorders are presumed to have a physical, internal basis (e.g., chemical imbalance, neurological impairment), thus rendering the defendant incapable of arriving independently at rational decisions concerning her or his actions. The underlying premise with this approach is that a physical basis makes the disorder beyond the individual's immediate control and, consequently, the defendant should not be held legally responsible for any criminal behaviors caused under these circumstances.

The medical paradigm is supported with more recent findings suggesting that mental illnesses (e.g., schizophrenia, bipolar disorder, and major depression) result from brain and/or biochemical abnormalities such as chemical imbalances (Arrigo, 1993a, pp. 13–17). Historically, most successful insanity defenses have been based on the presence of either psychosis (e.g., schizophrenia) or mental retardation (e.g., Goldstein, 1967; Perlin, 1994; Steadman et al., 1993). Thus, the legal community has continued to regard mental illness, in cases of the insanity defense, as a "sickness" that is more rightfully considered a medical condition (Szasz, 1987). While this model may rule out certain cases of pure psychological impairment (i.e., conditions without a physical basis) as *not* constitutive of psychiatric disease for juridical purposes, it still does not conclusively define the term. Indeed, the lack of consensus regarding the mental illness construct in relation to the insanity defense becomes even more apparent when noting that a number of jurisdictions have found that the presence of personality disorders and certain "syndromes" are sufficient for a successful insanity defense and acquittal (Melton et al., 1997, pp. 196–217).

For purposes of civil commitment, however, the term "mental illness" assumes a slightly different meaning than its use in the context of an insanity defense. Indeed, the criminal and civil definitions differ specifically in their respective purposes. The former is invoked as a legal defense by a presumably mentally ill person as a way to thwart wrongful criminal conviction. The latter is invoked by the State to justify involuntary hospitalization so that a presumably mentally ill person can receive much needed treatment.

Several commentators have noted that the legal and psychiatric communities favor a *presumption* of mental illness (e.g., Arrigo, 1993a; Scheff, 1984; Warren, 1982), when civil commitment determinations are in issue. Since involuntary hospitalization is intended to protect the individual either from harming him or herself, or from harming others in the community (Reisner & Slobogin, 1997), observers note that more latitude is justified when determining whether one is or is not mentally ill. The effects of such latitude, however, have been anything but justifiable. Indeed, legislative attempts to define mental illness have spawned more criticism and confusion than clarity and precision. Efforts to operationalize the construct have been woefully lacking, given definitional vagueness, circularity, and a general lack of limitations (Winick, 1995; Arrigo, 1992a, 1996; see also *Dusky v. United States*, 1960). For example, consider the following legal definition of mental illness from a 1982 Texas statute: "A mentally ill person is a person whose mental health is substantially impaired" (Melton et al., 1997, p. 307). This definition is unclear in that it could describe no one and everyone at the same time. More importantly, it is circular. Mental illness is established without providing any sense of what it is beyond reference to it (i.e., substantially impaired). Further, the term "mental health" as employed here is meaningless without some other construct of mental illness against which to judge it. While most legislatures (including Texas) have subsequently set forth more specific definitions, there remains a demonstrable and troubling degree of generality and, most often, a tautological component in most statutory definitions (e.g., Arrigo, 1993a, 1993b; Arrigo & Williams, 1999a; Winick, 1995).

Notwithstanding ambiguity and lack of specificity, the law has done little to provide detailed and operationally effective meaning for the construct of mental illness (Winick, 1995). Efforts undertaken by the law employ overly generic and broad categorizations or terminology that succumb to vagueness. For example, describing a person as mentally ill who is found incapable of meeting the "ordinary demands of life" (Melton et al., 1997, p. 307), requires that the phrase, "ordinary demands of life," be given clear and thorough explication. Unfortunately, this is rarely, if ever, accomplished in the legal arena. Rather, the precise meaning of mental illness is often left to the discretion of others. Indeed, the legislature's failed attempts to provide accurate definitions has left a void in state statutes, leaving individual courts with the responsibility of fashioning a definition for themselves (Arrigo,

1992a, p. 142). Generally, courts have decided to render determinations of mental illness on a case-by-case basis, informed only by the vague and general legislative guidelines provided by that particular jurisdiction (Perlin, 1999).

The problem courts confront, however, extends beyond definitional precision to an individual's Constitutional rights. In other words, "reasonably clear guidelines" (*Smith v. Goguen*, 1974, pp. 572–573) are necessary before the State can intrude upon individual liberty, including abridging one's freedom from restraint and unwanted invasions of body and mind. Recognizing that mental illness determinations potentially give rise to a host of intrusions (e.g., civil commitment, involuntary psychotrobic treatment), we submit that definitional precision with mental illness is absolutely necessary. Indeed, courts cannot and should not arrive at such decisions in an arbitrary or capricious manner (Arrigo, 1996). In response to this definitional dilemma, state courts have generally seen fit to rely upon the expertise of mental health professionals (psychiatrists, psychologists) for constructive input, arguably providing clarity on the meaning of mental illness and, thus, advancing the interests of (citizen) justice (Arrigo, 1993a).

We note that the law's relationship with psychology begins with this most fundamental of questions. Indeed, courts typically seek evidence or testimony from the mental health community, regarding the existence of mental illness in particular cases (Perlin, 1999). Interestingly, however, this deference establishes a certain dependency. In short, the law defers to psychology in matters that are, fundamentally, legal (Holstein, 1993; Scull, 1989; Warren, 1982). Thus, the expert opinion of mental health professionals becomes the decisive factor in most cases where mental illness determinations are in issue (Winick, 1995). While this reliance seems appropriate, the process is not without controversy, most notably in the area of definitional precision and clarity. Indeed, the psychiatric and psychological communities have displayed anything but consensus on the meaning of mental illness. In fact, medicine has pursued for centuries a more accurate explanation for psychiatric disease than has the law; however, its results have been no less discouraging (Scheff, 2000). With this in mind, we now turn to the psychological construct of mental illness and its impact on the law.

PSYCHOLOGICAL DEFINITIONS OF MENTAL ILLNESS

Psychiatry and psychology often use the term "mental illness" in a very broad sense to refer to a multitude of circumstances whose presence (or absence) amounts to a "treatable" situation or life condition. The meaning of mental illness in the psychological profession is very different from its significance in the legal community. In short, mental health professionals employ the term for purposes of evaluating, diagnosing and subsequently treating any number of disease or deficiency-based human ailments. The broad connotations of mental illness often serve a positive function; namely, they advance a certain inclusivity encompassing physiological problems (i.e., schizophrenia) as well as more general sociocultural concerns (e.g., depression). This inclusiveness assists the profession in making mental health treatment possible in psychiatric/psychological areas that might not otherwise constitute mental illness in a legal context.

For example, the *Diagnostic and Statistical Manual of Mental Disorders* (DSM-IV) (American Psychiatric Association, 1994) recognizes substance abuse as a form of mental illness, provided that certain diagnostic criteria are met. In the juridical sphere, however, the majority of State statutes specify that drug and/or alcohol abuse are not to be considered forms of mental illness for purposes of legal inquiry. Thus, in the interest of helpful intervention or treatment, recognizing substance abuse as a mental illness is conducive to the therapeutic aspirations of mental health professionals. Indeed, it allows a person experiencing a certain, identifiable condition to be treated. It is therefore in the interest of both clinicians and clients to conceive of mental illness as an "elastic" or overly inclusive concept (Winick, 1995, p. 554).

The American Psychiatric Association (1994) provides a working definition of "mental disorder" with the cautionary warning that ". . . no definition adequately specifies precise boundaries for the concept . . . [and] . . . like many other concepts in medicine and science, [it] lacks a consistent operational definition that covers all situations" (p. xxi). The diagnostic manual states that each of the included mental disorders "is conceptualized as a clinically significant behavioral or psychological syndrome or pattern that occurs in an individual and is associated with present distress or disability or with a significantly increased risk of suffering death, pain, disability, or an important loss of freedom . . . [which] must not be merely an expectable and culturally sanctioned response to a particular event" (ibid.). The DSM-IV excludes deviant behavior and conflicts that are "primarily between the individual and society . . . [unless] the deviance or conflict is a symptom of a dysfunction in the individual. . . ." (ibid.).

It is clear from this brief statement that mental illness is something of a pliant concept with clinical undertones. In other words, the use of the phrase "clinically significant" ensures that the definition covers certain wide-ranging conditions or experiential realities that provide the possibility of amenability to therapeutic and/or drug treatment. Thus, it is evident that psychology's conceptualization of mental illness benefits the psychological profession and their clients and is not intended to serve as a conceptual foundation for forensic purposes. Indeed, it is intentionally elastic, covering an array of possible behaviors, thought patterns, feelings, and so on, so that the mental health community may best serve its prospective patient population.

Psychiatry, however, has also, on occasion, developed position statements regarding the meaning of mental illness, specifically for forensic purposes. For example, when defining mental illness in relation to the insanity defense, the American Psychiatric Association noted that "the terms mental disease and mental retardation include only those severely abnormal mental conditions that grossly and demonstrably impair a person's perception or understanding of reality. . . ." (APA, 1982; Melton et al., 1997, p. 196). Thus, the proposed definition of mental illness in the forensic context is significantly more narrow.

Overall, however, we recognize that the psychological/psychiatric definitions of mental illness differ from their legal counterpart. Indeed, the mental health community understands the limits and dangers of adopting a broad and general (i.e., imprecise) description for the mental illness construct, especially when such indications are questioned in a court of law (Winick, 1995). In short, though, there is a clear difference between the psychological approach to mental illness and the legal approach. Mental illness refers to two different psychological states (i.e., syndrome/pattern of distress/disability and abnormal mental condition) in two different contexts (i.e., clinical and forensic). Given these realities, one might expect that the law would fashion its own definition(s) of mental illness, without deferring to the vagaries of the psychological community. Unfortunately, its failure to do so has contributed significantly to various critical appraisals of this psycholegal phenomenon, including the assessment that follows.

LIMITATIONS OF THE LEGAL AND PSYCHOLOGICAL DEFINITIONS OF MENTAL ILLNESS

The imprecision of legal definitions for mental illness and the over-inclusiveness of psychological conceptualizations for the same have far-reaching implications for the law-psychology interface. When psychological "experts" are given the power to make decisions that are theoretically legal in nature, there is a fundamental erosion of the justice system. Winick (1995, p. 555) notes that the breadth and imprecision of legislative attempts to define mental illness ". . . allow and mask arbitrariness and discrimination in the application of the law." The inherent capriciousness and unfairness found in legal determinations are compounded by the lack of specificity contained in psychological definitions, producing ". . . unavoidably ambiguous generalities in which [psychology] describes its diagnostic categories, [such that] the diagnostician has the ability to shoehorn into the mentally diseased class almost any person he [sic] wishes, for whatever reason . . ." (Livermore et al., 1968, p. 80). These are serious limitations, impacting the administration of (citizen) justice in the psycholegal sphere.

We note that deficiencies with legislative attempts to define mental illness are fully acknowledged by the legal system. Indeed, the fact that mental health specialists are called upon to provide forensic expertise (e.g., perform evaluations, develop diagnoses, testify as to one's mental status), makes painfully apparent the failure of the court system to assess fairly and adequately mental illness (Arrigo, 1996). Thus, we question whether the substitution of legal authority with expert knowledge is sufficient to ensure citizen justice.

We submit that the answer, in part, is found within the mental health community itself. Indeed, the DSM-IV includes a cautionary statement concerning its use in forensic settings:

> When the DSM-IV categories, criteria, and textual descriptions are employed for forensic purposes, there are significant risks that diagnostic information will be misused or misunderstood. These dangers arise because of the imperfect fit between the questions of ultimate concern to the law and the information contained in clinical diagnosis. In most cases, the clinical diagnosis of a DSM-IV mental disorder is not sufficient to establish the existence for legal purposes of a "mental disorder," "mental disability," "mental disease," or "mental defect." (APA, 1994, p. xxiii)

This statement has profound implications for decision making at the crossroads of law and psychology, particularly when the former defers to the latter for guidance in matters psychiatric. Not only does the legal system recognize its failure to produce a precise and, therefore, effective description for the mental illness construct, the psychological community acknowledges

the limits of its own standards when forensic questions are at issue. However, is this APA caveat exercised by psychologists performing forensic
evaluations, and is it embraced by those courts employing mental health
specialists who perform such assessments? As Melton et al. (1997, p. 197)
maintain: ". . . lawyers and judges often ignore DSM-IV's cautionary
injunction and demand that an expert give a diagnosis even when it is
not particularly helpful, in the belief that, without one, no 'mental disease or defect' exists." Thus, despite the limits of psychology's role in the
legal system—limits clearly recognized by both professional communities—
courts continue to rely on psychological input and, more significantly,
input that is often inconsistent with the goals of the legal system itself.

Where does this leave the law-psychology relationship? The answer to
this question is the focus of our subsequent critique. In short, the connection
between the two (e.g., psycholegal definitions of mental illness for forensic
purposes) is more uncertain now than ever before (Arrigo, 2000a). The
debates waged by the seeming lack of effective consensus have spawned a
number of social welfare problems, resulting, in the extreme, in the abandonment of persons with psychiatric disorders (e.g., Arrigo, 1993a; Isaac &
Armat, 1990; LaFond & Durham, 1992). Thus, we are led to ask the following: Does psychology have a role in responding to a question that is essentially legal? Why has the law been so unsuccessful in establishing a mental
illness definition of its own? Does a satisfactory conceptualization for this
construct even exist? We contend that chaos theory can provide some
helpful insights into these matters. Accordingly, we now turn to nonlinear
dynamical systems theory for direction in the controversial and contentious
matter of mental illness and its meaning.

CHAOS THEORY AND THE MEANING OF MENTAL ILLNESS

The element of chaos theory that turns to fractal geometry for instruction
into the nature of phenomena offers, perhaps, the most compelling story of
meaning in any context. Meaning is a timeless and enduring concept present in every culture and in every historical epoch (though philosophical
inquiries into "meaning" per se are a more recent phenomenon). The question of meaning or sense-making is related to inquiries about knowledge
and Truth in that meaning essentially considers what we know of ourselves,
what we know of the world, and, further, how this knowing is expressed,
understood, and used for human purposes. In our present age, the world is

often described through the use of words and other symbols. Thus, the question becomes: "What is the relationship between words and the world?" In other words, what does the expression "mental illness" tell us about the world we confront?

Accordingly, we maintain that the meaning of mental illness is fundamentally an issue of knowledge concerning psychological "being" employed for purposes of understanding an individual's reality. As such, it is best understood as a *fractal* phenomenon; that is, a reality that shares much with the lived nature of all things subject to human interpretation. We note that our application of nonlinear dynamical systems theory to the meaning of mental illness only addresses the chaos principal of fractal geometry. It is our contention that understanding meaning as an interpretive and flexible phenomenon best prepares the reader for the analysis in the subsequent sections of this chapter. At the outset, we wish to be clear: the fractal of chaos theory is not being used as a conceptual or methodological device by which some undisclosed Truth about the nature of mental health or illness will be suddenly revealed. Our position is that understanding the fractal nature of mental health serves only to bolster, if not extend, existing perspectives on its reality in relation to the social world of which it is a part.

Fractal Law: The Geometric Dimensions of "Health"

Geometry is about space. It intends to grasp such spatial phenomena as points, lines, angles, and surfaces in a way that allows for measurement and understanding of the properties of those phenomena. If one desires to understand the spatial relationship of a tree within the context of the greater area in which it lives, one traditionally relies on geometric theory and formulae. Measuring the space occupied by that tree, for example, requires that one approach it from the right perspective, remain conscious of the "unseen" portions that also assume space. More importantly, as chaos theory suggests, one must be aware that the tree does not exist in a perfect, three-dimensional world that may be accurately estimated by traditional geometric theorems or postulates. Rather, the space occupied by the tree depends, to a large extent, on the perspective one assumes in setting out to measure it.

Given this logic, we may also set out to measure or estimate the "space" that "mental illness" (or any illness for that matter) assumes in the larger context of "health." This chapter is about defining mental illness; that is, measuring it so as to understand its relationship in the larger social context (e.g., psycholegal sphere) in which mental illness exists. As we will see, however, measuring (and, thus, defining) this concept is not as simple as applying a standard geometric formula. Rather, much like the tree, we must be conscious of perspective. This being said, we will explore what we take to be several significant features of the mental illness-space relationship. In short, we will assess the geometric element of mental illness in society, psychology, and the law.

Presumptions of Objectivity and Absolute Truth

From the Enlightenment onward, meaning has been generally regarded as something to be uncovered. Thus it follows that the meaning of mental illness has always been thought to exist in a very certain, precise form. One's endeavors, then, should be directed toward scientifically investigating and subsequently revealing what this true meaning is. If it can be determined that mental illness refers, for example, to a condition related to an abundance of a given neurotransmitter in the brain, then we can define a mentally ill person as one who meets that requirement. Theoretically, however, while this approach promises a world in which understanding, prediction, and control will prevail, the reality is that mental illness and its meaning are not prone to willing, accommodating scientific retrievability and scrutiny. As Margolis (1980, p. 9) explains: "The idea that medicine . . . can claim to *discover* the natural norms or normative functions of human beings clearly depends on a premise that has yet to be supplied. . . ." In short, we have yet to discover or uncover completely or precisely the organic functioning of human beings—whether physical or psychological—such that a classificatory system based on these natural truth findings can be implemented. Indeed, the operation of the world as a *fractal* suggests that there may be no uncoverable, absolute truths. Rather, as Protagoras, the pre-Socratic sophist, once noted, "Man is the measure of all things" (Wheelwright, 1966, p. 239). Consistent with this and other historical accounts regarding the relative nature of phenomena, chaos theory supplements Protagoras's position, demonstrating how reality is a less-than-certain, less-than-objective experience.

Similarly, the legal system operates under the assumption of objective criteria for establishing certain truths (e.g., one is guilty or not guilty, competent or incompetent). These truths are organized as binary oppositions.

Essentially, they circumscribe existing reality within predetermined categories or "schemes of convenience" (Margolis, 1980, p. 6), and are introduced, not as demarcating absolute divisions of reality, but as promoting a necessary expedience (e.g., Boorse, 1975). To illustrate, a defendant can be either guilty or not guilty but not greater than, less than, or in between the two. For the legal system to function in an efficient and effective manner, these mechanisms of convenience are deemed necessary and appropriate.

This same logic applies to a determination of mental illness. According to the laws of mental health, an individual can either be ill or not ill (Arrigo, 1996). Falling into one or the other category can amount to liberty or its loss in a civil and/or criminal context. As we argued previously, however, the imprecision associated with the legal criteria for mental illness creates a situation in which no absolute method exists for ascertaining who falls into which category. This notwithstanding, the fluency with which the system operates depends on this classificatory scheme. In this instance, the inexactness of the law and its definition of mental illness conflicts with its own philosophy; that is, there is a need for organization, yet there is a failure to organize effectively. Why is there so much confusion?

Recall that chaos theory describes fractals as forms which are infinitely detailed. While confined to a finite area, closer examination reveals a reality which is infinite and immeasurable. The complexity of the fractal's form makes measurement, certainty, and absolute knowledge about its contents an impossible task. While mental "being" can never transcend natural boundaries (though the limits of these boundaries have yet to be ascertained), the play of difference within those boundaries is infinite. There exist endless possibilities for movement, endless qualities or states of being, and endless ways of measuring those states. To be sure, we can safely say that no two people are exactly alike. For example, if we attempted to place individuals into predefined categories of "healthy" or "ill," we would be met with a limited degree of success. Instead, it is better to describe this binary tension as a continuum with the two extremes representing the natural limits that humans experience psychologically. However, between these two polarities, we have an infinite range of variety, diversity, and ways-of-being, where no two persons are identified as absolutely similar. In other words, chaos theory tells us that mental health and mental illness do not exist per se. Rather, the fractal nature of psychological existence indicates that *there are only degrees of mental being* (Butz, 1997).

In their search for uncontested objectivity and absolute precision, both the legal and psychological communities embrace certain assumptions.

In particular, following the medical model of psychiatry, they accept that mental illness categorically exists, and that it is qualitatively and identifiably different from mental health (Al-Issa, 1982, p. 17; Arrigo & Williams, 1999a). To refute these assumptions, or, at least, to challenge the prevailing truths to which these assumptions have led, one need only consider the lack of contrast found between certain persons involuntarily hospitalized and their nonhospitalized counterparts. For example, Braginsky, Braginsky, and Ring (1969), upon observing schizophrenics on chronic wards, noted that "they did not appear to us to be the disoriented, dependent, and socially inept creatures that the textbooks described" (p. 29). Thus it follows, that if mental illness were qualitatively and identifiably different from mental health, one would expect that a sharp contrast would be present rather than what amounts to a continuum of mental functioning.

Recognizing the fallacy inherent in the dichotomous thinking outlined above, and consistent (somewhat) with the perspective of fractal geometry, Eysenck and Eysenck (1982; in Al-Issa, 1982) proposed a dimensional approach to mental illness. In other words, rather than health and illness representing absolute qualities, they suggested that pathology be regarded as merely an extension of normality or nonpathological behavior. Compatible with the criticisms of Goffman (1961), Foucault (1965), Laing (1969), Szasz (1961), and others, a dimensional or fractal approach would regard madness or insanity as potentially applicable to anyone and everyone. Indeed, since illness represents *merely movement* toward one pole of a continuum rather than something to be placed *at* one pole of a binary opposition, it should be measured accordingly. In this way, illness would be perceived in light of its relation to other forms of being and, thus, would be considered a point along a continuum rather than an "absolute label on a discrete point" (Al-Issa, 1982, p. 18).

We note that for the dimensional approach to illness to counter effectively the historical perception (i.e., scientific and medical approach) that searches for absolutes, the former must support its conclusions through persuasive exposition. Several prominent philosophical movements are worth reviewing here as they highlight the ways in which reality can be differentially perceived, depending on perspective. In addition, as we subsequently describe, these movements collectively represent a set of positions whose insights are generally consistent with nonlinear dynamical systems theory. These philosophical strains of thought include historicity and relativism, social constructionism, and perspectivism.

Historicity and Relativism

Attending to historicity and relativism allow for an approach to meaning that is sensitive to the historical and cultural influences under which interpretive endeavors occur. According to Gadamer (1975), historicity suggests that all knowledge and, thus, meaning is grounded in the prevailing conditions of a given epoch. There are numerous ways in which this historical conditioning might impact our conceptualizations of mental illness in society. For example, the prevalence of psychological depression during a period of economic stagnation may differ significantly from its prevalence during economic growth. Indeed, the availability of mental health care under a socialized system may encourage more individuals to seek treatment and, thus, the prevalence of mental illness may *appear* to be greater than under other systems. In short, the role that mental illness assumes in the consciousness of the age is readily affected by prevailing historical considerations (e.g., Morrissey & Goldman, 1986).

Perhaps most importantly, however, is the available knowledge or prevailing theoretical orientation in which we approach phenomena whose understanding is subject to various interpretations. This is the aspect of history that most concerned Gadamer and other social theorists of his intellectual persuasion (i.e., phenomenological). In short, the relationship between human beings and the quest for truth (e.g., what is expected, how it is approached, whether it is even wanted), is a product of the consciousness of an era. Though we may be aware that our conceptualization of a phenomenon is different now than from the past (and potentially from the future), we cannot escape the historical markers that anchor how things present themselves to our consciousness (Gadamer, 1975). All periods are beset by certain prejudices, biases, or what Heidegger (1962) called "foreunderstandings" of the world. Historical periods, however, are qualitatively different in that each is governed by their own, unique prejudgments. For example, as we have noted, the Enlightenment was a period marked by the search for absolute truths and objective knowledge about the world. This perspective (i.e., the belief that such understandings were available awaiting discovery), was merely the product of an historical frame of reference. Further, as we previously described , the disciplines of psychology and the law were, and continue to be, significantly influenced by this approach. Consequently, the quality of existence for those deemed mentally ill is contingent upon the given historical period and predominant theoretical mind-set in which one lives.

Relatedly, relativism maintains that knowledge and meaning are not only historically mediated, but also culturally bound. The philosophy of relativism has led society to question whether traditional Western conceptions of women, African-Americans, and the mentally ill as inferior rather than different is justifiable (Sarbin & Juhasz, 1982, p. 87). With regard to the latter, relativism holds that definitions and meanings associated with mental illness can and do vary between and even within cultures (e.g., Gaw, 1993). Indeed, consider, for a moment, the varying descriptions and interpretations assigned to persons who engage in nonheterosexist behaviors across cultures and even within various subcultures. More specifically, consider the different historical perspectives that have, in the latter twentieth century, significantly impacted changes in social (and, to a lesser extent, legal) perceptions of homosexuality.

To illustrate further the role of relativism in shaping knowledge and meaning, we can briefly examine contemporary Western perceptions of depression. As a culture, we are largely content to regard symptoms such as hopelessness and despair as expressions of illness that require treatment. However, early Buddhists would more than likely recognize the presence of such melancholy as the first step toward *nirvana*. The Buddhist doctrine acknowledges the pain and suffering that defines the life-world and this realization, on an individual level, is the first of the Four Noble Truths (*Samyutta-nikaya* in Thomas, 1927; *Dhammacakka Sutta* in Dhamma, 1997). This realization is then used to decrease attachment, desire, and craving for objects that merely promote temporary happiness within a larger cycle of suffering. The dispassion encouraged by Buddhism (de Silva, 1995; Marks, 1995), then, that stems largely from a melancholic recognition that life amounts to suffering, is a profound insight into the ultimate reality of the world and, consequently, the path that leads to the cessation of suffering (see also Berry, 1996). The Buddhist doctrine exemplifies the vast differences that can and do, at times, exist between cultures, concerning issues of psychological being.

Relativism in the social sciences grew largely out of the pioneering efforts of Ruth Benedict (1934). In drawing upon her anthropological field work, Benedict had the following to say about "abnormal" behavior:

> . . . [if a certain culture] chooses to treat their [persons displaying unusual behavior] peculiarities as the most valued variants of human behavior, the individuals in question will rise to the occasion and perform their social roles without reference to our usual

ideas of [adaptive and maladaptive behavior]. . . . Those who function inadequately in any society are not those with certain fixed "abnormal" traits, but may well be those whose responses have received no support in the institutions of their culture. . . . It springs not from the fact that they are lacking in necessary vigour, but that they are individuals whose native responses are not reaffirmed by society. (pp. 270–271)

Benedict anticipated many of the criticisms leveled against mental illness as a definitive construct by drawing attention to the need for cultural sensitivity in our understanding of various phenomena. For example, why might one culture value certain behaviors while another choose to confine involuntarily individuals displaying the same behaviors? Benedict's early work, as well as the relativist movement in psychopathology, which grew significantly thereafter, reaffirms the need for a fractal understanding of mental illness.

Thomas Scheff and the Social Construction of Mental Illness

The history of law pertaining to the mentally ill tells us something about the changing and fluid nature of this phenomenon. It also tells us something about the social climate in which these historical (i.e., regulatory) conditions were established and under which they assigned meaning to this elastic construct. To be sure, what we now term mental illness has not and, undoubtedly, will not remain stagnant. Rather, the presence of illness is as much related to sociocultural conditions and worldviews as it is to perceived reality as absolute and objective. Much like the distance between two points becomes greater or lesser depending on the angle from which one approaches it (cf. the "coastline" example of fractal geometry described briefly in the introduction), the precise meaning of mental illness can assume different characteristics, depending on the angle or perspective from which it is understood. The perspective from which mental illness or simply "difference" is approached hinges, to a large extent, on the prevailing sociocultural climate (e.g., world view, economic system, state of technology) of which it is a part.

Sociology has done much to advance our understanding of the sociocultural context in which mental illness is defined and substantiated. While mental illness is often regarded as a disease or sickness, it is also a violation of social norms. For example, persons who display extreme emotionality rather than measured reason, speak of "talking to the gods" rather than keeping such thoughts to themselves, or prefer the life of a street dweller to that of a home owner, are anomalies in our society; that is, the behavior and social conduct of such individuals typically is deemed inappropriate, abnormal, deviant, and, perhaps, dangerous (Arrigo & Williams, 1999a). Several prominent American and European theorists (e.g., Foucault, 1965, 1977; Goffman, 1961; Laing, 1967, 1969; Szasz, 1961, 1970) developed detailed and critical accounts for the meaning of mental illness as a social phenomenon. Whether one is inclined to regard this construct as entirely manufactured by culture and society or merely influenced by these forces, they nevertheless contribute to the meaning of mental illness and inform its psycholegal definition.

Perhaps the most acclaimed sociologist to propose a theory of mental illness was Thomas Scheff (1966, 1984, 2000). Scheff noted that all cultures have certain terms designating behaviors that are not congruent with the normal behavior of persons in that culture. Some nonnormative behaviors such as murder and incest are well defined and easily categorized (i.e., law violations). Others, however, are not so easily defined nor do they have explicit terms signifying what they are. These less-than-objective behaviors include such things as atypical displays of emotion and affection, or unusual interpersonal communication styles, etc. Unlike the previous examples of murder and incest, these behaviors are not governed by explicit rules and therefore this conduct is perceived as "weird," "strange," or "different," rather than as a distinct violation of (codified) rules. The social consequence for engaging in this behavior is not so much a function of physical harm or victimization; rather, its effect fosters an uncomfortable atmosphere for those who witness the conduct.

Scheff tells us that such "residual rule breaking behaviors" are attributable to different sources, depending on the sociocultural context. For example, ancient cultures often invoked theories of demonic possession to account for strange and bizarre behavior. Following the work of Freud (e.g., 1914, 1927) and others, however, more recent cultures have identified what they take to be the organic origins of these behaviors, claiming that they are manifestations of underlying psychiatric disease or illness. Determining who will become labeled in which way (e.g., demonic or diseased) depends on a number of factors, and none of them are constant or universal. Indeed, as Newman (1995, p. 191) observes when commenting on the architecture of mental illness:

The diagnosis depends on such factors as the identity of the rule breaker, the particular rule broken, the amount of strange behavior a community will tolerate, alternative explanations that might rationalize the behavior, and the social context within which the rule breaking takes place (see also Cockerham, 1992).

Thus, a homeless man who laughs himself to sleep while huddled in a cardboard box during the height of winter may be defined as mentally ill more quickly and routinely than a fifty-year-old attorney who cries publicly in the wake of a recent and painful divorce, following the loss of gainful employment. A poet living in an artist colony who exhibits behaviors that are normally regarded as inappropriate may be less likely to receive the mentally ill label (versus creative, talented, or genius label) than someone displaying the same behaviors and/or emotions in a religious or corporate organization. In fact, we are generally more inclined to regard such historical figures as Van Gogh and Baudelaire as men of ingenuity and profound creativity rather than as men of madness and danger, notwithstanding evidence of both. Even Freud, to some extent, recognized the socially constructed manner in which labels affix themselves to individuals. Indeed, as he described in his introduction to Dostoevsky's *The Brothers Karamazov*, "four facets may be distinguished in the rich personality of Dostoevsky: the creative artist, the neurotic, the moralist, and the sinner." Even in this brief passage we can glimpse how a brilliant novelist could just as readily be defined as a chronic psychotic. Consistent with Scheff (2000), our point is that a number of interacting sociocultural factors determine who will and will not be labeled mentally ill, despite similarities in the manifest behaviors of people.

For Scheff (1984), then, as with other social constructionists and labeling theorists, the origin or etiology of the behaviors, thoughts, and/or emotions is not as germane to sociological analysis as is the social reaction that the conduct elicits from those around the stigmatized individual. Indeed, elicited reactions ultimately determine whether a person will be defined as sick, deviant, mentally ill as opposed to some other, less consequential characterization. To be clear, Scheff (1966) as well as subsequent researchers in the sociology of mental illness (e.g., Kessler et al., 1994), have shown that the number of persons sufficiently free of symptoms generally associated with mental illness is less than 20 percent (Srole et al., 1962). In other words, the vast majority of persons, at some point during their lives, experience what would usually be regarded as symptoms of psychiatric disturbance.

This is one of the primary reasons why the mental health community has emphasized greater detection, diagnosis, and treatment of such illnesses as depression in recent years. Increasing our response to psychological problems (e.g., more facilities, educational awareness, availability of services) continues to be the preferred solution to this research finding on psychiatric disturbance. We submit that at a more fundamental level both our understanding of mental illness and our response to it are consistent with Scheff's (1966, 1984, 2000) view that the phenomenon is socially constructed.

The frequency with which persons experience symptoms of mental illness is prima facie evidence of the social reality of psychological illness. Scheff's (1966) conclusion is that, while the majority of individuals experiencing these symptoms as well as those around them simply rationalize or "explain them away" (Newman, 1995, p. 192), others with the same manifest symptoms but different social circumstances are labeled mentally ill and in need of treatment. Thus, fellow citizens, family members, coworkers, etc., upon observing strange or idiosyncratic behavior, may regard it as the product of stress, eccentricity, or physical illness, while those in other situations, in other cultures, and in other time periods, may be deemed mentally ill because of the same behavioral manifestations, resulting in involuntary confinement, treatment, or family, community, or societal ostracism. In short, what the social constructionist perspective tells us is that normality (and its binary opposition, abnormality) stem from one's ecology. This is not the same as implying that the behaviors themselves are not traceable to some organic or physical "cause"; rather, that those defined as mentally ill are so labeled because of the sociocultural context in which their conduct is interpreted.

Law and the Fractal of Mental Illness: Toward a Perspectival Approach to Meaning

If we accept the notion that conceptualizing mental illness is not as simple as applying some agreed-upon, objective criteria to a given individual, what consequences might this hold for the role that this phenomenon assumes in the legal system? At present, the legal system allows for two findings: health or illness (Arrigo, 1996). The law limits itself by insisting that reality be clearly defined and that it cleanly fit into predetermined categories. The existing definitions of mental illness (i.e., those of psychology and law) are useful to the extent that they advance the binary aspirations of the juridical sphere. In other words, criteria are useful to the legal system only if they absolutely define a person as either healthy or ill, well or sick. Thus, the multiple perspectives that define the fractal geometry of meaning ostensibly are of little value to these juridical aims. Indeed, finding an individual both mentally healthy and mentally ill, or healthy in some ways and ill in others, is of no value to the legal system, as it currently operates. However, given the fractal nature of psychological being, we contend that it would be more advantageous to adopt a fractal understanding of mental health. In other words, for legal purposes, embracing definitions of mental illness that allow for greater possibilities and more diversity in meaning would be more consistent with the interests of citizen justice.

A legal system in harmony with the fractal nature of reality would allow for, perhaps require, determinations of meaning outside of or beyond what they currently provide (e.g., guilty or not guilty, competent or incompetent, mentally ill or mentally healthy). Put differently, since mental wellbeing is about *shades* of health or *degrees* of illness, the law would do well to construct various meanings consistent with these amounts. This may include sensitivity to cultural and subcultural variations in meaning, as well as a reliance on each conceptualization as a sort of "mirror" from which to reflect on any one definition's shortcomings or misapplications. Clarke (1997, p. 28), for example, uses the phrase "corrective mirror" to describe this process of cultural reflection in light of other understandings of the world. We note, then, that assuming a fractal perspective would allow the horizon of possible legal meanings to expand in ways more compatible with the reality of psychological being. Embracing this strategy of the fractal would substitute the law's search for a precise definition with a series of definitions whose boundaries were loose and open to a variety of interpretations.

A precursor to the recent (postmodern) emphasis on appreciating and, perhaps, integrating cultural differences into civic life was Friederich Nietzsche. Nietzsche's (1887/1967, 1980) "perspectivism" reflects and, in fact, predates many of the same concerns we have discussed thus far, particularly in the area of knowledge and truth. There are no eternal facts (e.g., no mental illness that transcends historical context) and no absolute truths (e.g., no mental illness discernable through objective criteria). Without digressing too much into Nietzsche's philosophy (see, e.g., Schacht, 1983; Clark, 1990; Thiele, 1990; Nehemas, 1985 on Nietzsche and the perspectival approach to truth and values), it is important that we consider, at least provisionally, the implications of his insights. Nietzsche's perspectivism has been interpreted by some (e.g., Best & Kellner, 1997) as warranting a "multiperspectival vision" (ibid., p. 66). That is to say, if each perspective has its own truth, its own value, its own meaning, then the more perspectives we explore the less partial and one-sided our understandings will be. Applying this logic to mental illness, then, we see how embracing other perspectives and incorporating them into our conventional "either or" approach will move us toward the shades of meaning that fractal geometry argues are definitive of reality. If fractal geometry provides an answer in any form, it is a robust one that embodies the "multi-determined nature of existence and change" (Butz, 1997, p. 222). It is a form that distances itself from totalizing, categorical, and objective measures of truth, knowledge, and meaning, toward a more qualitative understanding of existence, one that validates the psychological being of individuals.

As we have seen, however, the psychological approach to mental illness—one that is nearly all-encompassing—is too inclusive for legal purposes. Yet the approach of the law has been to provide general, vague, and often ambiguous definitions, ultimately deferring to the wisdom of psychologists when one's mental state is in question (Arrigo, 1996; Perlin, 1999). More particularly, in cases of the insanity defense, the law has been generally exclusive to the extent that persons experiencing significant psychological adversity at the time of their offense have been deemed categorically mentally healthy (i.e., legally sane) because they do not fit into a preconfigured medical model conceptualization of mental disease or defect (Perlin, 1994). Chaos theory and fractal geometry suggest that neither approach (not exaggerated inclusivity nor rigid exclusivity) provides the definitional answers for mental illness that the law desires. Rather, the meaning of mental illness falls somewhere between these two. Its meaning must be sufficiently robust to include nonmedical understandings, yet sufficiently discriminating to prevent absolute chaos in the legal system. In short, searching for a definition of mental illness may be a futile exercise; such a thing, along objective lines, does not and can not exist. Rather, as we have shown, a qualitative understanding of the person and the sociocultural factors that give rise to our interpretation of the individual, are necessary to determine the fractal nature of one's (mentally ill) reality.

SUMMARY AND CONCLUSIONS

Recently, scientists studying the metabolic rate of animals discovered the "fourth dimension" factor that reveals the intricacies of this process as it relates to the mass of nonhumans (Couzin, 1999, p. 60). Consideration of the area that presents itself to the perspective of the onlooker is consistent with traditional geometry (e.g., two- and three-dimensional representations). However, accounting for (observable) surface area alone does not yield accurate answers as to why larger animals, for example, burn energy more slowly than smaller ones. To understand this complex phenomenon, that is, to yield accurate mathematical results, the equation must consider a fourth dimension. Where is this fourth dimension? The extra surface area is contained or, rather, *hidden* in the folds of the animal's skin. Like a coastline, a bird's-eye view does not reveal the intricate contours of the area under investigation. Rather, upon closer examination, there is an increasing complexity which makes accurate measurement nearly impossible. The skin folds of an animal (such as an elephant) could be said to have a fractal geometry: They hide a portion of the animal's mass and, consequently, frustrate attempts to account for that mass using traditional methods of mathematics.

What does this illustration from nature tell us about mental illness in relation to law and psychology, and the prospects for justice in the psycholegal sphere? Simply put, it tells us that, much like the elephant, psychological being has skin folds. These skin folds confound our attempts to measure precisely or even understand accurately this psychological being, especially in light of the goals of modern science and contemporary psycholegal practice (i.e., as a phenomenon conducive to objective classification and/or definition). In this chapter, we have discussed evidence of these skin folds, including sociocultural influences, political pressures, historical climate, and the like. Often, these factors are unstated themes, informing our understanding of mental illness beyond conscious awareness. Consequently, they significantly impact the way we approach deviance and difference in psychology, in law, and in society. Much like the skin folds on an elephant, their effects are generally unrecognizable or, at least, remain unaccounted for in psycholegal "equations."

To be clear, the fractal of chaos theory does not give us a definition of mental illness. It offers us nothing along objective lines that helps narrow the construct's boundaries for legal purposes. What the fractal tells us is precisely the opposite; namely, *there is no one definition of mental illness* (or two, or three, for that matter). Rather, conceptualizations of psychological being (i.e., mental health or illness) must account for the limitless perspectives from which such an experiential state can be approached. Any attempt to objectify psychological being is futile. A clear-cut, 3-dimensional world does not exist from the human vantage point. Instead, the world comes at us in dimensions of 2.25, or 1.76, or 1.23, etc. The picture we take away depends on the perspective from which we approached the subject/object.

This is not to suggest that mental illness does not exist or is not, in some way, discernibly different from mental health. What it does suggest, however, is that we cannot *categorically* rule out or rule in anything as evidence of the presence or absence of mental illness. Behavior that is "normal" or persons that are "in need of treatment" are realities that do not and cannot exist on paper (e.g., in a psychiatric manual or legal code). They are realities that are experiential, understood only from the unique perspective of the person experiencing them. There may be extreme cases that are less controversial; however, the majority of persons fall somewhere in between the extremes and are not easily placed into binary categories of psychological being. The fractal reality of human experience necessitates a similar understanding; that is, it requires a definition of mental illness that is colored, not in black and white, but in shades of grey.

Justice, then, like mental illness, must be mindful of the *degrees* of knowledge, experience, and truth that perforate our world. If the world is fractal, at least from the perspective of its inhabitants, so, too, must we say the same of justice. Accordingly, it must acknowledge and respond to the shades of reality that exist within (human) nature. Equations of justice that apply universal, objective, rigid laws to situations and citizens is necessarily (self)defeating. Thus, the extent to which psychology and law are prepared to embrace difference and, consequently, forego totalizing conceptions of reality, is the extent to which, following chaos theory and the fractal, the psycholegal establishment will promote justice and a just society.

CHAPTER FIVE

Dangerousness and Its Prediction

OVERVIEW. *A finding of dangerousness is, perhaps, the most elusive of determinations made in the psycholegal arena. It is elusive because accurate definitions for this construct have escaped the wisdom of legislators, and because predicting who will or will not be dangerous is a determination that has baffled the expertise of the mental health profession. Notwithstanding these shortcomings, the concept of dangerousness is pivotal to the loss of civil liberties that a citizen would otherwise enjoy. Indeed, several scholars have noted that the concept of dangerousness is "critical to at least fifteen different points of the decision-making process in the criminal justice and mental health systems" (Perlin, 1999, p. 102; Shah, 1978). For example, most often the law invokes the notion of dangerousness (coupled with a finding of mental illness) to justify involuntary civil commitment and/or sustained confinement of persons already subject to treatment against their will (e.g., Perlin, 1999; Reisner & Slobogin, 1997). In instances such as these, basic human rights (e.g., freedom from restraint, right to self-determination) are at stake, and defining the differences between those who are dangerous, potentially dangerous, and not a risk at all is crucial to the administration of psychiatric justice (Arrigo, 1996).*

At its core, the issue posed by this differentiation questions the conditions under which "the state [is] justified in using its power to infringe [upon] the liberty of the individual" (Shah, 1977, p. 91). Typically, the state is justified to exercise its authority in such matters when the person is a danger to oneself and/or to others (e.g., Reisner & Slobogin, 1997). In the case of the former, one's gross inability to meet basic standards of self-care or one's potential for self-injurious behavior (e.g., suicide) are of concern. In the case of the latter, the threat of physical harm to another wherein a plan has been fashioned in furtherance of the threat is cause for a dangerousness determination. In both instances (i.e., self-harm or danger to others), the well-being of the individual and the community at large are the interests that supercede one's individual rights to freedom (Feinberg, 1986, 1988). Applying this logic to persons who are mentally ill and dangerous is complicated because society has yet to find a sound justification for protecting the community from individuals known to be dangerous but not mentally ill. In other words, however logical the argument for confinement may appear, the psycholegal establishment has yet to identify accurately persons who are psychiatrically disordered but not dangerous and has, instead, seemingly collapsed the two, erring on the side of over-inclusive dangerousness determinations (e.g., Arrigo, 1996; Ennis & Litwack, 1974; LaFond & Durham, 1992).

The state's response to persons who are dangerous and mentally ill rests upon two broad assumptions: (a) The mentally ill are generally more dangerous than those not identified as such; and (b) the law has sufficient means to identify psychiatrically disordered individuals who are dangerous from those who are not (Arrigo & Williams, 1999a). We note further that the state tacitly assumes that the mentally ill can be treated effectively while confined, no longer posing a threat to themselves or to others once released into the community. This particular matter calls into question the expertise or competence of the mental health profession more generally.

In this chapter we examine the controversy surrounding the psycholegal concept of dangerousness. This controversy is twofold: first, similar to our analysis of mental illness in the previous chapter, dangerousness is subject to various ambiguities in meaning; second, and more significantly, we are interested in understanding the contentious issue of predicting dangerousness. We begin with an evaluation of dangerousness and its meaning in the legal context. Next, we review the manner in which psychology interprets this phenomenon, specifically for purposes of risk assessment determinations in particular cases. In addition, we consider the limits of prevailing legal and psychological interpretations of dangerousness and its prediction. On this point, we rely on chaos theory to guide our analysis, and critically examine how existing meanings for dangerousness advance or fail to advance prospects for justice.

DANGEROUSNESS AND THE LAW

Defining dangerousness has become as problematic a piece of legislative responsibility as defining mental illness (Cocozza & Steadman, 1978). Indeed, as Perlin (1999, p. 101) notes "no question in the area of the involuntary civil commitment process has proven to be more perplexing than the definition of the word 'dangerousness.'" In the legal context, the term refers to danger to oneself or to others as a result of an underlying mental disorder (see, e.g., *O'Connor v. Donaldson*, 1975; Note, 1974). If either determination is made, involuntary confinement follows. Statutory considerations of dangerousness are broad and, like those of mental illness, often yield little more than a general guideline, encouraging the legal system to rely on psychiatric evaluation and testimony to clarify the inadequate or limited language supplied by legislators. Several examples along these lines are worth noting.

Alaska's statute requires only that persons with mental illness be "likely to injure . . . others" to justify commitment (Melton et al., 1997, p. 308). Nebraska requires that a mentally ill person present "a substantial risk of serious harm" to self or others, and Wisconsin requires a "substantial probability of physical harm" (Schopp & Quattrocchi, 1995, p. 163) as a condition of civil confinement. While each of these standards is considerably vague, some states provide more specific statutory requirements for a finding of dangerousness. Florida's guidelines are instructive here as this state requires a "substantial likelihood that in the near future [the person] will inflict serious bodily harm on . . . another person as evidenced by recent behavior causing, attempting, or threatening such harm" (Melton et al., 1997, p. 308).

Each of the above cited instances relies upon statutory language, attempting to set a legal threshold for commitment based on danger to *others*. In the first three cases, expressions such as "substantial risk," "serious harm," "substantial probability," and "likely to injure," create a climate of uncertainty, one that pervades the dangerousness construct. Indeed, judges, mental health professionals, or communities in general may assign a meaning to "serious harm," for example, that could differ dramatically from what others would regard as either "serious" or "harm." Failing even to define "harm," Nebraska leaves open the possibility that it may assume any of several forms that rely on subjective interpretation (e.g., physical, sexual). The Florida statute, however, requires that "bodily harm" be present to meet the dangerousness criterion. This limitation is typical of many states in that harm to property and/or to the psyche do not constitute inflictions that justify a finding of dangerousness for legal purposes.

In addition, the Florida statute requires a *recent* demonstration of violence or threat of violence. This particular standard is generally referred to as the "overt act" requirement and has been adopted by a number of states. Pennsylvania defines an overt act as conduct that has occurred "within the past thirty days" (Melton et al., 1997, p. 309; Paczak, 1989). Some researchers contend that the overt act requirement safeguards against erroneous commitments. Indeed, a recent suicide attempt, for example, is a much more powerful indicator that a person might pose a threat to oneself than a conventional prediction unsubstantiated by demonstrable behavioral evidence (Levy & Rubenstein, 1996, pp. 31–32). We note that the overt act requirement has not been adopted by all states. The absence of uniformity across jurisdictions only further conflates and confuses the various meanings assigned to the dangerousness construct by legislative bodies (Perlin, 1999).

In confronting the semantic dilemmas associated with mental health law definitions for dangerousness, Brooks (1974) identified four variables that routinely factor into legal determinations of danger to self or others. These variables included: (a) magnitude or severity of harm; (b) probability of that harm occurring; (c) the frequency with which the harm may occur; and (d) the immanence with which the harm will occur. Brooks maintained that a satisfactory understanding of dangerousness (i.e., the ability to differentiate which persons legally pose a threat of harm) was possible when applying these variables collectively to individual cases. Perhaps the most instructive element of Brooks's typology was his emphasis on the interaction of the variables and the necessity to consider each case separately. As we subsequently explain, these elements of dangerousness are important to our treatment of it, especially from the perspective of chaos theory. For now, however, we note the seeming utility of Brooks' (1974) model (for other conceptualizations regarding the elements and dimensions of dangerousness see, e.g., Hiday, 1981; and Shah, 1977).

Thus far, our discussion of dangerousness has focused on one's (potential) harm to others. The related dimension to risk assessment determinations is whether a person poses a danger to him or herself. We note that the justification for each (i.e., danger to others or self) is subsumed under two different functions of the state (e.g., Perlin, 1999; Reisner & Slobogin, 1997). As we explain shortly, these state-mandated functions are often quite confusing and conflated as found in various legislative guidelines, and as articulated in sundry judicial decisions (Shah, 1977; Arrigo, 1996).

The involuntary confinement of individuals representing a danger to others is justified under the state's *police power* authority, and such determinations stem from the state's responsibility to protect the public (Perlin, 1989). The civil commitment of persons posing a threat to themselves is justified under the state's *parens patriae* power, and these decisions arise from the state's duty to care for individuals unable to care for themselves (Myers, 1984). Similar to our analysis of dangerousness when harm to others is posed, the threat of harm to self also warrants some brief commentary.

As a practical matter, the definition of danger to self is consistent with the definition of danger to others. Indeed, those states that provide only minimal explanation for the latter standard rarely provide sufficient explanation for the former standard (Schmidt, 1985). Every state statute calls for the commitment of persons who are suicidal. However, persons prone to such self-injurious behavior represent a fraction of the hospitalized population found to be a danger to self. Indeed, the remainder of this population includes "gravely disabled" individuals (Arrigo, 1996, pp. 68–71). Typically, gravely disabled citizens are not dangerous to others. Rather, they are unable to provide for their own basic needs (e.g., food, clothing, shelter) (Comment, 1983). This particular guideline poses unique problems for civil commitment determinations because it is not always clear whether one *cannot* provide or whether one *chooses* not to provide for their own basic welfare (e.g., *In the Matter of Billie Boggs*, 1987). Moreover, the imposition of treatment for persons considered gravely disabled, based on the *parens patriae* authority of the state, can amount to a Constitutional violation, impacting one's right to self-determination (Hermann, 1990).

In sum, therefore, the legal concept of dangerousness, much like definitions of mental illness, is somewhat controversial and unclear. Indeed, a finding that a person poses a danger to another, typically is not gleaned from behavior alone, except for certain recent overt acts which may be more indicative of an immediate threat to one or more individuals rather than some expression of an acute disorder. Similarly, one's potential harm to oneself is routinely the subject of sociopolitical interpretations (Hermann, 1973), thereby imbuing this finding with a somewhat arbitrary (rather than legal) character, calling into question the state's undisputed right to intervene in particular cases. Given these problems in the law, how, then, is the question of dangerousness and its meaning resolved? In part, the answer ostensibly resides in the domain of psychology. Accordingly, we now consider how this field defines (and predicts) dangerousness.

DANGEROUSNESS AND PSYCHOLOGY

The mental health profession has been the subject of considerable criticism since the concept of dangerousness was first introduced as a substantive criterion for civil commitment (Monahan, 1996). Psychology has been drawn into the fray because the legal system clearly and repeatedly depends on the expertise of the mental health profession to diagnose and predict dangerousness in the case of persons with psychiatric disorders. Indeed, these forensic specialists are called upon by the legal system, testifying as to the presence of mental illness and the prospects for future harm posed by a particular citizen. We have already discussed psychology's limits to define precisely the former construct. In the pages that follow, we intend to review how successfully the discipline engages in violence prediction. In other words, we are uniquely concerned with psychology's role in legal determinations of dangerousness. Accordingly, we briefly examine the mental health profession's twofold involvement in this controversy: (a) Is there a connection between mental illness and violence (i.e., the research dimension)? and (b) are sufficient tools available to forecast who will or will not be violent (the practical dimension)?

Mental Illness and Dangerousness: A Questionable Link

The relationship between mental illness and dangerousness or violent behavior is of notable concern for law and psychology scholars. Fueled, in part, by mass-media-generated stereotypes (Torrey, 1994), the mentally ill are portrayed as violent, homicidal maniacs in popular films such as *Psycho, Halloween, Silence of the Lambs,* etc. The MacArthur Research Network on Mental Health and the Law recently released a "Consensus Statement" describing this very process:

> "Mental disorder" and violence are closely linked in the public mind. A combination of factors promotes this perception: sensationalized reporting by the media whenever a violent act is committed by a "former mental patient," popular misuse of psychiatric terms (such as "psychotic" and "psychopathic"), and exploitation of . . . narrow stereotypes by the entertainment industry. The public justifies its fear and rejection of people labeled "mentally ill". . . by this assumption of "dangerousness" (Monahan & Arnold, 1996; quoted in Perlin, 1999, p. 114).

Given the public's limited knowledge of psychological disorders, it is not surprising that misleading stereotypes are perpetuated and endure (e.g., Steadman, 1981). Wahl (1987), for example, found that of those college students polled, fifty-two percent (52%) believed aggression, hostility, and violence were common characteristics of schizophrenia. Sentiments such as this inevitably contribute to the stigmatization of the mentally ill; however, the question for the psycholegal field is whether this type of student observation is justified.

A considerable amount of scientific scholarship has surfaced over the past two decades, endeavoring to better understand the mental illness-dangerousness relationship (e.g., Monahan & Steadman, 1994; Monahan, 1992; Swanson et al., 1990). Among mental health researchers, it is generally agreed that the psychiatrically ill are no more likely to commit violent acts than their nonmentally ill counterparts. This assertion derives, in part, from earlier investigations suggesting that the link between mental illness and violent behavior was minimal at best (e.g., Mulvey, Blumstein, & Cohen, 1986; Rabkin, 1979). Despite several subsequent studies claiming that this contention may be premature (e.g., Mulvey, 1994; Otto, 1992), the majority of research remains supportive of the original finding. The relative mental health of individuals makes "at best a trivial contribution to [one's] overall level of violence in society" (Monahan, 1997, p. 315).

Comparatively speaking, alcohol and drug abusers are far more likely to commit violent offenses than individuals with serious mental illness (Torrey, 1994). There is some evidence to suggest, however, that persons experiencing co-occurring disorders (e.g., persistent psychiatric illness and chronic chemical addiction) are significantly more likely to engage in violent behaviors than those who are not dual diagnosed (Reiss & Roth, 1993; Swanson et al., 1990). This finding may be particularly significant when considering that as many as thirty-three percent (33%) of persons with serious mental illness present with substance abuse issues (Reiss & Roth, 1993). This correlation does not make more valid the suggestion that mental illness alone contributes to violent behavior; rather, it further substantiates the link between alcohol/drug use and violent or dangerous behavior.

Recent research on the relationship between psychiatric disorders and dangerousness points to a correlation, but only within a small subgroup of the mentally ill population. In other words, the mentally ill as a whole are not more violent than the general population. Rather, a small percentage of the former may be more prone to violence (Monahan, 1996). Thus, the harmful acts committed by psychiatric citizens are attributable to a small minority of that population and their behavior should neither be generalized to the overall grouping of persons with mental disorders nor should this collective, in the aggregate, therefore be considered dangerous (Arrigo, 1996, 2000a). Torrey (1994), for example, suggests that this small minority of violent persons with psychiatric disorders may be identifiable. In short, he argues that persons with a history of violent conduct, a pattern of non-compliance with medication regimes, neurological impairment, and symptomology including certain types of delusions and command hallucinations are likely candidates for dangerous behavior. However, in response, Bell (1994, p. 711) maintains that Torrey's conclusions are "over-inclusive," justifying, perhaps, outpatient commitment, but not meriting a finding of dangerousness for purposes of involuntary civil confinement.

In sum, while the vast majority of persons experiencing mental illness are nonviolent and, therefore, not legally dangerous, researchers continue to search for indicators within subgroups of this population, establishing a firmer basis for the link between mental illness and dangerousness. Undoubtedly, these efforts will continue, especially given the role that the legal system has fashioned for the mental health profession (i.e., predicting who represents a threat to the well-being of society and/or to oneself). The vigor with which these studies are undertaken stems, in large part, from the mental health community's failure to generate reliable and accurate clinical assessments of dangerousness. As we subsequently explain, psychology's inability to predict consistently who poses a likelihood of future harm represents one of the most virulent criticisms leveled against the discipline and its wholesale involvement in the legal system.

Psychology and the Prediction of Legal Dangerousness

Mental health professionals often find themselves testifying in a court of law as to the presence of mental illness and the probability that a given individual will likely harm others or oneself. The ability of these forensic experts to predict dangerousness "to any acceptable degree of professional certainty" (Schopp & Quattrocchi, 1995, pp. 159–160) has been seriously challenged by social scientists and, consequently, psychology finds itself inescapably enmeshed in a contentious psycholegal debate (Grisso & Appelbaum, 1992). In general, the problem is twofold: the clinical assessment community has yet to demonstrate its ability to predict accurately who will be dangerous, let alone what the construct means; and the legal system, confronted with civil commitment determinations where questions of dangerousness are central to the outcome, lacks any viable alternative other than the expert testimony of forensic mental health specialists whose forecasting is already suspect. As such, a profound conflict exists between the demands of the law, and the limits of psychology when dangerousness predictions are at issue (Mossman, 1994a, 1994b).

Essentially, the forensic psychologist assumes two roles in the legal context when violence predictions are under consideration: diagnosis and prognosis. Diagnosis is the finding of legal mental illness (the topic of the previous chapter). Prognosis is the finding of dangerousness; that is, determining that a particular individual poses a threat of future possible harm to oneself and/or to others. Schopp and Quattrocchi (1995) suggest that a third function is embedded in the decision making of the forensic psychologist and term it a "normative" role. From a legal perspective this particular task is problematic because the mental health expert considers whether an individual is dangerous *enough* to justify confinement. Indeed, as Schopp and Quattrocchi (1995) observe, the normative component entails both a legal and moral determination that is principally, under our present system of justice, the responsibility of the legislature and the court.

Most scholars agree that the expertise of the clinician does not and should not extend to the point of decision making, involving legal and moral judgments (e.g., Wrightsman, 1997). Indeed, the skill of most forensic specialists is limited to descriptive concerns; that is, describing and explaining impairment, describing and explaining the risk of harm associated with that particular level of impairment, and describing and explaining the available treatment and possible effects of treatment given the level of impairment (Grisso & Appelbaum, 1992). Consistent with Schopp and Quattrocchi (1995), however, the determination of dangerousness also entails a normative component. In other words, while mental health experts provide the court with descriptive and explanatory information, legal and moral elements (e.g., whether the risk justifies curtailing liberty) also imprudently fall within the purview of psychologists (Holstein, 1993; Morse, 1982, p. 60). The court's reliance on psychology in matters that are fundamentally legal has profound implications for findings of dangerousness and determinations of commitment (Arrigo, 1996). Indeed, as we subsequently explain, the fuzziness with which the lines of responsibility are drawn between law and psychology, casts significant doubt on the role of the expert when questions of violence prediction are in issue. This is particularly the case when forecasting self-injurious behavior.

Psychology and Danger to Self: The Need for Treatment?

Psychology's role in defining and predicting dangerousness is more indicative of the discipline's need to understand one's likelihood of future harm to others. As previously noted, however, the law also allows for the involuntary confinement of persons thought to be a danger to themselves (i.e., suicidal or gravely disabled). Psychology's accurate forecasting of self-danger is important to our overall assessment because the majority of civil commitment cases are based on this finding and because this determination impacts one's right to refuse treatment. Thus, while the controversy surrounding dangerousness is most often linked to the prediction of violent behavior toward others, understanding its relation to nonviolent mentally ill persons facing preventative detention because of potential self-harm necessitates some attention.

According to the American Psychiatric Association's most recent guidelines on civil commitment, the goal of any assessment of danger to self or grave disability is to ascertain whether the individual

> . . . is substantially unable to provide for some of [one's] basic needs, such as food, clothing, shelter, health, or safety or will, if not treated, suffer or continue to suffer severe mental and abnormal mental, emotional, or physical distress . . . causing a substantial deterioration of [one's] previous ability to function on [one's] own. (Comment, 1983, pp. 674–677)

This proposed definition clearly acknowledges the need to understand whether a person is *psychologically* equipped to maintain one's own basic needs (Schmidt, 1985). The most obvious arbiter of such determinations is the discipline of psychology. These judgments are controversial, however, when questioning whose *values* or constructions of well-being underscore these decisions.

The single, most relevant assumption driving danger-to-self determinations is the need for quality care and treatment (e.g., Appelbaum, 1984, 1997). This assumption is a recurring theme throughout the present critique. Indeed, a concern for efficacious intervention informs psychology's decision making in relation to defining mental illness, ascertaining the presence of dangerousness to self (or others), reviewing the need for civil commitment, and evaluating one's right to refuse treatment. In the context of danger-to-self determinations, civil commitment follows if a person's mental illness gives rise to probable self-harm. In other words, one's psychiatric disorder must be such that if not treated it would amount to a level of distress and deterioration, consistent with the grave disability guideline (Comment, 1983; Schmidt, 1985). As a result, psychology forecasts who is likely to pose such a significant danger to oneself that the individual is (or will be) gravely disabled (e.g., *In the matter of Billie Boggs*, 1987). As we explain elsewhere (particularly in our application of nonlinear dynamics in chapters 6 and 8), these are matters that involve value judgments about the human condition and ongoing social interaction.

LIMITATIONS OF LEGAL AND PSYCHOLOGICAL
APPROACHES TO DANGEROUSNESS

The legal understanding of dangerousness is premised on the belief that the state has a duty to protect the community from dangerous persons and a duty to care for individuals unable to care adequately for themselves. We note, however, that it is difficult to describe with precision what constitutes a violent-prone individual from a legal perspective? Indeed, similar to defining mental illness (the other substantive criterion for involuntary confinement), legislatures have not yet articulated a meaning for dangerousness with any sufficient degree of clarity. As we have argued, definitions for this elusive construct vary significantly between states, and legislative revisions are not uncommon. These differing interpretations of dangerousness stem, in part, from inadequate understandings of mental illness and its relationship to violent behavior. Notwithstanding these shortcomings, the legal system is compelled to arrive at some conclusion when confronted with psychiatric citizens who potentially constitute a threat of harm to themselves or to others. Given this necessity, the legal community has generally seen fit to defer to the wisdom of the mental health profession, both for guidance and for clarification.

To the extent that the law's treatment of dangerousness is contingent upon reliable and valid scientific research, psychology assumes an important role in making sense out of statutory constructions for the same. Indeed, forensic specialists are called upon to assist the fact finder in a civil commitment determination. In a sense, then, the law and the legal profession are dependent upon psychological expertise when findings of dangerousness are in issue. In our analysis, we identified two prominent areas wherein the discipline's input has been constant: research explaining the link between mental illness and violent behavior (understanding dangerousness); and expert testimony assessing whether a given individual is likely to pose a future threat to oneself or to others (predicting dangerousness).

In both of these instances, the contributions of the mental health community have been woefully inadequate. Research clearly and demonstrably indicates that, in general, there is no conclusive link between mental illness and violent or dangerous behavior. Notwithstanding this finding, investigators continue to search for such a link. At the same time, psychology predicts dangerousness based on the limited clinical assessment knowledge it has at its disposal. As a result, forecasting is inherently suspect, lacking reasonable levels of accuracy and producing erroneous results. These failures have spawned considerable criticism, challenging psychology's involvement in the legal system on such matters altogether.

We submit that the extent to which psychology is called upon to contribute to the legal decision-making process is one that requires careful and thoughtful reconsideration. While it is generally accepted that courts tend to defer to the expertise of mental health professionals on issues of psychiatric disorder and dangerousness, psychology's inadequate understanding and unreliable predictions of dangerousness have become "established facts within the profession" (*Barefoot v. Estelle*, 1983, p. 12). Moreover, it is questionable whether the discipline should even be involved in decisions where civil liberties are at stake (Morse, 1982). Despite these controversial and contentious matters, psychology continues to involve itself in the prediction of dangerousness. In the following section, we further examine the "futility" that arguably describes these prognostication efforts. In other words, following our understanding of chaos theory, we critically explore why psychology has been so unsuccessful in its predictive endeavors to date.

CHAOS THEORY AND DANGEROUSNESS

In the previous chapter, we addressed the concept of mental illness as distinguished from mental health, employing a range of philosophical positions and augmenting them with insights generated by chaos theory and the fractal. Our examination was intentionally limited to a single principle, both to ease the reader into the material and to provide a necessary and helpful perspective from which to advance the more substantive critique that follows in subsequent chapters. Indeed, our contention is that fractal geometry is the best available "scientific" tool for understanding how meaning is to be approached.

In the present chapter, we expand our analysis by utilizing additional ideas found in nonlinear dynamical systems theory. As this chapter concerns itself not only with meaning but with the notion of forecasting, it will be useful to examine those chaos theory principles that contribute to our understanding of prediction. In brief, these concepts fall under the broad heading of ecology, including such notions as sensitive dependence on initial conditions, bifurcation, and iteration. By incorporating these particular ideas into our assessment of dangerousness, not only do we encounter a different perspective on violence prediction, but confront a different understanding of justice in the psycholegal sphere.

Reconceptualizing Dangerous "Behavior"

Shah (1977) tells us that one of the biggest impediments to defining and subsequently predicting dangerousness is our concept of behavior itself. In other words, behavior "is often viewed as stemming largely if not entirely from within the individual, that is, as derived from [one's] personality" (ibid., p. 105). Conflating behavior with personality is very problematic. Indeed, conceptualizing the former as an outgrowth of the latter creates a tendency "to view behavior as a fairly enduring, consistent, and even persistent characteristic" (ibid.). In the context of understanding dangerousness, then, this would mean that persons labeled as such would remain so because of previous harmful acts, indicative of the individual's personality. By the same token, no history of violent conduct would suggest that the person possessed a nondangerous temperament. The link that establishes dangerousness as a personality characteristic rather than a particular behavior has profound consequences for legal determinations of the same. In clinical circles, for example, the conviction that past conduct is the best indicator of future behavior has reached the status of near fact (e.g., Monahan, 1981, p. 1996). Thus, it is not uncommon for the forensic mental health specialist who assesses and testifies as to the dangerousness of a given individual to emphasize one's previous tendencies toward violence (or lack thereof) when arriving at a prediction.

Given the foregoing comments, we note that the process of defining dangerousness transitions from the identification of a *behavior* as dangerous, to the labeling of the *individual* as dangerous based on that conduct (Scheff, 1966). Foucault (1988) drew critical attention to this concern as well when he explained that

> [l]egal justice today has at least as much to do with criminals as with crimes . . . [F]or a long time, the criminal had been no more than the person to whom a crime could be attributed and one who could therefore be punished. . . . (p. 128)

Foucault's genealogical investigation marked the arrival of psychiatry into criminality by providing a new direction for the examination of mental illness and illicit conduct (Arrigo & Williams, 1999a). In particular, he argued that the focus of medical inquiry was on the *individual* rather than the *crime*. Foucault referred to this development as the "psychiatrization of criminal danger" (Foucault, 1988, p. 128), and linked its emergence with scientific efforts to comprehend the unreason or irrationality of mentally disordered people who committed unthinkable acts. The only way to make sense of these acts was to understand insanity as something hidden or as a *danger* that lay beyond the actor's control. Consequently, psychiatry created a crime; that is, it created the crime of mental illness which would carry with it the assumption of one's latent, concealed, repressed danger. As a consequence, psychiatrically ill people would thereafter be criminalized because of what they *represented* (i.e., a threat to society), rather than for what they *did*. Psychology's introduction into the legal arena, then, sanctions, produces, and legitimizes the causal link between mental illness and crime. Accordingly, dangerousness is equated with one's underlying personality (Arrigo & Williams, 1999a).

This shift in logic from behavior defined as violent to the individual designated as dangerous (and criminal) is problematic. Not only does this process produce unnecessary stigmatization (Gove, 1975; Scheff, 2000), it deprives otherwise harmless persons of their liberty (Arrigo, 1996; Morse, 1982). Further, to arrive at clinical predictions based on this line of inquiry may be seriously suspect. Indeed, "physically violent or other dangerous acts are usually rather infrequent, occur in specific situational contexts, and may not be representative of the individual's customary behavior" (Shah, 1974, pp. 677–679, 1977, p. 105). To understand this reasoning, we employ several principles contained in chaos theory.

Ecology, Sensitivity, and Stability

Chaos theory encourages us to view behavior in its ecological context. In other words, thoughts, feelings, impulses, physical states, and the like are determined, not by the individual alone, but by way of an ongoing and constant interaction with the environment. As a system, the individual is influenced by the various factors that impact the behavior of that system. Indeed, we cannot identify nor understand one's actions as separate from both internal and external variables. Internal variables may include the determinants of personality. Thus, for example, the extent to which an individual controls anger, handles stressful situations, makes rational decisions rather than succumbing to the influence of emotion or desire, hinges, in part, on his/her characterological make-up. External variables include those environmental factors over which the individual has little or no control. These include such wide-ranging factors as socioeconomic status, familial support/interaction, neighborhood stability, weather conditions, and any other variable that may play a pivotal role in one's behavior.

Chaos theory's principle of *sensitive dependence on initial conditions* furthers our understanding of this internal-external dichotomy and its impact on one's behavior. Recall the "butterfly effect" that we discussed in chapter 3 (i.e., the flapping of a butterfly's wings in China leads to violent storms off the coast of Florida a few weeks later). What this notion tells us is that the smallest effects—effects that are largely ignored if even realized—can have substantial impact on the system's overall movement or behavior. Further, the effect that eventually induces behavior could have occurred at some earlier point in time (e.g., days, weeks, months previously). This phenomenon occurs, for example, in cases of panic disorder where a panic "attack" may be traceable to a moderately stressful event that occurred several weeks prior to the incident itself. The influence of the earlier event is largely unrecognized and, thus, our understanding of the relationship between it and subsequent behavior (or thought/affect) is extremely difficult to ascertain.

While at times static and predictable, system behavior is prone to external influences which may cause the system to *bifurcate*. Recall that bifurcations in behavior can occur when an external stimulus perturbs a system to an extent beyond what the system can sustain. In other words, it becomes "knocked off balance" and its behavior is no longer static but moves somewhat unpredictably in response to the destabilization. If the system continues to lose stability, its behavior becomes increasingly disorderly and susceptible to more subtle influences. Seemingly stable behavior, for example, can quickly become unpredictable if its parameters change.

The "order-to-chaos" transition precisely describes, by way of sensitive dependence, bifurcations, and iteration (see below), this very process. A sensitive structure (e.g., a human being) may, quite unpredictably, fall under the influence of one or more external stimuli that distort the person's stability or state of equilibrium. As we have argued, the human being is a nonlinear system. Thus, the effects that various external stimuli have on a given individual are self-reinforcing. *Iteration* describes this "stretching and folding" process whereby outputs (i.e., psychological effects or manifestations of external input) are fed back into the system in a self-reinforcing manner. When not effectively managed by adequate coping mechanisms, for example, the effect can multiply *ad infinitum* or increase exponentially. We have seen as well that, when these effects become sufficiently disabling, the system can bifurcate and be propelled toward chaos. With regard to individual mental functioning, this might be thought of as the "breaking point" or the point at which dangerousness is realized.

Consider a man who appears to be in a stable state. The individual holds a steady job with a reasonable salary, has a stable marriage, extended family living nearby with whom he maintains favorable relations, and no history of behavioral displays that could be regarded as violent or contextually inappropriate. Now consider that one week ago the man received a call from a school administrator informing him that his 14-year-old son was caught selling drugs on campus, and two days ago his wife revealed that she had been, on one recent occasion, unfaithful to him. These may be considered perturbing stimuli in that the man's psychological and, perhaps, physical well-being will undergo a destabilizing change. The once stable man has entered a phase in which his behavior, influenced as well by his own thoughts and feelings, is marked by instability and disorder. In this situation, it is not clear whether the man will engage in violent or otherwise inappropriate behavior. What it does suggest is that he is more disposed to unpredictable behavior and conduct that may fall outside his normal range or pattern of interaction. Further, the $600 worth of repairs that his car had to undergo several weeks ago which seemed, at the time, little more than an inconvenience and an unavoidable expense, now has the potential to be much more meaningful. Indeed, the more unbalanced his psychological state is, the more sensitive he becomes to external influences, and the more likely the man is to manifest behaviors that are not customary for him.

What all of this suggests is that ultimately ecological concerns are of equal, if not greater, significance than the internal or psychic influences that impact individual behavior. Whatever characterological traits may be identifiable and traceable to an individual, the complexities of social life, as described by such chaos principles as iteration, sensitive dependence, and bifurcation, are of such sufficient magnitude that they render a precise diagnosis of psychological state informative only to a limited degree. As the hypothetical indicates, the susceptibility of human psychology to ecological influences leaves behavior largely unpredictable and routinely subject to unforeseen deviations or bifurcations. In the next chapter, we will examine the extent to which this sensitivity and consequent unpredictability informs (or should inform) current civil commitment practice. For now, however, the selected principles of chaos theory we utilized suggest that *any* conception of human conduct must necessarily acknowledge the limits of imbuing this behavior principally or exclusively in the individual.

An Ecological Perspective on "Dangerousness"

Given the previous analysis, it is plausible to conclude that the man in the hypothetical will act dangerously. However, much like Shah (1977) cautioned and Foucault (1988) explained, it is imperative that interpretations of one's behavior not be attributed solely to underlying personality. Indeed, it is crucial to assess the influence of external stimuli when engaged in a clinical forensic evaluation for dangerousness. Collectively, we regard these external stimuli as ecological variables; that is, factors whose influence is manifest in the individual's ongoing relationship with his/her environment.

Behavior must be conceptualized as a manifestation of personality and the contextual influences (e.g., social, cultural, environmental, political, situational) of which one is a part (Shah, 1977, p. 105). The MacArthur Risk Assessment Study has shown some movement in this direction (e.g., Monahan, 1997; Monahan & Steadman, 1994). In assessing risk factors, the study attempts to incorporate a wide variety of variables. These variables are categorized into four interrelated domains: dispositional (e.g., age, race, gender, class, personality, and neurological factors); historical (e.g., family, work, mental health, violence, and juvenile delinquency); contextual (e.g., social supports, stress, physical environment); and clinical (e.g, current symptoms, drug and alcohol abuse, and level of functioning). Following the tenets of chaos theory, the movement *toward* an ecological understanding of violence risk assessment by the MacArthur Research Network is a step in the right direction. Indeed, by considering a broad array of external variables, there is a recognition that behavior exists only in conjunction with influences outside the individual's own personality.

Accordingly, behavior can be reconceptualized from an ecological perspective as an *interaction*. As physical and social scientists remind us, nothing in the world, at any level, occurs without some form of interaction. The existence of water requires atomic interaction; the onset of a storm requires interaction among atmospheric conditions; the stability of an economy requires interaction between production and consumption; and spousal violence requires some degree of interaction (sexual, psychological, physical) between partners. Beyond these immediate interactions, however, there are innumerable others. For example, not only does crime (e.g., armed robbery) require the interaction of victim and offender, but it is also situationally contingent on such variables as time of day, amount of light, presence of potential witnesses, presence or absence of law enforcement, etc. If there are even the slightest of variations in these circumstances, the robbery is not likely to occur at that particular moment (e.g., Calder & Bauer, 1992; Cornish & Clarke, 1986).

It should be noted that most systems settle into patterns of behavior over time. These patterns are called *attractors*. Without moving too far into a discussion of this principle (see chapter 7 for a more detailed exploration of attractors), a couple of comments are warranted. First, while these patterns are discernable, they are subject to perturbations from without. We have mentioned the principles of bifurcation and sensitivity to initial conditions in this context. Even a seemingly small change in the system's relationship to its environment may be sufficient to disturb it, throwing it into a new attractor or new pattern of behavior. Thus, while one could argue that individual behavior generally conforms to certain discernable patterns, this position obtains only to the extent that both intrapsychic and ecological variables also remain in a fairly static and predictable state. Thus, for example, researchers have enjoyed some success in predicting the near future (e.g., weather trends/conditions for a period of several days), given these patterns of behavior. Even these short-term forecasts are, at times, inaccurate. Moreover, long-term predictions (including predictions of individual behavior), are largely futile endeavors, especially if some degree of accuracy and reliability are desired.

Thus, it is better to conceptualize behavior as an interaction between the individual (i.e., one's personality and internal factors) and the social-environmental context (i.e., external factors) of which one is a part. These external factors may serve as stabilizers encouraging order, or as destabilizers encouraging disorder. As Shah (1977, p. 105) reminds us, individual behaviors vary in form, frequency, and magnitude. Contributions from without inevitably exert an influence on the range of possible behaviors as well as on the form, frequency, and magnitude with which these actions are undertaken at any given time. This is particularly relevant when reconsidering Brooks' (1974) four variables identified for violence prediction purposes: the severity, probability, frequency, and immanence of potential harm. Each of these four variables cannot be considered outside of the interaction between the individual and his/her environment. Having said this, we question whether environmental factors can be integrated into the "dangerousness equation" with any degree of reliable accuracy. This is the subject of the next section.

The Fallacy and Futility of Prediction

Chaos theory informs us that nonlinear systems (e.g., individual persons) "behave according to properties that can be defined only through examination of the collection of the system components, not through reductionist study of any one system component" (Ruhl & Ruhl, 1997, pp. 418–419). Some behaviors are the product of what can be termed "emergence." Emergence may be generally construed as a process whereby something (e.g., a behavior) appears that would not otherwise be describable, given the defining parameters of the system (ibid.). In other words, it is the manifestation of a behavior that one would not be able to predict based on what is observable or available through examination of the individual (i.e., one's traits or personality) alone. This is the result of the limitless influence of interacting variables on the individual at any given time.

Shah (1977, p. 106) asserts that "efforts to understand, evaluate, predict, prevent, and treat an individual's violent or otherwise 'dangerous' behavior should not concentrate *solely* upon discovering or uncovering aspects of an individual's personality. . . ." Instead, he suggests that "it is also very important to give very careful attention to the particular physical and social environment and the situational contexts in which certain types of behaviors are displayed" (ibid.). This is a cautionary statement regarding the clinical evaluation instruments used to predict dangerousness, and the extent to which forensic psychologists should make such determinations absent the insights of sociology. However, the value of Shah's warning ends here. Indeed, even if socioenvironmental factors were considered, predictive efforts would largely be futile. Further, notwithstanding the MacArthur Network initiative and its attempt to include broader variables for forecasting dangerousness (including contextualizing factors), efforts to *predict* violent behavior accurately (as opposed to *understanding* it more fully) are likely to be in vain.

Chaos theory tells us that the behavior of a system (e.g., individual), while sometimes static and predictable for short durations, is ultimately prone to periods of disorder and, consequently, is unpredictable in the long run. In general, this is because the external influences on behavior in the "real world" are unpredictable. Indeed, while efforts to "understand, evaluate, predict, and prevent" may be met with a limited degree of success in experimental laboratories, the world of ongoing human social interaction is far too complex for adequate comprehension. Both the "new science" of nonlinear dynamical systems theory and the conviction and optimism that fueled the Enlightenment age, have hampered our ability to recognize fundamentally how the disorderly order (i.e., chaos) of systems and of society makes nearly impossible our attempts to predict the world and events in it with any appreciable degree of accuracy.

Indeed, to realize fully the relationships necessary for precise prediction, we would have to grasp completely the association between and the effects of every interaction that influences a given individual or system. As Cohen and Stewart (1994) observe, the problem is that "if the effect of any particular interaction is tiny, we may not be able to work out what it is. We can't study it on its own, in a reductionist manner, because it's too small; but we can't study it as part of the overall system, because we can't separate it from all the other interactions" (p. 182). Thus, understanding the effects of every intrapsychic and ecological variable as well as their various interactions is the necessary prerequisite for accurately predicting the behavior of any nonlinear dynamical system, including people. As applied to the phenomenon of forecasting who will or will not be dangerous, what this means is that the complexity of the world limits and, perhaps, eliminates any hope that we may have for reliable, long-term predictions, including events as mundane as the weather forecast to events as impactful as one's likelihood to harm oneself and/or others.

Dangerousness, Prediction, and Civil Commitment

While we have thus far concerned ourselves with what chaos theory would acknowledge as the *futility of prediction*, we have not addressed the preciseness of measurement necessary for a psycholegal finding of dangerousness in the interest of civil commitment. In other words, while chaos theory informs us that, given ecological influences, accurate forecasting is impossible, to some extent the law has addressed this very matter. In short, the law recognizes the limits of prediction; nevertheless it continues to rely upon this forensic practice for decision-making purposes. Why? The answer is complicated as it calls into question the prevailing philosophical assumptions under which the legal system operates (Arrigo, 1996). By asserting and privileging the Constitutional need to protect individuals from themselves and/or others (see the following chapter for more), the law willingly allows imprecision to guide its judgments. Indeed, while the uncertainty of psychiatric opinion was the very basis upon which the legal community was criticized and, subsequently, was asked to *raise* its standard of proof in civil commitment cases, the juridical response used this very uncertainty as justification for a *lower* standard of proof (Levy & Rubenstein, 1996, p. 31).

The precedent case on this matter is *Addington v. Texas* (1979). In *Addington*, the United States Supreme Court recommended the "clear and convincing" standard as a necessary and plausible measure of proof in civil commitment cases (Perlin, 1999). The Court recognized the need for due process protection when deprivation of liberty was at stake. Thus, by proposing this procedural guarantee, it took an important step in this direction; however, the Court did not grant civil commitment detainees the same procedural right it availed to criminal defendants (i.e., "the beyond a reasonable doubt" safeguard). The Court maintained that by requiring such a stringent standard in involuntary hospitalization cases, it would "completely undercut efforts to further the legitimate interests of both the state and the patient . . . served by civil commitment" (ibid., p. 430).

As a practical matter, this means that due process requires that the clinician's predictive efforts need only meet a seventy-five percent (75%) degree of legal certainty for dangerousness determinations (e.g., Stone, 1975). If this standard is reached and is coupled with a finding of mental illness, then civil confinement follows. Conviction of criminal defendants, however, is based on the procedural standard of proof, amounting to beyond a reasonable doubt. What this means is that the trier of fact must be *at least* ninety percent (90%) certain that the defendant is guilty, in order not to abridge his/her due process rights.

The relationship between predicting dangerousness and the clear and convincing standard of proof is noteworthy here. In short, in order to meet due process requirements in civil commitment cases, forensic psychologists/ psychiatrists must be able to forecast that a person is dangerous (i.e., will commit a future harmful act to self and/or to others) with a seventy-five percent (75%) level of certainty or, more correctly, a seventy-five percent (75%) *level of success*. Interestingly, however, current estimates suggest that mental health professionals are able to predict dangerousness with an accuracy rate falling somewhere between less than chance to moderately better than chance (e.g., Mossman, 1994a, 1994b). Despite what some claim is improvement or, at least, the undervaluing of predictive success (Lidz et al., 1993), the undeniable and undisputed conclusion is that experts are not able to forecast future violence anywhere approximating the seventy-five percent (75%) success rate required by due process standards. This basic criticism of clinical assessment practice is profound, notwithstanding the more obvious philosophical contention that persons facing a loss of liberty (even in civil cases) should be granted protections equal to those facing confinement because of criminal conduct (e.g., Arrigo, 2000a ; Morse, 1982).

Cocozza and Steadman (1976, p. 1101; 1978) suggest that attempts to commit individuals civilly based upon a finding of dangerousness, requiring an accuracy rate anywhere above fifty percent, is "futile." This statement is consistent with our analysis of prediction from the stand point of chaos theory. We were led to examine the standard of proof question so that we could consider just how pointless dangerousness forecasting is, following chaos theory. Accordingly, we submit that they are *too futile* to be the basis of civil commitment. As we have noted, the law acknowledges the imprecision and error with which clinical predictions of dangerousness are made, adopting, in response, a lower standard of proof in order to arrive at such findings. In conjunction with accuracy studies, chaos theory tells us why prediction is hopeless even when only a reasonable degree of accuracy is required. The ecology impacting the human system (e.g., sensitive dependence on initial conditions, bifurcations) significantly limits prospects for understanding what impacts behavior. Thus, we conclude that *any* standard of proof or, more accurately, *any* civil commitment reality that includes a finding (i.e., prediction) of dangerousness as a substantive criterion is demonstrably opposed to the promotion of justice.

Danger to Self, Grave Disability, and Civil Commitment

Before we discuss more fully the issue of civil commitment in the next chapter, it is worth revisiting, at least briefly, the concept of danger to self or grave disability in the context of chaos theory. For the most part, the arguments advanced concerning the inadequacy of prediction are equally applicable when the object of injurious conduct is the self or another. The primary difference between the two lies in the type of danger to which one is exposed. Danger to others implies violent behavior; danger to self implies self-neglect or something more akin to negligence than overt action. Thus, it is important to note that, in the context of grave disability (or its jurisdictional equivalent), predictions are informed less by what an individual will or will not do, and more by an evaluation of the quality of his/her life.

In the following chapter and in our cast study analysis (chapter 8), we systematically consider the problem of assigning value to the quality of one's life based on "common sense" understandings of appropriateness. For now, however, it may be helpful to recall the concept of the fractal that was described in the previous chapter when exploring chaos theory's contribution to the meaning of mental illness. This same logic applies to the phenomenon of dangerousness. Indeed, identifying persons based on the "distress and deterioration" or the "severely impaired" standard of self-danger (APA, 1983) is a more obvious example of the labeling process at work (Arrigo, 1996, p. 29). In other words, for instance, individuals who prefer to dwell in the streets or to live in shelters might be defined as suffering from deep psychological trauma, giving rise to perceived abnormal functioning (i.e., the decision to be homeless). Consequently, society's reaction to the street dweller may amount to insisting upon "a need for treatment" to stave off his/her inevitable deterioration. Indeed, this may be articulated as the only humane response to persons who might otherwise "rot with their rights on" (Appelbaum & Gutheil, 1979, p. 308; Gutheil, 1980, p. 237). As we have seen, however, socially constructed definitions of humaneness, appropriateness, normalcy, and so on, are not always equivalent with the lived experiences of others. Again, we examine this notion more closely in the next chapter.

SUMMARY AND CONCLUSIONS

The pre-Socratic philosopher Heraclitus is thought to have once said that "you cannot step twice into the same river, for other waters and yet others go ever flowing on" (Wheelwright, 1966, p. 71). Following this observation, attempts to predict the effect of stepping into the river based, for example, on a previous experience would be futile: waters change and, consequently, the experience must change with them. Thus, an historical encounter that was once considered harmless may not be so regarded in the future. Similarly, an historical encounter that was once defined as dangerous may not be interpreted as such at another, later time. While Heraclitus was not a psycholegal scholar, he does predate (by more than two thousand years) our understanding of the "universal flux" that defines the world in which we live. The fluid nature of reality in itself should be sufficient to give us some pause or apprehension about our predictive endeavors. More specifically, the manifold influences, however subtle, that impact this ever-changing reality signify just how unlikely forecasting dangerousness, much less life, truly is.

Heraclitus is also reputed to have written that "seekers after gold dig up much earth and find little" (Wheelwright, 1966, p. 69). It is unfortunate that the legal system has shown a preference for the findings (i.e., opinions) of "gold diggers" when questions of precious human liberty are at stake. Indeed, the unreliability of expert testimony has encouraged some scholars to suggest that forensic clinicians should never attempt to predict dangerousness (Grisso & Appelbaum, 1992). Unlike the diagnosis of mental illness which, despite our considerations in the previous chapter, continues to lie closer to the psychologist's expertise, forecasting something as elusive as dangerousness can not advance the interests of justice. Indeed, it is defined vaguely by most legislatures and the reality of this construct is that it is subject to nonlinear and ever-fluid ecological forces that make its precise prediction impossible.

We are all cognizant of the impact that significant events or stressors can have on our lives. To some extent, we are also aware that more subtle phenomena (e.g., outdoor temperature) can likewise affect our behavior, notwithstanding our (limited) knowledge of their influence at the time. What is apparent when we consider the everyday involvement of chaos theory and its principles in our lives is how seemingly insignificant events can substantially move us to behave this or that way. In fact, much of the time we are not even made aware of their impact. Instead, we think, feel, behave, and live through their imperceptible, but powerful, influence.

What does all of this portend for law, psychology, and justice? In this chapter, we addressed the role that dangerousness and its prediction assume in the psycholegal sphere. To facilitate and to inform this analysis, we utilized several principles of chaos theory, including iteration, bifurcation, and sensitive dependence on initial conditions. The implications of our critical assessment are twofold: first, the law has failed to communicate clearly and precisely to psychology what it means when inquiring about the dangerousness of certain individuals or classes of individuals; second, clinically predicting anything as sensitive to external influence as behavior (including one's likely harm to self or others) is a futile exercise. The former matter, although noteworthy in its own right, is a semantic concern beyond the scope of our analysis. The latter point was substantially challenged and debunked, given the professed, though inadequate, expertise of those who engage in such forecasting determinations. Indeed, when the acclaimed violence expert John Monahan wrote that, for mental health professionals, ". . . our crystal balls are terribly cloudy" (quoted in Levy & Rubenstein, 1996, p. 30; see also *Barefoot v. Estelle*, 1983, p. 920), he may have been better served using the phrase "terribly unstable," given the quixotic nature of being human.

Undoubtedly, there are patterns of behavior that persons settle into over time. Moreover, there are, unquestionably, less-than-subtle signs available on occasion to warn us about one's likelihood of harm to self or others. However, the latter phenomenon is the exception to the rule and the former is valuable only to the extent that the pattern does not shift as a result of variables beyond the immediate control of the individual and others in direct contact with that person. By employing the insights of chaos theory, we have shown how behavior can be perceived only in relation to the myriad of interactions that directly affect it. Thus, dangerous conduct must not be attributed to one's personality but, instead, must be attributed to the interaction of countless (past, present, and future) factors, at a given time. Unfortunately, this particular understanding is not a light that shines on Monahan's "crystal ball."

What we inescapably conclude, then, is that the civil commitment of individuals presumed or predicted to be dangerous, is a practice that results both in the abrogation of liberty where such abridgment may be unjustified, and the bestowal of freedom where such a provision may be unwarranted (i.e., the person may indeed represent a threat to harm him/herself or others). If justice requires that we do not deprive persons of liberty, freedom, and the right to self-determination under *arbitrary* guidelines, then the practice of violence prediction must be acknowledged as thoroughly inconsistent with the establishment of a just society. Indeed, as chaos theory suggests, justice demands that we respect the unpredictability and indeterminacy that governs the behavior of individuals and/or collectives. It remains to be seen whether such respect is afforded psychiatric citizens subject to involuntary hospitalization. This matter is examined in the next chapter.

CHAPTER SIX

Civil Commitment

OVERVIEW. *The previous two chapters addressed the meaning of mental illness and the concept of dangerousness (and its prediction) respectively. The controversy surrounding these two psycholegal matters is significant as findings of both considerably impact involuntary civil commitment determinations. This particular judgment results in a deprivation of liberty as one is confined, against one's will, to a psychiatric hospital. Thus, by necessity, the decision to commit requires that the systems of law and psychology jointly and interactively function.*

Unlike criminal offenders who find themselves confined as a consequence of violating the law, persons institutionalized in psychiatric facilities are not generally found to have committed wrongs against society. Indeed, the decision to hospitalize is based on a clinical prediction of likely self-harm and/or danger to others, and not on any acts which require criminal sanctioning (Perlin, 1999). Thus, given the absence of any demonstrable law violation, the decision to commit and, thus, to deprive a person of his or her autonomy, raises a number of ethical questions about this finding and its psycholegal justification (Arrigo & Williams, 2000).

The ethical dynamics of civil confinement have given rise to several competing perspectives within the legal and psychiatric communities (e.g., Arrigo, 1993a, pp. 12–23). Indeed, proponents of civil commitment suggest that a temporary loss of freedom, liberty, and self-determination is warranted to protect the community from unstable individuals who may engage in behaviors considered injurious to themselves, others, or, in some states, one's property (e.g., Chodoff, 1976; Treffert, 1985). Staunch opponents of civil commitment, however, thoroughly reject the logic of confinement. For example, employing the language and conceptual framework of antipsychiatry (e.g., Guattari, 1984), supporters of the wholesale abolition of involuntary hospitalization draw attention to the adverse effects of institutionalization (Goffman, 1961) and labeling (Gove, 1975; Scheff, 1984; Warren, 1982), the questionable reality base of mental illness (Szasz, 1961, 1963, 1987), and the role of social, economic, and political forces, impacting our definition of psychiatric illness and our understanding of civil confinement altogether (e.g., Deleuze & Guattari, 1977; Foucault, 1965, 1977; Laing, 1967, 1969; Marcuse, 1966).

    There are a number of other perspectives that fall along this continuum of protective confinement versus absolute liberty (e.g., mainstream legalists, civil libertarians). We note, however, that the level of disagreement surrounding the appropriateness of civil commitment is appreciable. In addition, notwithstanding mild or extreme arguments for or against involuntary hospitalization, it is the legal system, informed by the mental health community, that must balance the civil liberties of psychiatric citizens against the community's right to be protected from (potential) danger.

    In the present chapter, we explore the much debated phenomenon of involuntary civil commitment. In particular, we examine its social standing in contemporary society. Similar to our previous analysis on dangerousness and mental illness, we consider the legal and psychological approaches to confinement. Further, we identify and assess the limits of both. These shortcomings encourage us to question whether justice is or is not promoted through the practice of civil commitment. Along these lines, we rely on several principles found within chaos theory to guide and substantiate our analysis.

THE LAW OF CIVIL COMMITMENT

Civil commitment refers to the involuntary hospitalization of individuals who are in need of psychiatric treatment and/or in need of detainment because they are thought to be mentally ill and to represent a threat of harm to themselves and/or the community of which they are a part (Perlin, 1999). Civil commitment is state-sanctioned and, thus, the state reserves the right to determine who meets the criteria for institutionalization. In other words, where there is any question or challenge concerning one's psychiatric illness and dangerousness, the decision to commit is ultimately made by a court of law. Therefore, the role of the mental health professional is, theoretically, to *assist* the state in determining whether an individual is psychiatrically ill and likely to be violent toward him/herself and/or others. In practice, however, courts have almost unfailingly deferred to the wisdom of the clinical forensic community on such matters (e.g., Holstein, 1993; Reisner & Slobogin, 1990).

    Given that the civil commitment process, at least in theory, is fundamentally governed by the law, there are several notable legal components to civil confinement that warrant some attention. We already examined the substantive criteria for involuntary hospitalization in the two previous Chapters. Both mental illness and dangerousness to self and/or others must be shown before an individual may be subjected to a deprivation of liberty.

In the present chapter, however, we focus on the jurisprudential bases of commitment; that is, *why* the state exercises (or should exercise) its decision-making power to involuntarily commit a citizen. At the outset, we note that our discussion will be historical mostly as the existing criteria for commitment are the result of a number of smaller reforms and criticisms, occurring chiefly throughout the latter half of the twentieth century.

Jurisprudential Bases for Civil Commitment

The authority of the state to confine individuals who meet the substantive criteria for commitment stems from two separate, but often interrelated, functions (e.g., Arrigo, 2000a; Myers, 1983/1984; Perlin, 1999; Reisner & Slobogin, 1997). The first justification is the "police power" authorization in which involuntary hospitalization is legally sanctioned for persons believed to be a danger to others. This mandate provides states with "a plenary power to make laws and regulations for the protection of the public health, safety, welfare, and morals" (Note, 1974, p. 1222). The second justification is the *parens patriae* authorization and is applicable to cases wherein the person is believed to be a danger to him/herself. *Parens patriae* represents the paternal function of the state. These two standards mark the jurisprudential basis for commitment in the United States today. Although reviewed somewhat provisionally in chapter 5, both the police power and the *parens patriae* authorization require some additional explanation in order to understand more fully the rationale for curtailing individual freedom for the sake of state interests.

The *parens patriae* (literally, "the parent of the country") function is paternalistic in nature (Feinberg, 1988). It stems from feudal England and is intended to allow the state (then the King) to perform its traditional role of guardian for persons "incapacitated," including minors or persons with a mental disability (Levy & Rubenstein, 1996, p. 16; Melton et al., 1997, p. 300). Its primary purpose in England was to protect the property interests of those individuals who had lost the use of their rational capacities (Grob, 1994; Myers, 1983/1984). Thus, the state assumes the parental role and, consequently, the power to make decisions for persons unable to do so themselves (Reisner & Slobogin, 1990). In the United States, it was not until the mid-1800s that this practice was widely observed (e.g., Melton et al., 1997). The dawn of involuntary confinement, based on the state's *parens patriae* authority, occurred simultaneously with the birth of the asylum

(Rothman, 1971). While asylums were often warehouses for the violent mentally ill and other "undesirables," it was also commonly believed, especially by social reformers of the time, that the "cure" for insanity (i.e., mental illness) lay in moral treatment which could best be accomplished within the confines of the asylum (Grob, 1994; Rothman, 1971, 1980).

By the twentieth century, however, medical advances and scientific breakthroughs created an air of optimism concerning the efficacy of treatment regimes for the mentally ill (e.g., Arrigo, 1993a; Grob, 1994; Isaac & Armat, 1990). Given this increased optimism, many of the early reforms in commitment law were driven by a desire to make civil confinement decisions _easier_ to accomplish (Melton et al, 1997, p. 299). Indeed, up until the 1970s throughout a majority of the states, if a physician certified that an individual was mentally ill and in need of treatment, civil commit followed (Dershowitz, 1974). States routinely deferred to medicine for scientific guidance and relied on psychiatry for clinical expertise, fueling the mental health community's interest in solving psychiatric disease (Grob, 1994). At the same time, however, the absence of legal safeguards spawned large-scale human rights violations (Arrigo, 1996). In short, persons with mental illness facing involuntary confinement were rarely given the same rights that their criminal offender counterparts received (Appelbaum, 1997).

In the 1970s, the lack of legal protections afforded persons with psychiatric disorders began to change. While the _parens patriae_ power of the state had always been regarded as the jurisprudential basis for civil commitment (e.g., treating those who needed treatment, helping those who needed help), this conviction was now questioned. In challenging the medical or disease model of intervention itself, critics helped alter popular sentiment concerning the character of mental illness (e.g., Szasz 1961, 1970). The relationship between the public's perception of wellness and illness was exploited in the mainstream press and culture (Grob, 1994), such that the courts were sufficiently persuaded to enact warnings about findings of mental disease and their generalizability (e.g., _Jackson v. Indiana_, 1972; _Lessard v. Schmidt_, 1975). For example, the suggestion by Scheff (1966) that psychiatric illness was merely a socially constructed means of controlling unwelcomed but harmless deviants became suitably meritorious such that this logic helped inform several significant mental health law rulings. Thus, in short, the need to redress the inadequate statutory definitions for mental illness found support in the legal system itself. This legal remedy was deemed necessary in order to protect persons subjected to involuntary hospitalization who failed to meet the medical community's standards for normal, human behavior (Isaac & Armat, 1990).

In addition to the criticisms surrounding the meaning of mental illness, consumer groups, social activists, and public interest attorneys drew attention to the perceived inhumanities of the psychiatric facilities themselves (Grob, 1994). In particular, the unsanitary and unhealthy conditions of overcrowded mental hospitals were censured, and the loss of individual rights that accompanied the individual's commitment to these new "asylums" was challenged (e.g., Arrigo, 1993b; Stone, 1975). Existential themes, including "alienation," "institutional dependency," "disempowerment," as well as concern for long-term stigmatization became fertile ground for wholesale objection (LaFond & Durhman, 1992; Scheff, 2000). As a result, a panoply of legal rights and reforms were established for the institutionalized mentally ill (e.g., the right to refuse treatment, minimally adequate standards in treatment), in their struggle for dignity and humanity (Arrigo, 1996; Isaac & Armat, 1990).

Indeed, a number of legal challenges arose in response to the manner in which persons were committed against their will. In short, critics of civil commitment argued that the agents of the state (i.e., hospitals and psychiatrists) should not maintain a position of absolute authority in the decision-making process (Grob, 1994). Given that persons civilly committed were deprived of freedom in much the same way as criminal offenders, it was felt that they should enjoy the same due process protections. The most significant dimension of this criticism, in relation to the jurisprudential basis of confinement, is that mental illness and need for treatment alone were increasingly regarded as insufficient for civil commitment determinations (Myers, 1983/1984). In other words, the *parens patriae* power of the state as *sole* justification for commitment was questioned (Arrigo, 1993b). Instead, it was proposed that involuntary confinement be regarded as a police power function (Isaac & Armat, 1990). To support this contention, observers noted that persons with mental illness should not only need treatment but should also pose a danger to others (see Note, 1974 on the history of confinement and the necessity of an overt act).

The Constitutional limits of involuntary civil commitment surfaced in the 1970s, notwithstanding its widespread practice throughout the United States and much of its history (Perlin, 1999). For example, in the landmark decision of *O'Connor v. Donaldson* (1975), the Court considered the plight of a 55-year-old man hospitalized against his will for 15 years, without specific treatment for his illness. The hospitalized individual was not believed to be a danger to himself and/or to others, and appeared capable of earning a successful living outside the confines of the treating facility (in fact, upon his eventual release, Donaldson obtained a job in hotel administration). The Court ruled in favor of Donaldson. In doing so, it established clearer boundaries for state commitment power. The Court held that "a State cannot constitutionally confine without more a nondangerous individual who is capable of surviving safely in freedom by himself or with the help of willing and responsible family members or friends" (*O'Connor v. Donaldson*, 1975, p. 576). Other similar precedent-setting cases helped pave the way for the plethora of mental health law reforms that followed (e.g., community-situated treatment, *Lake v. Cameron*, 1966; procedural protections, *Lessard v. Schmidt*, 1975; the right to treatment, *Rouse v. Cameron*, 1966; medical and Constitutional minimal standards in treatment, *Wyatt v. Stickney*, 1972).

Thus, by the 1970s there was a movement away from committing the mentally ill where the basis for this determination was merely a need for treatment (Reisner & Slobogin, 1997). Consequently, by this time period, the first steps toward requiring a finding of dangerousness were taken. The basis for commitment shifted from the *parens patriae* doctrine toward the state's police power authority. It became increasingly necessary to demonstrate that individuals suffering from a psychiatric disorder were, in some sense, a danger to themselves and/or to others if they were to be involuntary hospitalized. As we described in the previous chapter, legal danger assumes two forms today: likely harm to others; and likely harm to self or grave disability. These two expressions of dangerousness, when coupled with a finding of mental illness, represent the contemporary justification for civil commitment in the United States.

PSYCHOLOGY AND INVOLUNTARY CIVIL COMMITMENT

The role of the mental health professional in civil commitment determinations is a complex, controversial, and uncertain issue. As previously discussed, at one time the medical community held almost complete and unbridled authority in confinement decisions. With the movement toward a more legalistic rather than medical decision-making orientation (e.g., affording legal rights to the committed and potentially committed), the role of the clinician was, theoretically, reduced and minimized. In practice, however, the majority of state and federal courts still rely considerably on expert forensic opinion when reviewing specific civil commitment cases. The extent to which clinical forensic assessments and/or testimony factor into legal judgments varies from state to state and court to court. This not-withstanding, we note that treating psychiatrists/psychologists who once had the power to commit on their own are now relegated in the confinement process to a role that necessitates specific interaction with the legal system. To be clear, mental health professionals provide evaluation and diagnostic information unattainable through a legal proceeding otherwise devoid of such evidence. However, the forensic mental health specialist generally does not possess the requisite knowledge of the law to reach complete decisions about a matter (i.e., civil commitment) whose fundamental character is legal. Accordingly, the role of the clinical forensic expert in such determinations is one of complexity, controversy, and confusion.

What then does the mental health professional do or contribute in cases of involuntary hospitalization? The answer is manifold. The treating psychologists/psychiatrists are not responsible for civil commitment decisions. Judgments such as these are made by fact finders (e.g., an administrative law council, jury, judge). Forensic specialists do, however, evaluate, diagnose, and recommend treatment, including extended involuntary hospital confinement. Having said this, it is not uncommon for clinicians to infringe upon the territorial responsibilities of fact finders, or for fact finders to relinquish their own responsibility, showing considerable deference to the opinion of the treating physician (Warren, 1982).

Precisely because the substantive criteria for civil commitment are unclear and the statutory language fails to provide measurable guidelines for the same, the expert opinion of mental health professionals assumes a definitive role in the decision-making process (Perlin, 1999). Thus, while a determination to hospitalize someone involuntarily has always been, in principle, a legal matter, it more closely resembles a clinical judgment in practice (e.g., *Youngberg v. Romeo*, 1982). This decision to defer to the wisdom of mental health experts would be less controversial if the psychological community embraced the same understanding of mental illness, dangerousness, and commitment espoused by the law, and if the research community generally agreed upon, through reliable and valid replication studies, its assessment of these constructs. Regrettably, however, law and psychology vary considerably on these controversial matters (Arrigo, 2000a), and the scientific establishment has yet to offer compelling and/or incontrovertible empirical support for its own research findings on these very contentious issues (Durham & LaFond, 1985; LaFond & Durham, 1992).

Generally speaking, the mental health profession (especially psychiatry) assumes a need-for-treatment approach in matters of patient intervention (e.g., Appelbaum, 1997; Levy & Rubenstein, 1996). In other words, while the law provides certain safeguards against the denial of one's human rights and freedoms, treating physicians and/or clinicians concern themselves with the type and quality of care necessary for those found to be in need of medical intervention (e.g., Appelbaum & Gutheil, 1981; Treffert, 1971) Thus, it is not surprising that psychologists prefer to *treat* rather than to *protect* the mentally ill. This treatment preference is clearly recognized in cases of involuntary confinement. While the legal community balances the *parens patriae* and/or police powers of the State against the liberty rights of psychiatric citizens, the mental health establishment assesses mental illness, predicts dangerousness, and recommends a need-for-treatment (i.e., involuntary hospitalization) in particular cases.

A need for treatment (e.g., psychopharmacological care) carries with it the conviction that (temporary) confinement would be in the best medical interests of the patient. Further, the purpose of civil commitment is to address those symptoms that give rise to self-injurious behavior or conduct harmful to others. Thus, the psychological community views hospital intervention as largely therapeutic and appropriate. Indeed, through drug and related therapies, individuals suffering from a psychiatric disorder can eventually function meaningfully and productively within society (Arrigo, 1993a, pp. 13–17; Chodoff, 1976). Accordingly, treating physicians, psychologists, psychiatric social workers, and other mental health professionals view their role as assisting persons so that they can care for themselves. This is where expert (clinical forensic) opinion becomes useful and important to the court system.

Indeed, the practical role of the psychologist is to offer an informed opinion regarding one's need for treatment as the basis of a civil commitment recommendation. Fact finders "weigh" this testimony in reaching a judgement about confinement. Generally speaking, however, courts often demand that mental health professionals provide more conclusive information about the likely dangerousness of an individual, or provide a more precise explanation for a clinical finding of mental illness. Instances such as these place a considerable burden on the forensic expert, ostensibly shifting the legal focus of civil commitment to one that is clinical. Thus, we see why mental health professionals may believe their role extends beyond what is expected of them (i.e., assess, predict, diagnose, recommend), venturing forth into fundamentally legal terrain.

LIMITATIONS OF LEGAL AND PSYCHOLOGICAL APPROACHES TO CIVIL COMMITMENT

Despite the movement toward ensuring the civil liberties of persons with mental illness that has marked the late twentieth century in the United States, many commentators still provide arguments and evidence of a contrary nature (e.g., Arrigo, 1993, 1996). The main thrust of these criticisms differs little from those of the past. Essentially, the civil commitment of persons who have engaged in no criminal wrongdoing is viewed as a barbaric practice that strips and denies individuals of their humanity. Further, opponents of involuntary hospitalization observe that the primary difference between confinement today as opposed to some 50 years ago is that the established Constitutional safeguards are a step forward in theory only. In other words, while persons facing civil commitment are availed more substantive and procedural rights, there is little observable difference in practice (Levy & Rubenstein, 1996).

For example, Appelbaum (1997, p. 140) notes that despite initial optimism about increased legal safeguards against arbitrary confinement, proving that significant changes in commitment *practice* are the result of changes in commitment *law* has been difficult. Further, although findings of dangerousness are now necessary for involuntary hospitalization, many studies show no change in rates of civil commitment following legal reforms (ibid.). In addition, the population of civilly committed individuals, both demographically and diagnostically, has changed little, if any, since Constitutional safeguards for the mentally disordered were enacted (Levy & Rubenstein, 1996).

While many reformists insist on more precision with definitions of psychiatric illness and dangerousness, a discernable statutory vagueness remains making confinement decisions no less arbitrary than in the past (LaFond & Durham, 1992). Despite the limits placed on the mental health professional's role in civil commitment decisions, these restrictions are, at best, infrequently acknowledged. In short, the indecencies and inhumanities perpetrated against the mentally ill have merely grown more surreptitious (Grob, 1994). The appearance of justice, fueled by a panoply of well-intended legal protections, has not amounted to justice in practice. Indeed, the myth that the mentally ill are diseased, deviant, and dangerous remains (Arrigo, 1996; Szasz, 1961, 1970), and society, law, and the psychological community tend to perceive, treat, and punish them as such (Arrigo, 1997a; Scull, 1989).

In part, the persistence of this myth is linked to the failure of decision makers to acknowledge and endorse thoroughly the wholesale reforms in mental health law. For example, judges and other nonclinically-trained decision brokers rely on commonsense notions of who should be committed (e.g., Applebaum, 1997; Hiday & Smith, 1987; Warren, 1982). Further, researchers suggest that many decision makers apply intuitive criteria in cases of involuntary civil commitment, even when the guidelines of the law lead elsewhere (Applebaum, 1997, p. 143; Holstein, 1993). Moreover, lawyers may be less adversarial than anticipated when pursuing the release of mentally ill patients, choosing, instead, to follow their own instincts about particular clients (Arrigo, 1993; Poythress, 1978; Warren, 1982). Finally, as noted previously, mental health professionals are typically driven by intuitive clinical instincts. Indeed, the primary interest of the psychologist lies in efficacious, quality treatment, not in the careful consideration of the laws that are intended to shape the contours of the clinician's opinions (Applebaum, 1997, p. 143).

In theory, the rights afforded the psychiatrically disordered and the limits placed on mental health professionals are considerable steps in the right direction. As a practical matter, however, these reform efforts lack substance. Both the legal and mental health systems reach beyond their respective "zones of authority" in matters of involuntary confinement, subjecting far too many psychiatric citizens to arbitrary civil commitment determinations. Without legal safeguards, psychologists would involuntarily hospitalize individuals who did not meet the clinician's standard of mental health, however (subjectively) defined. Without psychological input, the law would confine individuals who appeared to be different (e.g., weird or strange) and seemingly dangerous, absent convincing clinical evidence that the individual was ill or was in some way unable to live outside the bounds of an institution. Unfortunately, both of these situations are far too common in everyday civil commitment practice (Levy & Rubenstein, 1996). As a consequence, law and psychology, although authorized to attend to the very human problems posed by civil commitment, come disturbingly close to manufacturing a psycholegal response anchored by the philosophy of social control (Arrigo, 1993b). In other words, fixed ideals regarding behavior and the policing of deviation from these ideals are the cornerstones of confinement, and the psycholegal sphere functions to ensure absolute compliance (Isaac & Armat, 1990; Szasz, 1963).

It is often noted in psychology that everyone is diagnosable; that is, everyone can be situated within categories of psychological illness. There is a significant degree of truth to this statement. Indeed, the "perfect picture of mental health" does not and cannot find embodiment in any human being. Of course, this leads us to conclude that everyone can, at some time, benefit from psychological treatment, in one form or another. Where, then, is the line drawn between mental health and psychiatric illness? The answer ostensibly is found within the law. The legal system creates a distinction between those who *need* treatment for mental illness (i.e., the person will act violently without it), and those who would merely benefit from treatment. As we have seen, however, this line is not drawn with much confidence and, consequently, it is often difficult to articulate in specific cases.

CHAOS THEORY AND CIVIL COMMITMENT

Our application of chaos theory to the matter of involuntary civil confinement largely relies on a single thesis; however, this notion has established itself as the basis for much criticism in the area of mental health law and policy. The thesis states that confining individuals against their will when they have committed no criminal wrongdoing is, in effect, a method of social control. In other words, involuntary hospitalization is a legally and medically justified means of shaping an individual's moral or hygienic standards, life goals, mode of productivity, and thinking, feeling, and being so that these are consistent with the values society has set for itself. From this perspective, civilly committing the mentally ill is a means of policing public hygiene (Foucault, 1965, 1977), and of ridding society of its undesirables (Arrigo & Williams, 1999a). The social control thesis implodes the very definition of mental illness. Consistent with our critical commentary found in chapter 4, we argue that mental illness is nothing more than deviation from social norms (as opposed to physical illness which is better regarded as a disease of the body). If our contention is correct, then psychology's efforts to "cure" mental illness are merely attempts to promote socially sanctioned conformity. Civil commitment, then, is an extreme form of this promotion (i.e., the conformity of society is seriously threatened or compromised by the thoughts and/or behaviors of persons with persistent and severe mental disorders).

If civil commitment is defined as an exercise in controlling the quantity and quality of difference that pervades society, then chaos theory contributes to our understanding of this phenomenon. In short, what it offers us is an alternative and more natural conceptualization of health itself. Additionally, chaos theory identifies the consequences of controlling social boundaries as an artificial mechanism to ensure conformity and a shared (i.e., linear) perspective on individual and collective (mental) health. Thus, more than contributing to the definition of psychiatric illness and the meaning of dangerousness (and its prediction), nonlinear dynamical systems theory enables us to see how social control impacts several artifacts of culture and society (e.g., civil commitment). We begin our analysis by investigating, somewhat provisionally, the social control thesis that pervades Michel Foucault's writings. This French social theorist and historian provides a fertile theoretical backdrop against which an examination of law and psychology's role in disciplining difference through confinement can unfold. Thus, our subsequent discussion of several chaos theory principles necessarily follows our presentation of social control as applied to matters of civil commitment.

The Social Control Thesis

Over the course of his life, the twentieth-century French philosopher Michel Foucault proposed a critique of institutions (e.g., psychiatric hospitals, prisons) that drew attention to the unseen or surreptitious motivations of criminal and/or civil confinement. Foucault's critique is consistent with the social control thesis (Arrigo & Williams, 1999a). In brief, he perceived institutionalization as a means of isolating and, thus, controlling the disenfranchised elements of society. Policing undesirables amounts to eliminating the inevitable and natural differences that pervade society. Law and psychology contribute to the policing or control of difference. Knowingly or not, they ensure that their respective knowledge about civil commitment assumes the form of truth, embodying a specialized power (i.e., juridical and medical) to determine whose freedom will be abrogated, when one's thought/behavior is deemed incompatible with the normative social order (e.g., Arrigo, 1996).

Foucault (1988) described psychologists and psychiatrists as "functionaries of social order." In this context, mental health professionals are agents of the state which, in turn, is driven by the demands of the majority and its moral sensibilities. The growth of the mental health profession (e.g., psychiatric social workers, mental health clinicians, psychiatric nurses), as both pillar and exemplar of the social order, has bridged medical and police practices wherein the distinction between the two often is blurred. This is particularly the case when psychologists or psychiatrists determine who does or does not need involuntary hospitalization for treatment purposes. Indeed, this particular function is not appreciably different from the police officer who patrols the streets, maintaining public order when stopping, detaining, and arresting citizens who violate the criminal law. If we expand this analogy consistent with Foucault (1965, 1977), we see how the psychiatric hospital becomes a prison for those who commit civil rather than criminal wrongdoings (Arrigo, 1996; Szasz, 1977).

As Foucault (1988) observed, however, the difference between the two lies in an important distinction: being perceived as a dangerous individual versus engaging in injurious behavior. As he explained:

> [W]hen you look closely at the penal code . . . *danger* has never constituted an offense. To be dangerous *is not an offense*. To be dangerous *is not an illness*. It is not a symptom. And yet we have come . . . to *use* the notion of danger, by a perpetual movement backwards and forwards between the penal [law] and the medical [psychiatry/psychology]. (1988, p. 191)

Foucault concerned himself with the advent and subsequent deployment of the concept of the "dangerous" individual; a notion that, as we have seen, continues to be a source of psycholegal controversy seemingly without foreseeable closure. As we noted in chapter 5, the arrival of psychiatry into criminality allowed for an examination of several links between mental health and violence. Of particular interest to Foucault was the degree to which attention could be shifted away from the crime itself to the *individual* responsible for the crime. It is here where danger, as a characteristic of individuals, established a permanent role for itself in the analysis of crime and society. Criminal wrongdoing is committed by individuals who are dangerous (i.e., possessing the characteristic of dangerousness) and, thus, the identification of such individuals allows for the possible prevention of crime. According to Foucault (1988), psychiatry provided a means to understand illicit behavior and to prevent future harm—to the extent, that is, that mental illness could be correlated with dangerousness and dangerousness with criminality.

Consequently, Foucault (1988) argued that psychiatry *created* a new crime; that is, the crime of mental illness (Arrigo & Williams, 1999a). In searching for psychological explanations for illicit conduct, the (likely) danger that the mentally ill represented came to constitute a crime in itself. If mental illness was linked to criminal behavior such that psychiatric citizens were potentially dangerous to society, then this association justified control over disordered individuals to prevent future violence and likely social problems from occurring. Thus, the introduction of psychiatry into the legal arena solidified the perceived causal link between mental illness and crime, making the control of such a union a legitimate psycholegal practice in the interest of society (Grob, 1994).

Society and the Control of Difference

How we define dangerousness and how it is subsequently handled by psychology and the law is influenced decidedly by power relations (Shah, 1977). While almost any individual could, at specific times or under certain circumstances, fit the criteria for dangerousness, persons who do typically embody stereotyped characteristics of dangerousness (Isaac & Armat, 1990; Levy & Rubenstein, 1996). For example, ethnic and racial minorities, persons of low socioeconomic status, and individuals with limited educational achievement are treated much differently than those with political and economic influence for commitment purposes (Shah, 1977). Individuals with the former constellation of personal and social features become identified with dangerousness and its meaning in ways that the latter grouping of persons do not (Scheff, 2000). Indeed, we are unlikely to witness a dangerous, though socially and economically self-sufficient, individual confined in the same institution under the same conditions and stipulations as a sexual psychopath without such means (Shah, 1977, p. 106). Based on these observations, some researchers conclude that the operative jurisprudential bases for civil commitment in the United States are merely conflated attempts to disguise the primary objective of socially controlling the feared and misunderstood masses (e.g., Arrigo, 1996; Kittrie, 1971; Scull, 1989; Shah, 1977; Szasz, 1977). Chambers (1972) has even suggested that, in addition to providing care and treatment and preventing harm to individuals and the community, we should add a fourth function of civil commitment: concealing the social element that evokes a feeling of uncomfortableness in the community (see also Williams, 1999).

Other evidence for this thesis is found within the vagueness of state and federal civil commitment statutes that can be manipulated to suit a particular occasion or purpose (e.g., In the Matter of Billie Boggs, 1987). Despite the dangerousness provision that was intended, in part, as a reform measure to ensure that civil commitment not be used for purposes of social cleansing (LaFond, 1981), the flexible nature of many statutes allows for concepts such as grave disability to justify the commitment of nondanger-ous individuals (Schmidt, 1985). For example, researchers have demon-strated that many persons thought to be in need of treatment but not found to meet the dangerousness criterion, are committed on the basis of grave disability or inability to care for self (Cleveland, Mulvey, Appelbaum, & Lidz, 1989). What this suggests is that there are multiple approaches to civil commitment, allowing clinical or legal intuition to negate the standards or criteria set forth by the law. If social control is indeed a motive in some, if not many, civil confinement cases, the inadequate statutory language per-mits this goal to be accomplished despite the absence of a finding of danger to oneself or to others (Arrigo, 1993b).

Thus, the process of civil commitment often bears little resemblance in practice to its mental health law articulation. Why? As we suggest above, social norms, moral sentiments, myths, and fears all help fashion the legal order. Ultimately, the law is shaped to fit prevailing social sentiment (Appelbaum, 1997, 144–145), and it is modified in light of social demands. If the law fails to present itself as consistent with these sentiments and demands, it is molded accordingly in everyday interactions. Civil commit-ment is a compelling illustration of this phenomenon. The limits of the psycholegal sphere in matters of involuntary hospitalization substantiate this conclusion as well. It is in this context, then, that social control is achieved surreptitiously. Indeed, a society fueled by fear of the unknown (e.g., mental illness, dangerousness) is unlikely to allow this element of uncertainty much room to mold civic life. Thus, the mental health and jus-tice systems, as powerful institutional emblems of prevailing societal norms, function to maintain conformity and to police difference.

Chaos, Social Control, and Mental "Health"

The social control thesis provides an important perspective from which to pursue the topic of involuntary civil confinement. What chaos theory offers is a conceptual glance at the role of disorder in society. In other words, nonlinear dynamical systems theory considers whether disorder (e.g., differ-ence, nonconformity) should hold a place in the social order and, more importantly, whether it must hold a place there as well. Thus, in the con-text of law and psychology, the question to ask is whether society should attempt to "cure" mental disorder through therapy, drug treatment, and/or involuntary hospitalization. Matters such as these draw attention to one of the most important principles of chaos theory for social scientific analysis; namely, the attractor. In the sections that remain, we examine civil commitment arguing that, as an expression of social control, the current practice is consistent with the point attractor of chaos theory. In addition, however, we offer an alternative approach, invoking the logic of the strange attractor.

Point Attractors and Social Control

Recall that the point attractor (or fixed-point, single-point) encourages a system to approach a stable end state in an effort to maximize equilibrium conditions and minimize the effects of disorder that could propel a system into far-from-equilibrium conditions. In other words, the diversity that represents a system in its natural dynamic state is compelled toward a point of stasis or rest, counterbalancing the natural effects of disorder that would otherwise define a diverse system. The end-state of the system is homogenous, stable, and applied to the system's components with displays of sovereign control. The example of the swinging pendulum shows this sovereignty; that is, the pendulum has no choice but to settle into a very specific dynamic that is defined by the "magnet" of the point attractor. The point attractor, then, exemplifies control, or an attempt at control, over systemic behavior.

Similar to the magnetic effect of the point attractor described in the example of the pendulum, we can observe comparable types of control in social relations. The manner in which law and psychology function in civil commitment determinations is a representative example. Psychiatric hospitals can be regarded as institutions that remove disorderly elements from society. These disorderly elements include a certain diversity (e.g., gravely disabled citizens, the psychiatrically disordered and dangerous, the homeless mentally ill) that inevitably defines any society governed by a natural dynamic. The aim of civil confinement is to treat, heal, and/or cure this disorder such that individual order may be restored and the possibility of ensuing chaos significantly diminished. Thus, involuntary hospitalization serves two interrelated functions: (a) to keep disordered individuals safely away from society; and (b) to employ medicolegal knowledge (cf. Foucault's power-knowledge thesis) to correct the difference that disorder embodies.

Contemporary civil confinement, then, may be regarded as an effort to normalize the mentally ill (Kittrie, 1971). Normalization in this context is metaphorically equivalent to the effects of the point attractor. Psychology draws all diversity to it by identifying and defining all individuals who deviate sufficiently from normal social behavior (APA, 1994). In addition, it subsequently channels or attempts to coerce, through therapy, drug treatment, and the like, these disordered individuals toward an end state that is consistent with the socially accepted conceptualization of health or healthy behavior (e.g., Grotstein, 1990; Moran, 1991). Successful treatment means that the individual is reinstated into the increasingly homogenized whole of society; failure means that the individual continues to be confined against his or her will such that the disorder (i.e., difference) the person represents does not impact or influence the outside world to some greater or lesser extent.

The suppression of disorder, through the state-sanctioned mechanism of civil confinement, is one of the most harmful, yet insidious, forms of social control in contemporary society today (see Butz, 1993a,b; Grotsetin, 1990 for applications to therapy). Psychology's primary function is to ensure that social homogeneity is maintained. The law's principal function is to legitimize such determinations through the instrumentation of the time-honored practice of deference to clinical forensic experts in matters psychiatric. Thus, the psycholegal sphere ensures the magnetic effect of the point attractor in commitment findings. Entire ways of being are limited to predefined parameters of appropriate thought, behavior, feelings, values, impulses, and the like (e.g., Arrigo, 1994, 1996c). The medicolegal attractor draws humanity to an end-state that represents preordained and delimited notions of normalcy, health, morality, and conformity on both individual and social levels (Williams, 1999).

The point attractor's magnetic energy is a means of ensuring that social parameters are well defined and maintained. Stifling behavior that threatens these preexisting boundaries allows the system (i.e., society) to avoid the otherwise inevitable periods of disorder and, perhaps, chaos that intermittently arise. Healthy individual functioning, then, is linked to healthy social functioning which amounts to an orderly society free of the corruptive influence of alternative ways-of-being. Thus, civil commitment serves to eliminate the unpredictable (i.e., the uncontrollable, corrupting behavior) that is the nemesis of an orderly society. But while the point attractor, sustained by civil commitment, attempts to guarantee social accord, the more provocative question concerns the very definition of health itself. In other words, is the order that is imposed upon society a healthy phenomenon? Do the various mechanisms of order (e.g., psychology, law, and civil confinement) contribute to or fail to advance the pursuit of a healthy society? In order to examine these questions more fully, we turn to another attractor in chaos theory; namely, the strange attractor.

Strange Attractors and the "Healthy" Society

The lesson that the attractor, and, more generally, nonlinear dynamical systems theory, provide can be briefly summarized in the following statement: order and health are not synonymous. Order is not necessarily healthy, and health does not emerge from a highly organized world. Order, in fact, restricts the room that a system has to breathe; that is, to adapt, to change, and to become something more in tune with the greater environment of which it is a part. Unlike point attractors, strange attractors represent this possibility of change and growth. They provide an unrealized vision of a society without the strict control embedded in the operation of the point attractor, yet one that maintains a dynamic conducive to individual and social well-being. While the point attractor advances our critique of existing (point) dynamics (i.e., the social control thesis), the strange attractor considerably moves us into the realm of what could be.

The strange attractor is a governing force whenever systems are at far-from-equilibrium conditions, or whenever there exists a conspicuous absence of tight control and fixed order. The statement that there *is* an attractor that governs chaotic systems suggests that disorder, and society without strict measures of control and public hygiene, are not what we routinely think them to be. Rather, the order-within-disorder thesis of chaos theory finds its fullest explication in the notion of the strange attractor.

The dynamics of the system governed by the strange attractor ensure, among other things, that the system never repeats the same behavior or path of motion. Instead, the system remains within broad, natural boundaries of movement while enjoying limitless possibility for movement within those boundaries. On a micro-level (i.e., local, everyday), the system's behavior appears random and unpredictable. On a macro-level (i.e. global, structural), patterns emerge and the system appears loosely ordered (i.e., unpredictable), but not random and not without its *natural* order, including definite boundaries.

What does the strange attractor of chaos theory specifically tell us about the mentally ill and the law-psychology interface? The system of medical justice tends to deny the nonlinearity that is inherent in human behavior. As we have argued, behavior is unpredictable and mostly unmanageable. If notions of "appropriate" conduct are too closely or narrowly demarcated, disorder will not only be present, but it will define society as a whole. The psycholegal sphere would be more attuned to the natural reality of being human if it was prepared to "accept variations around a theme" (Young, 1992, pp. 448–460). These variations are theoretically linked to the nonrepetitive, endlessly varied dynamics that govern the patterned behavior of the strange attractor. Again, we note its movement never traces the same path twice, but always stays within the boundaries naturally developed around the "theme."

The point attractor, as exemplified by the psycholegal system of control, draws human behavior and social being *to* a theme rather than letting it naturally fluctuate *around* a theme. As individuals are, at best, only vaguely similar to one another and never completely identical, this "strange" theme is more appropriately one of general well-being. In contrast, the theme under which the psycholegal system operates is one of predefined standards of constrained well-being. As we have noted, these standards are inevitably influenced by prevailing societal notions of who a person should be and how the individual should function.

By predefining and normalizing reality (attraction to a single point), psychology and the law make certain assumptions that are, in some cases, not only false but unjust, yielding injurious and devastating results. Civil commitment exemplifies this point. For example, a mildly depressed individual may be "in need of treatment" (e.g., therapy, antidepressant medication), yet the person may rarely be subjected to hospitalization involuntary. Contrastingly, the diagnosis for some paranoid schizophrenics may indicate that the patient is "out of touch" with reality, subjecting the person to a loss of liberty. When the point attraction of the psycholegal sphere, with its categorical assumptions about well-being, becomes operative in practice, the nonlinear dynamic that the strange attractor naturally embodies is dismissed. In other words, all roads to mental health do not converge on a single point (i.e., the predefined parameters of normal well-being). Instead, all roads follow their own path, creating their own patterned dynamic within a natural or organic range that more or less encircles the point of normalcy.

In the context of our example, this means that while a paranoid schizophrenic may be less "in touch" with normal life than a depressed individual, the person's highly elaborate and idiosyncratic perception of the world may be highly functional. Conversely, the depressed individual, while seemingly closer to the ideal of mental health, may be significantly debilitated by his or her experiential reality and, consequently, unable to function effectively in the world. What is important to understand, then, is that all persons have a unique road or pattern upon which they travel. While some paths may tend more toward the agreed-upon point of normalcy, wellness, and health, these paths are not necessarily more conducive to a functional experiential reality.

The point attractor of law and psychology, then, is in fact a dangerous reality. Through the mechanism of civil commitment, the point attractor insists that persons travel down the linear road of conformity. Psychological treatment is a coercive attempt to chorale stray individuals, placing them back on this uniform road. Reality, however, often tells us a different story about allegiance to this road and the extent to which those who travel it are more equipped to withstand the perturbations of life than those finding their own way. Indeed, consider the following quote from the Supreme Court's decision in *O'Connor v. Donaldson*:

> May the State confine the mentally ill merely to ensure them a living standard superior to what they enjoy in the private community? That the State has a proper interest in providing care and assistance to the unfortunate goes without saying. But the mere presence of mental illness does not disqualify a person from preferring his home to the comforts of an institution. Moreover, while the State may arguably confine a person to save him from harm, incarceration is rarely if ever a necessary condition for raising the living standards of those capable of surviving safely in freedom, on their own or with the help of family or friends.
>
> May the State fence in the harmless mentally ill solely to save its citizens from exposure to those whose ways are different? One might as well ask if the State, to avoid public unease, could incarcerate all who are physically unattractive or socially eccentric. Mere public intolerance or animosity cannot constitutionally justify the deprivation of a person's physical liberty. (1975, p. 575)

The *O'Connor* Court clearly recognized the value of difference and the importance of letting it be. In doing so, the Court established a powerful precedent for civil commitment theory and practice. What is implied in this decision, but not expressly stated, is what the strange attractor tells us about difference: Not only should it be appreciated, but difference is *necessary* for the continued growth and well-being of society and its members. Without it, social being becomes static. Chaos theory tells us that something static is something dead, or something that will soon be dead. To adapt sufficiently to the disorder and change that the natural world hurls at individuals, people must have a distinctively robust and diverse quality. Point attractors eliminate disorder. In the psycholegal sphere they quash the difference that psychiatric citizens embody. Civil commitment, as the instrument of socially regulating difference, promotes homogenized selves, static being, and controlled order. According to chaos theory, these are not the pathways that lead one to the road of (emotional) health; rather, they are the sign posts of psychological death.

(Controlling) Chaos in the Psychiatric Courtroom

In addition to the broad social realities that inform the process of civil commitment are several notable procedural dynamics. The social control thesis represents a staunch criticism of the established jurisprudential basis for involuntary hospitalization. Relatedly, however, a decision to institutionalize (or not) must be reached. This decision is the procedural reality of civil commitment. Thus, despite the assorted clinical evaluations, the various forensic testimony, the detailed rebuttal evidence, and the like, a standing protocol exists to determine who will be subjected to involuntary confinement.

The decision-making process specifically addresses the substantive criteria for civil commitment; including, a finding of mental illness and a determination of dangerousness. The arena in which these proceedings take place is the psychiatric courtroom (Arrigo 1996a, 1996c). Although research on the dynamics of civil commitment proceedings are generally lacking (Arrigo, 1993, p. 23), several important studies can be identified (e.g., Holstein, 1988, 1993). Perhaps the most influential of these investigations is Warren's (1982) fictitiously named "Metropolitan Court" study. Warren's ethnographic research on the civil commitment hearing and process has several notable implications for mental health confinement law, particularly given our assessment of chaos theory. Chapter 8 details many of these implications in relation to the precedent case of *Boggs* (1987). However, for purposes of our review of the strange attractor in this section, we suggestively consider several of these matters.

"Shared Commonsense" in the Court of Last Resort

Generally speaking, shortly after one's initial confinement, the involuntarily hospitalized citizen is granted an administrative hearing to determine whether, under the law, the person should be released or not (Perlin, 1999). In this sense, then, the committed person or petitioner appears before the "court of last resort" (Warren, 1982). The purpose of this hearing is to assess whether the individual remains mentally ill such that he or she continues to be a danger to self and/or to others (Reisner & Slobogin, 1997). Persons who are successful in their petition are released from involuntary confinement and persons who are not successful are institutionalized for an extended period in a psychiatric institution or some other long-term care facility (Arrigo, 1993, p. 39). We question *how* these decisions are made and the manner in which chaos theory facilitates our understanding of this process.

Following Brooks' (1974) analysis on legal and psychiatric decision making, Warren (1982) argues that the perspectives these professionals bring to the courtroom are not always mutually accommodating. Indeed, significant ideological differences impact the clinician-attorney relationship such that each is suspicious of the other's interpretive scheme and system of values (Warren, 1982, p. 138; Wrightsman, 1997). We have tried to draw attention to some of these differences throughout our critique. Perhaps most important for our analysis is the science and treatment orientation of psychology/psychiatry versus the doctrinaire and rights-based approach of the law. Given these clear differences, how, then, are mutually agreeable decisions reached (e.g., a determination to extend or not inpatient psychiatric treatment)?

Recognizing the disparate (and conflicting) nature of the physician-attorney relationship, Scheff (1984) explains that decisions in civil commitment hearings are often mediated by a *shared commonsense model* of mental illness. This cooperative understanding is dominant in decision making, regardless of specific psychological (e.g., diagnostic classifications) or legal (e.g., statutory definitions) understandings (Warren, 1982). As others have noted, the commonsense approach is the "anchor which settles any trace of scientific or juridic uncertainty in confinement matters" (Arrigo, 1993, p. 24).

These shared meanings are influenced by the prevailing conceptions of mental illness and dangerousness that act as "simplifying heuristics" (Perlin, 1999, p. 17), under conditions of uncertainty. Indeed, employing commonsense understandings in clinicolegal matters of uncertainty may be intimately related to heuristic fallacies (ibid., p. 22). In other words, shared ideas tend to override whatever factual data may otherwise present itself. For example, in discussing dangerousness Perlin (1999, p. 102) suggests that "few other concepts . . . inspire the same 'I-know-it-when-I-see-it' attitude" (see also Perlin, 1994). Warren (1982), too, provides a similar analysis for the meaning of psychiatric illness, indicating that clients are viewed by their attorneys as "sick" or "crazy," consistent with medical (i.e., psychiatric) interpretations (see also Holstein, 1993). This same logic applies to civil commitment decisions reached in the psychiatric courtroom (Arrigo, 1993). Indeed, deference to agreed-upon meanings of confinement, informed by psychiatry's understanding of mental illness and dangerousness, shape administrative outcomes in the court of last resort (Warren, 1982). Zealous client advocacy, featured prominently in criminal proceedings, gives way to an accommodating and shared model of psychiatric justice in matters of civil commitment (Holstein, 1993). Thus, the question that remains is how can chaos theory help change this commonsense and shared decision-making approach operative in the court of last resort?

"Attracting" Shared Commonsense

The phrase "shared commonsense" evokes images of mutual understanding; of two or more individuals coming to some equitable or, at least, agreed-upon position on a given issue. However, behind those images are other impressions, ideas, or beliefs, representing what is *lost* in the course of reaching a settlement or coming to a resolution. For example, when three people maintaining positions A, B, and C respectively agree, through discussion and debate, on position D, the unique and distinct value that points A, B, and C embody is lost or, at least, diluted. In a sense, then, shared commonsense understandings represent the *elimination of difference*.

As we have argued, there are many ways in which the elimination or denial of difference can be detrimental to a society and individuals within it. As the point attractor of chaos theory explains, the process of eliminating difference occurs when its denial *appears* to be in the best interest of the greatest number. Within the court of last resort, the result of this process is the loss of alternative meanings.

We note further that this shared, commonsense understanding (e.g., of mental illness and dangerousness) should not be confused with a dialectic in which the tension of different perspectives produces a new synthesis. Instead, the agreed-upon and accommodating model of psychiatric justice, yields civil commitment outcomes based on preexisting interpretive schemas (Holstein, 1993). Thus, rather than incorporating different clinical and legal positions into a new synthetic understanding, the psychiatric courtroom and the administrative hearing exclude and/or dismiss those viewpoints that are inconsistent with the commonsense understanding of mental illness and dangerous, as informed by the wisdom of psychiatric medicine (Warren, 1982). As a result, the articulation of distinctive or dissenting perspectives are deemed socially unacceptable, as they transgress the boundaries of the civil confinement proceeding which signifies cooperation, compliance, and expedience (Arrigo, 1993).

Thus, we see how the procedural dynamics of commitment, consistent with its structural reality, endorse an insidious form of social control. In order to reach a decision in a specific case, participants in the psychiatric courtroom harbor some preference for "attracting" all accounts of situational knowledge to shared, cooperative, commonsense versions of psychiatric justice (Arrigo, 1996). As previously noted, we explore this decision-making process in much greater detail in Chapter 8. For now, however, the reader is encouraged to consider the possible ways in which chaos theory's point attractor operates in the court of last resort. For example, do the sociopolitical assumptions upon which the practice of civil commitment is based translate into or otherwise inform the confinement decisions that are made on a daily basis? If so, what do they portend for the psycholegal practice of involuntary hospitalization and the prospects for citizen justice in the psychiatric courtroom? These very weighty matters warrant a careful assessment and await our critical attention.

CONCLUSIONS AND IMPLICATIONS

The civil commitment of persons with mental illness has a long tradition in modern society. From the inception of the asylum to the more "humane" psychiatric hospitals of the present day, isolating mentally disordered citizens from the general population for purposes of patient treatment and/or society's protection has been a routine practice. The generally acknowledged reason for confining such citizens is because they suffer from a mental illness that requires treatment and because they are dangerous either to themselves and/or to others. Whether this is correct in any particular case is irrelevant, especially when we consider the broader matter of who defines mental illness and who conceptualizes dangerousness. A finding of psychiatric illness and dangerousness requires a framework within which to make these judgments. This framework can be traced to psychology's efforts to understand mental health and the law's attempts to safeguard the liberty rights of individuals and the larger society.

Determining who fits into a mentally ill classification and/or predicting who fits into the violent category requires that individuals be judged. But what standards are used for these judgments? Critics of involuntary confinement argue that the existing criteria are not objective; rather, they are the products of professional opinions which, in turn, are products of cultural norms. Thus, opponents of institutionalization adopt the thesis that civil confinement is yet another mechanism of social control; that is, a means of keeping the undesirable element in society in a desirable (i.e., normative) place.

Chaos theory contributes to the social control thesis. Chaos theory tells us that mechanisms of social control are similar, in effect, to the point attractor. The fixed or point attractor encourages behavior to achieve a stable end-state conducive to order. Moreover, nonlinear dynamical systems theory tells us why this degree of order is, in fact, *unhealthy* for social systems. Indeed, health is defined by the ability to adapt, change, and accept variations, and to incorporate them into one's conduct. This type of attraction is termed "strange" by chaologists. However, the strange attractor is not disorderly. Instead, it encourages systems to achieve a natural or organic organization; that is, an order arising from within itself. In other words, external forces that impose order are unhealthy precisely because they are coercive. A more constructive approach to the natural disorder defining living systems (including society and people) is to impose very little order and to let organization emerge on its own.

In the case of civil commitment, the psycholegal system assumes the task of imposing order on society and its citizens in the name of justice. By involuntarily hospitalizing those individuals who do not meet prevailing social ideals for productivity, morality, normalcy, etc., the exogenous powers of the clinicolegal apparatus define, in effect, the contours of medical justice. In doing so, however, chaos theory tells us that what is achieved is not a more just and humane society but, rather, a more narrow path leading to death. Being "normal," as articulated by the constraints of the psycholegal system, is not normal. Indeed, difference, diversity, and change are the framework of a healthy society. In this sense, then, affirming life means encouraging disorder to flourish and insisting that prevailing social norms change in the face of it.

Justice, then, requires difference. In other words, the extent to which diversity characterizes a society is the extent to which a society is healthy, prosperous, adaptive. Rigidly or tightly controlling the contours of society encourages justice to assume a constricted posture that does not allow for the process of adaptation, change, and growth to occur. Thus, justice is not something derived from prevailing popular (and professional) opinion. This notion of what is just can be traced to Plato (1973), who claimed that everyday "appearances" of justice (i.e., just acts) are merely shadows of something greater and more significant for social life. A similar critique of popular opinion can be found in Kant's (1784/1983) notion of "enlightenment" and Nietzsche's (1887/1967) concept of "herd morality." In sum, then, civil commitment, as a prevailing manifestation of social control, is based on assumptions embedded within popular culture, dismissing difference and, consequently, failing to promote justice. Chaos theory, however, suggests that justice, as an abstract and undefined (Platonic) "Form," is something more akin to a strange attractor.

CHAPTER SEVEN

The Right to Refuse Mental Health Treatment

OVERVIEW. *Perhaps the most prized of all human possessions is the safety of one's body and the security of one's mind. If either is appropriated, altered, or jeopardized in any way, the experience of being human and uniquely oneself is inevitably diminished. When Descartes proclaimed his famous maxim "Cogito ergo sum," he established a fundamental relationship between existence and the cognitive capacity of thinking. Indeed, following his logic, the absence of thought gives us reason to doubt our very being. We may also infer, then, that if one's thought processes are reduced, stifled, or otherwise lessened in some manner—while we may still surmise our existence—our very humanity is called into question. This notion is not as outlandish as it may sound at first. In particular, this assumption is linked characteristically to persons who are mentally ill, developmentally disabled, or in some way "less fortunate" than others.*

Interestingly, we do not generally raise similar criticisms when the diminished capacity to contemplate, analyze, or conjecture for oneself is the result of biological or physiological conditions. In other words, when the capacity to think, feel, and be is altered, on some level, by exogenous factors (e.g., illicit drug use), we are often less quick to log this objection. In some cases, these exogenous forces are even considered beneficial; that is, worthwhile methods to enhance our existence. In most instances, however, our interaction with them is voluntary, representing part of our existential journey and struggle for human happiness.

It is precisely at this point that the importance placed on freedom from intrusive exogenous influences becomes paramount. If we forego our search for happiness in thought, feeling, and action by deferring to that which is prescribed, the journey is no longer of our own making. It may be that our body remains intact, but the processes to which our body is subjected are no longer of our own choosing. Instead, our natural rhythms are harnessed under the influence of outside forces that attempt to mold our bodily functions, directing them to something presumably more appropriate, healthy, or acceptable in the larger social world of which we are a part.

When these forces are orchestrated by the system of psychology, they include various therapy interventions and psychotropic medications. Moreover, when psychology acts under the auspices of the law, its methods have an unsettling similarity to the fictional, mind control fantasies portrayed in such utopian texts as Anthony Burgess's Clockwork Orange or Aldous Huxley's A Brave New World. While these therapeutic techniques are often touted as warranted for the well-being of individual citizens and the public at large, they represent one of the most contentious and volatile of matters at the crossroads of law and psychology today.

This chapter explores the controversy surrounding one's right to refuse mental health treatment. At issue are the conditions, if any, under which forcible intervention (e.g., therapy or medication over objection) is (constitutionally) permissible. Consistent with our previous application chapters, we examine the legal and psychological approaches to mental health treatment (and its refusal), mindful of each perspective's limitations. Unlike the chapters on mental illness, dangerousness, and civil commitment, however, we begin with a review of psychology's position on treatment. This adjustment makes sense, especially since it is first necessary to understand what treatment is before one can reasonably comment on the legal grounds upon which it may be refused. Thus, our orientation to psychiatric intervention is as prudent as it is expedient, especially in light of the current chapter's goals. We conclude by applying selected chaos theory principles to mental health treatment refusal. In this context, we assess whether nonlinear dynamical systems theory tells us something more or something other about prospects for justice at the law-psychology interface than prevailing clinicolegal interpretations.

PSYCHOLOGY AND TREATMENT ISSUES

An underlying theme throughout our critique of psychology and the mental health profession, is the adoption of a need for treatment approach to mental illness. In other words, the prevailing assumption among clinicians is that persons found to be psychiatrically ill are, in fact, in need of some greater or lesser therapeutic care and intervention. Although originally committed to *understanding* the human mind and individual conduct, psychology has become synonymous with *treating* the human mind and the variety of behavioral oddities and conditions that characterize our existence. How is this treatment accomplished? The answer lies in the methods devised by the discipline, techniques that include some degree of personal intrusiveness and, consequently, some potential abuse for individuals exposed to them. The extent to which psychiatric citizens can exercise their treatment refusal rights with invasive medical intervention is a legal matter to be discussed in a subsequent section of this chapter. For now, however, we provide an overview of several more popular treatment modalities and the shared assumptions that govern most of them, including the goals and motivations of mental health intervention.

Treatment Modalities: Psychotherapy

The notion of treatment is an increasingly complex and ever-changing part of our society. Indeed, within the mental health care industry alone there exists a near unlimited variety of so-called treatments with which to intervene therapeutically in the lives of individuals in need. The specific techniques that concern us are those interventions related to the involuntary treatment process, including those authorized by the law. To facilitate this investigation, it will be helpful to explore the primary means by which treatment is accomplished in the mental health community. Generally speaking, this occurs through psychotherapy alone, or in conjunction with psychotropic medication or other drug therapies.

Psychotherapeutic intervention is the most common form of treatment undertaken on behalf of persons with mental illness. Notwithstanding the presence of additional types of treatment (e.g., psychotropic medication), psychotherapy represents the most lauded and administered of interventions among mental health circles today (Isaac & Armat, 1990; Szasz, 1977). For purposes of our exposition, psychotherapy refers to all intervention that is premised upon the healing relationship, involving interaction between therapist and patient. As Corsini (1995) defines it:

> [psychotherapy is] a formal process of interaction between two parties . . . for the purpose of amelioration of distress . . . relative to any or all of the following areas of disability or malfunction: cognitive functions (disorders of thinking), affective functions (suffering or emotional discomforts), or behavioral functions (inadequacy of behavior). . . . (p. 1)

The use of the term malfunction in Corsini's definition reveals something quite profound about psychology and one of its core assumptions. In short, the discipline proposes to influence the lives of individuals by changing attitudes, beliefs, and behaviors, and by providing insight into the problem-causing situation and/or symptoms that are etiologically significant (see, e.g., Weiner, 1975). While the specific means of ameliorating the distress that ensues varies consistent with the theoretical orientation(s) of the therapist, the clinician typically attempts, through verbal interaction, to "correct" (i.e., treat) the individual's presenting problem by "readjusting the disordered personality" (Rychlak, 1981, p. 32). In other words, notwithstanding the specific malady responsible for creating disorganization in the psychological makeup of an individual, psychotherapy intervenes to *control* or *reorder* the disarray.

The most common psychotherapies are conceptually grounded in either the psychoanalytic or cognitive-behavioral tradition. This is not to suggest, however, that a particular therapist would not elect to rely upon other perspectives on their own or in some combination, given the specific presenting issue. Rather, we draw attention to the fact that psychotherapies are united by the same general motivation: treatment and/or cure. Thus, in some very meaningful way, the methods by which these are accomplished is often less significant than the end result.

Following Freud (1914, 1927) and his epigones, psychoanalytic therapies have a Platonic (1973) character, given their emphasis on conflict or competing forces within the psyche or soul. The goal of psychoanalytic therapy, compatible with Platonic thought, is to gain insight into one's conflicts and reinstate reason or rationality as the governing force in one's decisions. Indeed, Plato's description of the "well-ordered soul" continues, in a modified way, to be the philosophical foundation of psychoanalytic treatment as it stresses order over disorder, and the elimination of disarray in the pursuit of happiness.

Cognitive and behavioral therapies are often used in combination with one another. In their pure form, behavioral therapies emphasize learning principles, and, thus, "teach adaptive behavior or modify maladaptive behavior by means of systematic manipulation of the patient's environment" (Winick, 1997b, p. 41). Cognitive therapies identify and explore the "dysfunctional interpretations" (Beck & Weishaar, 1995, p. 230) of one's world which are thought to be responsible for the individual's maladaptive thought processes and actions. The general project of cognitive-behavioral intervention is to modify one's thoughts and, as a result, to adjust the person's behavior stemming from those thoughts, through the use of behavioral techniques (e.g., positive and negative reinforcement). This form of psychotherapeutic treatment encourages the client to rely continually on these alternative, more adaptive thoughts and behaviors throughout the life course.

As previously indicated, notwithstanding some important philosophical differences, all therapies are motivated by a perceived curative function (see, e.g., Rychklak, 1981). Persons presenting as mentally disordered in any number of ways are, in a sense, thought to be afflicted by illness and disease. Of course, curing illness is the driving motivation behind medicine, psychiatry, and most models of psychology. If this illness manifests itself in behavioral, cognitive, or affective abnormalities, then the goal of therapy is to change or, at the very least, to control such irregularities. Indeed, Carl Rogers acknowledged the power of the therapist to "mold" individuals, causing them to become "submissive and conforming" beings (Rogers & Skinner, 1956, p. 1063). In many psychotherapeutic situations, the power of the clinician is such that ". . . the therapist may gain a degree of control which is more powerful than that of many religious or governmental agents" (Skinner, 1953, p. 383). Thus, given such power and influence, it stands to reason that the possibility for abuse and/or misuse is abundant. Indeed, consistent with the objections raised by the social control thesis (see chapter 6 for more), we question where the line is drawn between therapeutic treatment of deviant behavior and social control of deviant behavior that is not therapeutically initiated (e.g., Breggin, 1975; Winick, 1997b). This concern is especially poignant when we realize that the goals of psychotherapy, at least in institutional settings like psychiatric hospitals and prisons, are routinely set by the therapist rather than the patient, and often without the client's participation in the decision-making process (e.g., Rogers & Skinner, 1956, p. 1063; Winick, 1997b, p. 39).

Treatment Modalities: Psychotropic Medication or Drug Therapy

The clinical community introduced psychotropic medication in the early 1950s in the form of antipsychotic and antidepressant drugs (see, e.g., Baldessarini, 1980). In contrast to the verbal/behavioral interventions found among traditional psychotherapeutic methods, the use of psychotropics emphasized chemical treatment which directly or indirectly altered brain functioning and, consequently, individual behavior. The effectiveness of these new drugs in responding to the symptoms of psychosis "revolutionized state mental hospital systems" (Gelman, 1984; Perlin, 1999, p. 368). The revolutionary nature of these curative chemical agents was, in part, a reflection of several substantive changes they produced (Arrigo & Tasca, 1999). For example, the duration of hospitalization for persons with mental illness decreased, treatment took place in the community rather than in inpatient settings, and the need for institutionalization abated (Grob, 1994; Talbott, 1978). Indeed, the census at state hospitals showed a drastic reduction in the years following the advent of antipsychotic drugs (Perlin, 1989).

For a brief period of time following the discovery of these medications, treatment results were encouraging. Indeed, positive effects, discernable on both individual and social levels, included: the elimination or minimization of psychosis and its major symptoms (e.g., hallucinations); a decrease in the rates of recidivism; the movement toward deinstitutionalization; a reduction in the average length of hospital stays; and a diminished sense of fear and/or anxiety among friends and family members of psychiatric citizens (Davis & Cole, 1975; Perlin, 1999, p. 369). Soon thereafter, however, these beneficial outcomes were seriously questioned, especially when evaluated alongside the antitherapeutic effects that were quickly and prominently materializing (e.g., irregularities in sleeping, sexual drive, appetite) (Brooks, 1987).

The "dark side" of drug treatment produced "physical, emotional, and mental side effects that diminished the person's quality of life" (Arrigo, 1996, p. 80). The limits of psychotropic medication spawned decades of criticism among researchers, clinicians, public interest attorneys, and patients' rights advocates (Appelbaum, 1997; Rapoport & Parry, 1986). Despite these objections, the medications were (and are) used as an alternative to other treatment modalities. Today, for example, it is estimated that as many as ninety-eight percent (98%) of all mental health intervention in state hospitals is organic in nature, necessitating psychopharmacological therapy (Perlin, 1999).

Given the problems posed by drug therapy, it is not surprising that the overwhelming majority of treatment refusal cases implicate psychotropic medication (Arrigo & Tasca, 1999). More specifically, these cases focus on the major tranquilizers or neuroleptics commonly used to treat schizophrenia (Melton et al., 1997, p. 350). While the mental health community has enjoyed some success in treating schizophrenia and other psychotic disorders by prescribing neuroleptics, the injurious and debilitating side effects of their use cannot be too readily overlooked or dismissed. Indeed, although somewhat different depending on the drug administered, harmful effects include: akathesia (restlessness, fidgetiness); dystonia (muscle spasms); fatigue; headache; and constipation (ibid.). A more serious consequence of neuroleptic use that has drawn substantial clinical attention is the onset of tardive dyskinesia (Bromberg, 1982). Tardive dyskinesia is characterized by involuntary movements in the tongue, jaw, or extremities. Beyond a certain point it is irreversible and it occurs in approximately twenty percent of patients (Bowes, 1956). Finally, though rare, neuroleptic malignant syndrome has been known to occur in some patients. Neuroleptic malignant syndrome is characterized by any of several severe physical symptoms and, in thirty percent of cases, results in death (Melton et al., 1997, p. 350).

The most abusive cases involving the use of psychotropic drugs are those in which medications are employed as a means of restraint or coercion (see, e.g., *Davis v. Hubbard*, 1980; *Rennie v. Klein*, 1978; *Washington v. Harper*, 1990). In these instances, treatment is either secondary or is tangentially a factor in the decision to administer drugs to patients (Arrigo & Tasca, 1999, pp. 8–13). Instead, psychotropics are prescribed in the interest of staff convenience and not as a therapeutic method by which to address mental illness (e.g., Brooks, 1987, p. 351). Our point is not that this abusive practice is commonplace in mental health facilities; rather, we acknowledge that "chemical restraint," as a form of drug therapy, does occur, and, accordingly, it warrants some critical attention when questions of treatment refusal are raised (e.g., Arrigo & Williams, 1999b). This is precisely the point at which the law intervenes. However, before considering the legal response to psychotropic treatment and one's right to refuse it, some commentary on the goals of mental health intervention are warranted.

The Goal(s) of Mental Health Intervention

We have very provisionally addressed several of the more prevalent treatment modalities. Although certainly not mutually exclusive, each is unique in treatment approach, yet similar in motivation (i.e., the elimination of mental illness). What is less distinctive about these modalities is their shared assumptions regarding the *goals* of therapeutic intervention. In other words, while each form of treatment endeavors to facilitate the realization of one's wellness or health, each psychotherapeutic intervention adopts a similar understanding of what that wellness represents.

The modalities we examined assume that treatment is something *given* to someone in need. Indeed, mental health intervention is rarely questioned in light of the conviction that treatment professionals are *providing* something that is needed and, generally, wanted by the one receiving that help (Arrigo & Williams, 1999b; Williams & Arrigo, 2000a). Psychology intervenes to treat (i.e, repair, heal, normalize) the patient's illness, believing that it is something the receiver desires to have corrected. In this context, then, psychological treatment does not lend itself to critical interrogation. Rather, the operative assumption is that the mental health community provides a service, a benefit, in the interest of the patient, whether or not the treated individual recognizes that the intervention is warranted or needed. Thus, the core premise under which psychiatric care and intervention unfolds is one's need for treatment. This assumption is not based on an assessment of the patient's subjectively articulated interests, but rather, on psychology's objective understanding of what illness, health, and treatment constitute, and what any reasonable patient would desire under similar circumstances (e.g., Scull, 1989; Szasz, 1963, 1970, 1977).

The assumption that treatment, knowingly or not, is a beneficial service to patients is exemplified in the notion of "thank you" therapy (Stone, 1975). Observers of thank you therapy contend that some persons subjected to psychiatric confinement and treatment against their (initial) will, subsequently come to appreciate the mental health intervention. Indeed, retrospectively, they realize that treatment was in their best interest and are grateful for the intervention. Other commentators, however, are skeptical of this position. For example, Beck and Golowka (1988) reported no evidence of the thank you therapy sentiment in sixty-two percent (62%) of the cases they examined. In other words, a clear majority of persons civilly committed still objected to receiving such treatment even after they arguably were restored to "order." This finding is consistent with the psychological motives for intervention; namely, persons are thought to want treatment and the elimination of illness, pain, and suffering even if they do not explicitly realize it or state that they do at the outset of the commitment process (Kane et al., 1983; Schwartz et al., 1988).

The goals of treatment, then, are compatible with the broader assumption of paternalism, underlying mental health practice and the law-psychology interface (Arrigo, 1993b). Paternalism is evidenced both explicitly in treatment modalities and implicitly in the unspoken objectives of treatment. Through specific treatment modalities, we see that psychology/psychiatry attempt to alleviate distress or overt symptomatology. Additionally, however, mental health professionals assume the role of identifying which thoughts, emotional states, and behaviors fall outside the bounds of normative, pro-social conduct. Psychology, then, functions to treat mental abnormalities or aberrations, consistent with prevailing community norms, across a continuum of "craziness" (Arrigo, 1996). Mindful of this continuum, the gift of psychotherapeutic intervention is most conspicuous in the classification and diagnostic manual of mental diseases (APA, 1994). Psychology, then, effectively assumes both a diagnostic and mediating function with regard to social hygiene. Indeed, identifying and treating disorderly persons constitutes the ultimate goal of mental health intervention in all its forms. While the law has, to some extent, supported this objective, it also has raised significant concerns about psychological treatment and one's right to refuse it. It is to these matters that we now turn.

THE LAW'S CHALLENGE TO PSYCHIATRY

The law concerns itself with liberty interests, impacting both individuals and communities. The involuntary psychiatric treatment of citizens, whether in community or institutional settings, raises important jurisprudential questions about the rights of individuals to refuse such psychotherapeutic intervention. The law's involvement in treatment refusal matters can be traced, more or less, to the inception and subsequent utilization of antipsychotic medication in the 1950s (Arrigo & Tasca 1999, pp. 3–7). Before the onset of psychotropic drugs, the available and varied interventions rarely presented a legal problem to the mental health community. For example, for some time psychosurgery (e.g., frontal lobotomy) was considered a legitimate treatment technique, garnering little legal interference when performed in particular cases. Indeed, it was not until the significant side effects of neuroleptic medications were discovered that the law saw fit to protect the rights of individuals, seeking to curtail or avoid altogether the debilitating consequences of drug therapy (e.g., Appelbuam & Gutheil, 1979; Grob, 1994; Isaac & Armat, 1990).

As previously noted, psychotropic interventions for several disorders, including schizophrenia, initially appeared to be successful in alleviating symptoms of mental illness (Denber, 1967). Sometime thereafter, however, the serious side-effects associated with these medications led researchers to question their efficacy, particularly in situations where patients did not agree to drug treatment (Gelman, 1984). As a result, a number of important legal cases surfaced, encouraging state and federal courts to consult the Constitution for a resolution to the problem of involuntarily medicating individuals.

Overall, we note that the law pertaining to one's right to refuse treatment is exceedingly complex (Winick, 1997b). This complexity can be traced to the law's failure to define, with any significant detail, the boundaries of this right. While the Constitution does not expressly place restrictions on the treatment of individuals *per se*, the legal justification for objecting to it is drawn from several relevant Amendments, including: the Eighth Amendment's prohibition against cruel and unusual punishment; the First Amendment's guarantee of freedom of expression, including the right to think; the Due Process clause of the Fifth (federal) and Fourteenth (State) Amendments; and generally the right to (mental) privacy, autonomy, and bodily integrity. The full and detailed scope of these objections is well beyond the thrust of our project on chaos theory and justice at the law-psychology divide. This notwithstanding, several summary comments on these Constitutional matters are warranted, as they delineate the contours of the law's response to mental health treatment and a citizen's right to refuse such intervention.

Early Cases and the Eighth-Amendment Controversy

The earliest case law involving the right to refuse treatment implicated the First and Eighth Amendments, and challenged the use of drugs as *punishment* in aversive conditioning programs (e.g., *Rennie v. Klein*, 1978). The Eighth Amendment of the United States Constitution prohibits the state from inflicting "cruel and unusual punishments." Thus, for persons involuntarily treated in the mental health system (or for those receiving said treatment through the correctional system), the principal question is whether psychological/psychiatric intervention is punishment (Arrigo & Tasca, 1999). In response to this matter, Winick (1997b, p. 223) suggests that "to the extent that at least some of the more intrusive treatment techniques are experienced as painful or distressing, they may be regarded as 'punishments. . . .'" Given this logic, the issue is whether the Eighth Amendment's prohibition against cruel and unusual punishment applies to noncorrectional settings (e.g., state mental hospitals), and, more specifically, whether mental health treatment can, under certain circumstances, amount to punishment for purposes of Eighth Amendment scrutiny.

The applicability of the Eighth Amendment to civil treatment settings such as mental hospitals was upheld in several early court decisions, only to be rejected in several more recent cases (Winick, 1997b, p. 225). This early litany of court rulings disallowed the use of psychotropic or related drugs in aversive therapy prison programs, and when administered involuntarily in state psychiatric hospitals (*Knecht v. Gillman*, 1973; *Mackey v. Procunier*, 1973, on aversion programs in prison; *Scott v. Plante*, 1976, on state hospitals). However, none of these cases was decided by the U.S.

Supreme Court. In fact, the Court has yet to provide sufficiently clear and reasonable guidelines to compel lower courts to render judgments one way or another. Instead, the notion that various kinds and levels of civil treatment may violate the cruel and unusual punishment clause of the Eighth Amendment remains a controversial and undecided matter in mental health law (Arrigo & Tasca, 1999).

Indeed, the Supreme Court historically has found the Eighth Amendment applicable only in criminal punishment cases (*Ingraham v. Wright,* 1977). However, the Court has held that some punishments exist that ". . . though not labeled 'criminal' by the State, may be sufficiently analogous to criminal punishments . . . to justify application of the Eighth Amendment" (ibid., p. 669 n. 37). Whether or not some treatment in mental health hospitals and juvenile detention facilities is analogous to (cruel and unusual) intervention in correctional settings, has not been made explicit by the Court (Winick, 1997b, p. 226). Thus, it is difficult to discern whether the Eighth Amendment is applicable to cases involving psychiatrically hospitalized individuals.

The law makes very clear, however, that persons in mental health settings are not to be punished in the legal sense (Stefan, 1993). Decisions made in treatment settings are to be made in the interest of the recipient; that is, in terms of the patient's potential psychological and/or physical benefit, without reference to any nonhealth related concern (see, e.g., *Knecht v. Gillman* and *Mackey v. Procunier* on aversive conditioning programs in prisons). Controversy arises, however, when the punitive effects of psychiatric treatment are called into question. In other words, what is the law's position on mental health intervention whose effects could be construed as punishment?

In part, guided by the opinion in *Bell v. Wolfish* (1979), the administration of psychotropic drugs, behavioral therapy, and the other therapeutic methods that constitute a justifiable treatment program is *not* subject to Eighth Amendment challenges (Winick, 1997b, p. 230). Rather, cruel and unusual punishment provisions apply only in cases where a clear punitive purpose is demonstrated (i.e., the treatment is *not* obviously in the interest of helping the recipient), the dosage of psychotropic medication is excessively high, or the treatment provided is entirely ineffective and, thus, not justifiable as an intervention technique in that particular instance (ibid.). Arguably, this logic applies to inpatient hospitals not directly associated with a correctional institution, outpatient programs, and treatments availed to prisoners by way of community initiatives (ibid.).

Rennie and the Current Status of Right to Refuse Treatment Law

Perhaps the most significant right to refuse treatment case is *Rennie v. Klein* (1978). Although the United States Supreme Court ultimately remanded *Rennie* for reconsideration, given its decision in *Youngberg v. Romeo* (1982), *Rennie* embodied what the district court maintained was the "grossly irresponsible" way in which psychotropic drugs were administered (*Rennie*, 1978, p. 1301). The Court's position in *Rennie* was fueled, in part, by an increasing number of instances where drug administration amounted to staff convenience only (*Davis v. Hubbard*, 1980), and/or advanced punitive purposes (i.e., punishment and control) rather than efficacious treatment (Arrigo, 1996). In some cases, staff increased the drug dosage as a retaliatory response for uncooperative patients, ignoring serious side effects and withholding necessary additional medications to address these consequences (*Rennie v. Klein*, 1978). In addition, a growing concern for psychiatry's inability to diagnosis with any reasonable degree of accuracy surfaced (Ennis & Litwack, 1974; Szasz, 1977). This concern for clinical prediction was thought to be necessary, especially in light of the significant adverse effects of psychotropic medication. For example, some researchers argued that as many as forty percent (40%) of diagnosed schizophrenics were, in reality, *mis*diagnosed cases of bipolar disorder (Litman, 1982). Moreover, even if one conceded accuracy in diagnostic efforts, ascertaining appropriate dosages for patients was routinely considered a matter of trial and error (Plotkin, 1977). These and others professed misuses and abuses of psychotropics spawned not only increased public awareness, but increased legal attention in matters of mental health treatment and one's right to refuse it.

The original intent behind the establishment of the right to refuse treatment for mentally disabled persons was to affirm the autonomy of the individual, thereby placing final decision-making power in the hands of the patient (Winick, 1997b). However, the practice of treatment refusal is far less consistent with this intent. Indeed, several important limitations to this right exist. For example, one's right to refuse treatment is curtailed in cases where incompetency is a factor, the patient poses a danger to self or others, or when an emergency situation arises (Roth, 1986). In effect, then, some commentators conclude that mentally disabled persons have a right to *object* to treatment (Arrigo, 1996; Brooks, 1987). This objection ensures a case review by hospital staff to determine the necessity of treatment, while providing, in a very limited way, an affirmative right to refuse such treatment. Therefore, final authority in treatment decisions remains firmly in the hands of the attending psychiatrist and treatment team (Roth & Appelbaum, 1982).

A legal challenge to involuntary treatment focuses on whether the reason and judgement utilized by hospital decision maker(s) was sound, and not necessarily on an effective argument, describing the best interest of the patient (Arrigo & Tasca, 1999). Authority may be questioned only in instances where medical intervention deviates from "substantial professional judgement" (*Youngberg v. Romeo*, 1982, p. 309). In effect, then, there is a presumption of validity regarding the judgment of those professionals responsible for a patient's treatment (Perlin, Gould, & Dorfman, 1995). We note that the *Youngberg* Court did not provide clear and detailed guidelines, defining what constitutes a departure from "substantial professional judgement." Generally speaking, however, three situations may exist where treatment deviates considerably from accepted medical practice: (a) no judgment was exercised at all; (b) judgments were made by unqualified persons; and (c) judgments were made based on factors not relevant to treatment interests (e.g., budget, available resources) (Stefan, 1993). The latter of the these instances includes those cases where treatment is administered solely in the interest of staff convenience and/or merely for the purpose of punishment and control (ibid.).

Summary

What can we make of treatment refusal law and one's right to exercise it? Without compelling and decisive Supreme Court opinion, we can only reach general conclusions. Cases such as *Rennie v. Klein* (1978) and *Rogers v. Okin* (1980) proposed procedural due process rights for mentally disabled persons, amounting to a hearing right. Further, the decision in *Rennie* provides some limits related to treatment not performed or administered on the basis of substantial professional judgement. Court rulings such as these were intended to protect patients from mental health treatment abuses (e.g., drug therapy for staff convenience or as punitive action). However, the right to refuse treatment appears to be nothing more than a formal right to object to it. Indeed, exceptions to this right are granted with incompetency cases, emergency situations, and when the patient is a danger to self or others. Thus, as a practical matter, mental health intervention decisions are typically made under the direction of the attending psychiatrist and the treatment team. As a result, most jurisdictions place minimal limitations on many commonly practiced treatment modalities, even though patient involvement in them may not be entirely voluntary.

LIMITATIONS TO LEGAL AND PSYCHOLOGICAL APPROACHES

In the case of treatment refusal, the law-psychology debate is akin to the civil commitment controversy. That is to say, while the public intuitively recognizes that citizens have a genuine liberty interest in avoiding involuntary treatment, society also maintains that, in some cases, involuntary psychotherapeutic intervention is necessary and, hence, justified (Melton et al., 1997, p. 350). As with most issues in the psycholegal sphere, the manner in which treatment refusal is conceptualized telegraphs the configuration of mental health law and policy. Thus, similar to our previous investigations, there is considerable dispute about whether the controversy principally revolves around legal or medical authority.

Consistent with the philosophy of psychiatric medicine in general, clinicians tend toward the need for care and treatment approach (Scull, 1989). Thus, it follows that mental health intervention, including, where necessary, involuntarily treatment, is believed to be in the best medical interest of the patient. For the psychological community, then, treatment refusal is typically perceived as a *product* of mental illness, further justifying the need to intervene with the consent (or lack thereof) of the individual in question (Winick, 1997b). Further, in cases where patient objection to treatment is noted, the medical model of intervention and clinical decision making recommends that the law assess Constitutionally based refusal requests, consistent with the patient's need for quality care and efficacious treatment (e.g., Appelbaum & Gutheil, 1979, 1981). Indeed, critics of large-scale treatment refusal rights contend that legal objections (e.g., due process and other liberty infringements) do nothing more than *interfere* with the patient's interests (e.g., Brooks, 1987). Thus, psychology, similar to the law, claims to advocate zealously and genuinely on behalf of the psychiatric citizen. The essential difference, of course, is in the *definition* of patient/client interests.

The law, in contrast, emphasizes its affirmative duty to protect citizens against individual liberty, autonomy, and self-determination intrusions. These are interests that, in theory, are applicable to every human being, regardless of mental (dis)ability (Morse, 1978, 1982). Accordingly, for the legal profession, the issue is one of law and morality to be decided by fact-finders (Melton et al., 1997, p. 350). This position does not imply that the law therefore concerns itself with protecting the interests of mental health citizens in *all* cases. Indeed, the legal sphere is subjected to sundry and competing ideological considerations (e.g., Milovanovic, 1994). For example, the "law and liberty" approach to mental illness is liberal in nature, possessing fundamental interests in protecting the rights of the individual. Conversely, the "law and order" approach to psychiatric disorders is utilitarian in design, embracing core interests in safeguarding the community/society from danger (see, e.g., LaFond, 1981; Morse, 1982). Notwithstanding these different ideological frames of reference, both the law and liberty and law and order models insist that rights-claiming occurs within the juridical arena (Arrigo, 1996). In addition, though, the law may, on occasion, solicit opinions from other domains (e.g., psychology), concerning the nature of these broad mental health consumer interests in specific cases.

In relation to the exercise of treatment refusal rights, the mental health profession has objected to the law's questionable stance as protector of patients' rights. In short, critics of the law contend that the expansion of rights afforded the mentally disabled is often counterproductive to the medical agenda which provides effective treatment to individuals in need. Indeed, for psychiatrists and other treating clinicians, the real issue is quality care and not the "right to rot" (Appelbaum & Gutheil, 1981, p. 199). Moreover, commentators indicate that ensuring one's precious liberties can place significant limits on the quantity and quality of available treatment options (Gutheil, 1980). In this context, then, the law interferes with the *professional duty* of mental health care providers to treat effectively psychiatrically disabled persons (Cichon, 1992). To be clear, law's initial foray into the domain of psychiatry was in response to the abominable conditions found in the asylums of old (Grob, 1994; Myers, 1983/1984; Rothman, 1971, 1980). While psychology, in principal, does not object to the humanization of mental health treatment, several need-for-treatment proponents contend that providing a "right to rot" is as repulsive as the asylum era of the past (Appelbaum & Gutheil, 1979; Gutheil, 1980; Treffert, 1971). We note that this theme of abandonment is not without merit (Isaac & Armat, 1990), particularly among those on the psychology side of the treatment debate (Arrigo, 1993a).

Thus, in short, neither law nor psychology has been able to ascertain and implement a reasonable, workable solution to the right to refuse treatment polemic (Winick, 1997b). The medicolegal divide continues to inform, though apparently without much agreed-upon closure, courtroom decisions impacting psychiatric citizens. We question whether the legitimate perspectives of law and of psychology truly bring us any closer to understanding mental health treatment (refusal), and its array of individual and societal implications. We contend that chaos theory and selected principles contained within it may be informative in this regard.

CHAOS THEORY AND THE RIGHT TO REFUSE (MENTAL HEALTH) TREATMENT

Human behavior is complex, yielding little certainty as to its origins, patterns, and methods. Without question, physiological systems play a significant role in shaping thought, emotion, and action. Yet how are we to understand these systems? While seemingly enigmatic, we feel quite strongly that there is an inherent pattern to the way physiological systems operate. For example, the heartbeat of the human being, while not always perfectly rhythmic, shows enough regularity that we conclude there is some driving pattern at its core. For the most part, identifiable patterns such as these are true not only of our general physiology, but of our entire experience of being human as well. Chaos theory directs our attention to why regularity and order exist amidst seeming disorder and randomness.

Fundamentally, chaos theory explores the ways in which systems *change* (Morrison, 1991; Barton, 1994). This is why it is also called nonlinear *dynamical* systems theory. Indeed, the purpose of chaology is to examine the effects that various internal and external forces have on systems over time and, further, to assess the ways that these systems respond to these forces. In many instances, linear analysis is quite useful for this purpose. For many *natural* systems, however, linear models are not equipped to take account of the sudden "jumps" that often define the behavior of complex systems such as human beings. On these occasions, it is necessary to employ *nonlinear* equations.

Nonlinear dynamics allows for a necessary level of scrutiny targeted at those seemingly unpatterned behaviors that define natural systems. Each principle of chaos theory has a role in this type of analysis. Summarily, we recall that external stimuli may induce a loss of "balance" in a system (due, in part, to the system's *sensitive dependence on initial conditions*, making it prone to disturbance by minor inputs). This imbalance may be complicated by the procedure known as *iteration* in which the imbalance essentially feeds into itself, creating greater levels of disturbance. In some cases, these greater levels of imbalance encourage the process of *bifurcation*. Bifurcation occurs when the behavior of the system is no longer steady, but is somewhat unpredictable. A defining characteristic of nonlinear systems, however, is that they tend to "settle" into patterns over time. Thus, the concept of *attractors* shows us the various ways (generally one of four points) in which the ostensibly unpredictable behavior of a system settles into a more predictable (at least globally) order.

This notion of "settling" is the order-out-of-chaos thesis, characteristic of chaotic dynamics and is the focus of the present section. It is best described by a process known as *self-organization*. In short, notwithstanding what may appear as extreme levels of disorder, nonlinear systems (including people) tend to reorder themselves in ways consistent with other natural systems. This *adaptation* has significant consequences for the right to refuse mental health treatment controversy. Indeed, self-organization critically directs our attention to the manner in which psychology has come to treat disorder through methods that may be defined as unnatural (e.g., psychotropics).

We note that our subsequent chaos theory investigation of mental health treatment (and its refusal) focuses exclusively on the modality of psychotropic medication. This is because the majority of (legal) objections raised pertaining to forced or otherwise coercive treatment question the need for and utility of this type of intervention. We contend, however, that our analysis is relevant to other modes of treatment as well (e.g., psychoanalytic and cognitive-behavioral therapy), although only in an implicit or indirect way. Indeed, the principle of self-organization and its logic is applicable to an array of treatment modalities. Following chaos theory, the only difference among these interventions is the extent to which a given treatment interferes with the individual's natural capacity to adapt to disorder. The level of interference is correlated with the level of treatment intrusiveness. If the intervention is exceptionally invasive (e.g., forced medication), the interference is high. If the intervention is minimally intrusive (e.g., a particular psychotherapy), the interference is low. Thus, our assessment of self-organization is (and should be) applicable to other modes of treatment, not expressly reviewed in this section

Further, we recognize that our presentation of self-organization and its application to mental illness may appear, at times, to be overly inclusive. It is not our intention to portray this chaos theory principle as germane to *all* individuals nor as appropriate in *all* circumstances. Rather, self-organization is a natural or organic alternative to psychotropic medication in the majority of cases where drug therapy is usually employed. The extent to which our position on self-organization can reasonably address persistent and severe psychiatric disorders is a research question beyond the scope of the present inquiry. Thus, our analysis is descriptive, rather than prescriptive, especially in relation to increasing degrees of disability.

Mental Health, Psychotropics, and Self-Organization

Self-organization is a process in which a pattern *emerges* within a system without external assistance. In other words, a system exhibiting disorderly behavior will come to exhibit, without aid beyond its own means, orderly behavior over time. This process is one that is intuitively antithetical to the manner in which individuals, under the influence of psychotropic drugs, come to an orderly (i.e., healthy) state from a disorderly (i.e., ill) condition. At this juncture, it is important to consider both the process of self-organization that naturally occurs in living species, and the artificially imposed organization that represents the preferred treatment method throughout much of the mental health care industry.

Psychopharmacology and the Linear Paradigm

Butz (1994, p. 692) describes the deployment of psychopharmacology (i.e., medication prescribed by mental health professionals) as ". . . the portent of mechanistic linearity with its self-ascribed ability to control and predict human behavior [through] drug intervention." There are several important ideas embedded in this statement. First is the concept of linearity. As we have indicated throughout our critique of mental health law, human behavior (indeed, the behavior of *all* living systems) is prone to nonlinearity. For example, in our discussion of civil commitment, we described the point attractor as emblematic of the psycholegal system to impose order and linearity on psychiatric citizens. We also demonstrated that there are generally two erroneous assumptions regarding the imposition of linear behavior: (a) Since human beings are governed more naturally by the laws of chaos rather than order, any project attempting to assure global and local order by "fixing" the parts (i.e., the person's soma and psyche) that "break" (i.e., becoming mentally ill or disorderly), will necessarily fail to some greater or lesser degree; and (b) since mechanistic functioning (i.e., tight, rigid order) is unhealthy to the human condition, any excessive amount of it, expressed through linear behavior, would not be wanted or valued by the public at large. Indeed, generally speaking, some degree of nonlinearity, unpredictability, and difference is healthy for a society of adaptive, self-organizing, and evolving beings.

Butz's comments on psychopharmacology are significant for a related reason. The prediction and control of human behavior ensures, by way of imposition, that linearity defines individual conduct and social action. The linear paradigm is a mechanistic view that has dominated science since the Enlightenment. In the psychological sciences it is detected in the research algorithm of observe, describe, predict, and control (Butz, 1994, p. 694; Kerlinger, 1979). The mechanistic argument typically works as follows: (a) Homeostasis is the most desirable state; (b) instability is dangerous because it encourages the system to move away from homeostasis; and, therefore, (c) through measures of control we can (and should) guarantee that behavior stays within those limits (i.e., parameters) conducive to homeostatic conditions (ibid.). The mechanistic thesis assumes that, without such measures of control, the entire system (in this case the whole of society) will fall apart and cease to exist in its most desirable form.

Psychotropic drugs are a definitive example of how such a control-driven task might be carried out successfully in the treatment arena. Although behavioral constraints exist in the form of laws, rules, regulations, and other possible sanctions, people are granted some degree of choice. However, intervening in one's mental functioning through the forced administration of psychotropic drugs removes this element of choice. In legal terms, involuntarily medicating someone erodes or displaces many of the rights (e.g., self-determination, freedom of thought) that otherwise allow for some fraction of individuality and choice. In a sense, then, the censorship imposed by forcibly treating a citizen is twofold: (a) It challenges one's hypothetical right to *be* mentally ill; and (b) it challenges one's hypothetical right to adapt to mental illness or engage in a more natural self-healing process. The former point was discussed in previous chapters (see chapter 4 especially). The latter observation is the focus of the present critique. As we subsequently describe, both objections are important in a therapeutic context. For now, however, a brief review of self-organization theory and its relevance to the emotional health of human beings is in order.

Revisiting Self-Organization Theory

Butz (1994) traces the roots of self-organization theory to Bertalanffy's (1968) influential "general systems theory." Ludwig von Bertalanffy was a theoretical biologist who conceived of organizations or systems as *organisms* that needed to remain open to their environment in order to achieve appropriate relations with their respective environments and in order to ensure survival (see also Morgan, 1997 on organizations as organisms). Within his theory of systemic behavior and change, Bertalanffy (1968) identified two fundamental states which define an organism: steady and transformative. The first of these (steady state), described the operation of an organism as somewhat stable in relation to its environment. The second of these (transformative state) referred to a system that had been perturbed by external influences and was removed from its steady or stable condition. This movement away from stability, however, was described as the "passage-way to a more *adaptive* steady state" (Butz, 1994, p. 694; emphasis added). The second of these states is important to chaos theorists generally, and to our investigation of stability, order, and mental "health" functioning in the face of drug treatment in particular.

The major contributor to self-organization theory was Ilya Prigogine (see Prigogine & Stengers, 1984). In Prigogine's work, the optimal point at which adaptive capacities occur is at far-from-equilibrium conditions. In other words, as disorder increases and comes to define a system's behavior, the system moves into a state in which it is able to adapt and reorganize itself, given the disruptive influences to which it has been exposed. Butz (1994, p. 694) succinctly describes this process as follows: ". . . at one time a system has a steady state that is adaptive for the current situation and then something new comes along, perturbs the system, and it 'bifurcates' or is 'knocked off balance' by a stimulus." Following this perturbation, the system's state is no longer sufficiently adaptive for its "new" situation. It must reorganize to account for this change in circumstances.

The value of self-organization theory is in its description of how a system reorganizes to adapt to new circumstances. Indeed, according to this chaos theory principle, the organism adapts to change without relying on external assistance. For example, consider, the human body's response to physical illness. If infected, the body's temperature may rise as a response to the illness. If the body's temperature rises above a certain point, other bodily functions may change to counteract this increase in temperature (e.g., perspiration and heavy breathing) (Morgan, 1997, p. 40). All of these responses to illness occur naturally without the infected individual encouraging or insisting upon these reactions. In other words, the self-organization is an organic process of adaptive responses to perturbing stimuli located within, rather than outside, the particular environment in question.

Thus, what self-organization theory teaches is that *within* periods of chaos (or far-from-equilibrium conditions), a nonlinear system will not proceed necessarily to a state of utter disarray where it no longer is able to maintain sufficient "health." Rather, the organism will respond to systemic challenges by moving into a state where adaptive capacities are higher and the system itself is best able to reestablish (mostly) a steady state. This is the process of self-organization as defined by chaos theory. It remains to be seen how the adaptive capacities of human beings as complex, nonlinear systems would interface with mental health treatment. This subject is explored in the next section.

Self-Organization in the Context of (Mental Health) Treatment

At this point, it may be somewhat obvious that a tension exists between the assumptions of psychopharmacology and self-organization theory. In short, the treatment of mental disorders through the administration of psychotropic drugs largely assumes that an organism (i.e., a mentally ill person) must return to a state of equilibrium or stasis and, further, that this may require coercive intervention to ensure one's expedient recovery. This presupposition is particularly true of psychiatrically disordered persons subject to criminal sanctions whose competency must be restored for purposes of a trial, a sentence, or an execution. In these cases, society has a vested interest in returning one to a state of mental health as quickly and as efficiently as possible (Arrigo & Tasca, 1999; Winick, 1997b). In this context, then, "pushing through" chaos (Chamberlain, 1994) is the principle assumption governing the use of drug therapy.

The conviction of psychopharmacology is antithetical to the logic of self-organization. Indeed, "pushing through" chaos to restore order is most closely linked to the mechanistic paradigm discussed in a previous section of this chapter. It is an approach that relegates people to the status of machines that occasionally require fixing. Psychotropic drugs are the best method known to modern medical science wherein this "repair work" can occur effectively and efficiently. In contrast to chemical intervention, the approach of self-organization theory contends that, similar to all living systems, human beings in a state of disorder must be granted time and opportunity to adapt or self-organize into stronger individuals. This philosophy parallels Nietzsche's (1995) conceptualization of the "will to power" in which the health of an individual is defined, not by the absence of "illness," but by the amount of illness it has and can *overcome*. Overcoming aversive situations (e.g., perturbing influences from the environment, including illnesses), can be beneficial in that they allow the individual to grow into a stronger, more adaptive being, better equipped to confront other, similar perturbations in the future. Rather than classifying illness as a problem to be fixed, the organismic approach to health regards illness as a natural development in nonlinear systems, requiring time and space for the self-organizing process to occur successfully.

Thus, we see how treatment, in the form of psychotropic drugs, may produce adverse, stifling effects rather than healing, reparative outcomes. In endorsing this position, Butz (1994, p. 695) ponders the following:

> If one [administers] a psychopharmacological agent and it does stop the chaotic patterns, have we not also wiped out the seeds of a more adaptive psychological order—an order that may have taken days, weeks, months, or even years to develop in the complex electrochemical organization of the brain?

Thus, we note that psychotropic medication, employed as involuntary treatment, may be intrusive and life-negating rather than liberating and life-affirming in two important ways: (a) The coercive aspect of it removes and/or displaces the individual's right to choose and to make determinations about his or her own immediate future; and (b) the effects of the drug can disengage the self-organizing, adaptive processes that would otherwise occur on a natural and, arguably, healthier level. The stasis achieved by psychopharmacological agents is therefore nonadaptive. In other words, while stasis may be achieved or reestablished, this stability is not the type of order that is conducive to pro-social human life. Instead, it is counterproductive, especially since the individual is not given a chance to adapt to his or her circumstances as part of the continual evolutionary process (Butz, 1994, p. 695).

The Structure of Organization: Attractors Strange and New

The process of self-organization requires that we review yet another principle of chaos theory. This is the concept of attractors or, more specifically, the *strange* attractor, a notion previously examined in the context of civil confinement. Given our analysis thus far, it is reasonable to question whether an individual, diagnosed as mentally ill for medicolegal purposes, might regain a state of health experienced prior to the onset of illness. In other words, what would this new, more adaptive order look like? Consistent with its position on mental health and illness more generally, chaos theory does not rely upon normative standards as a basis by which to respond to this query. Thus, rather than suggesting that a person suffering from psychological disturbance would be able to retrieve a normative, homeostatic state of mental being without psychiatric intervention, chaos theory reexamines prevailing conceptualizations of health and wellness. It is in this context, then, that both the process of self-organization and the strange attractor principle are informative.

Health as a Point Attractor

We have already discussed, to some extent, the commonly shared belief that health is the *absence* of disease; that is, the absence of disorder. Conventional medicine embraces the "allopathic" tradition; that is, it typically concerns itself with the suppression of symptoms or the identification of conditions that give rise to disease and disorder (Butz, 1997, p. 72). Indeed, the treatment protocols of both medicine and psychiatry adopt this orientation. For example, exhibiting high blood pressure levels will most often ensure a drug prescription to suppress such disorder in the body. Similarly, symptoms of depression, if sufficiently disabling, will usually result in a patient prescription for antidepressant medication to suppress the natural thoughts and feelings that otherwise embody one's melancholic state. The treatment-of-choice is that therapy which most effectively and efficiently countervenes disorder and restores order.

As we have noted, however, this order is akin to the point attractor that chaos theory describes. Fundamentally, it is not an order based on the individual's need to establish a unique harmony within which to exist psychologically; rather, it is an order based on prevailing sociopolitical descriptions of regularity, maintenance, and conformity, commonly understood as the absence of disease and the elimination of disorder when it arises (Arrigo, 1996). Thus, the concept of health as it informs treatment is based on a linear and mechanistic conception of how it should reveal itself; namely, as the absence of illness.

In contrast, a less common description of health is found in chaos theory. It echoes Nietzsche's (1995) appreciation for an organism's ability to *overcome* illness and, in a sense, *assimilate* that experience of dis-ease into a new conceptualization of the organism's existential reality. In light of chaos theory's position on illness and health, then, the question posed about one's ability to regain a state of health prior to the onset of illness essentially is misguided if not altogether moot. Indeed, the treatment of mentally ill persons is oriented by a tradition that seeks to suppress disorder and, thus, return an individual to an orderly state. For example, psychotropic medications override the physiological mechanics of the body and, for all practical purposes, *impose* health upon an individual. This imposition, especially when it amounts to medication over objection, is, as we have demonstrated, an attempt to treat illness in a linear fashion that is the very antithesis of self-organization. Chaos theory suggests a nonlinear overcoming of disorder, including the subsequent onset of a new, more adaptive order. This self-organizing standard does not fall within the limits imposed by the point attractor. Thus, it may not appear as health in the sense that it is not defined by an absence of illness. Rather, it is best understood within the confines of the strange attractor.

(Orderly) Disorder as Constitutive of Health

We have proposed that self-organization theory offers a description of order-out-of-disorder. That is to say, the theory provides an account of a process that arguably defines, for purposes of our investigation, a healing protocol that individuals come to experience over time. Conceptually speaking, while the process itself may be more or less intellectually sound, we have additionally questioned what it ultimately produces as a practical matter. In other words, based on chaos theory, we contend that this new, more adaptive order will not be readily assimilable into society's prevailing understanding of stasis, regularity, conformity. Indeed, our interest is in explaining a self-organizing process that is the result of a nonlinear transformation from disorder to *orderly* disorder.

Self-organization theory, then, encourages us to reformulate our conventional understanding of (mental) health and disease for reasons of individual autonomy as well as for institutional objectives, including treatment goals that promote the psychiatric citizen's best interests. Characterizing the health of an individual may amount to a description of disorder, but the person's psychological reality may be, nonetheless, quite orderly. This is the concept of orderly disorder: behavior that merely appears as disorderly when, in fact, it can more accurately be conceptualized as orderly, given chaos theory's revised formulation of it. The strange attractor tells us that there may be local, everyday disorder, unpredictability, irregularity; however, over time, a global, systemic pattern to the person's behavior emerges that is more ordered, predictable, regular (Arrigo, 1994).

To illustrate, let us recall the scenario of two individuals where one is mildly depressed and the other is schizophrenic. Prevailing psychological assumptions about treatment typically lead us to regard the latter individual as more disabled (i.e., disordered and ill) and, consequently, more in need of treatment than the person's mildly depressed counterpart. Thus, the schizophrenic is far more likely to be subjected to intervention in the form of psychotropic medication, including involuntary treatment even if the patient objects. However, when health is reformulated in light of the strange atttractor, we may find that the schizophrenic is far more organized psychologically and better equipped to meet the emotional and physical demands of everyday life, within or outside an institution, than we had believed. This is especially the case when a thought and behavioral pattern emerges over time that, although somewhat different from prevailing sensibilities of appropriateness, nonetheless amounts to a noninjurious and self-sufficient way of living in the world (e.g., *In the Matter of Boggs*, 1987).

Moreover, the extent to which disorder affects the psychological well-being of the schizophrenic or mildly depressed person is dependant, at least in part, on the individual's health (in Nietzsche's sense of the word). Consequently, the linearly defined models by which psychology and the law understand disorder may be antithetical to the interests of *both* psychiatric citizens. In short, the mildly depressed subject may be unable to bear the full weight of disorder while the schizophrenic may be perfectly capable of doing so within an elaborate, but effective, orderly disorder. In this case, the schizophrenic's psychological existence constitutes a naturally (self) organized and adaptive reality, whereas the mildly depressed subject has not integrated, as of yet, his or her disorder into a globally functioning, more accommodating order.

This example is not intended to suggest that schizophrenia is not a disorder that requires treatment, including the administration of psychotropics. It also does not suggest that depression is, in all cases, more serious or disabling than psychotic disorders. Rather, as a hypothetical, the illustration draws attention to the *individual* nature of mental health and the need for an individualized approach to the (non) treatment of mental illness. More specifically, however, this individualized approach to treatment requires some understanding of the self-organizing process and the relative, temporal position of the person within this process. The example intends to call into question the need-for-treatment approach, particularly the coercive use of drug therapy for individuals who appear to be disorderly and object to forced medication. Thus, consistent with the present chapter, the example affirms an alternative understanding of one's right to refuse treatment, especially for those who are categorically defined on the basis of their disorder alone.

IMPLICATIONS AND CONCLUSION

Through the use of chaos theory and its sundry principles, we have briefly developed an objection to the administration of mental health treatment when the intervention involves the surrendering of one's adaptive capabilities in the interest of expediency. Nonlinear dynamical systems theory tells us that, following certain events or periods in a person's life, the onset of disorder is not only natural but, in most cases, inevitable. Of course, the character of these events directly impacts the nature of the disorder and, consequently, the extent or severity of mental disability. We have not addressed whether our understanding of self-organization theory is applicable to *all* cases of psychiatric illness. This is a research question necessitating further investigation beyond the scope of the present study. However, self-organization theory does indicate that the order-out-of-disorder phenomenon applies to all natural systems (including the human system) in all but the most extreme manifestations of chaos. We employed this logic in our critical assessment of mental health, drug treatment, and one's right to refuse it.

We are aware of the reordering process that occurs in all of our lives following events or experiences that induce disorder (e.g., extreme periods of psychological stress). Additionally, in our own lives we recognize how this new "order" somehow makes us feel stronger, healthier than our old selves. The established adage, "If I can get through this, I can get through anything," is certainly relevant here. Granted, we are not generally referring to disabling psychotic episodes. Nevertheless, the theoretical process is the same. Indeed, there are many instances of psychosis, for example, that might lead us to conclude that the mental functioning of a schizophrenic is somehow orderly, despite the fact that the *appearance* of that order may seem unusual. Chaos theory affirms our intuitive feeling about these and other similar situations.

In regard to the law, affirming a right to refuse treatment seems therapeutic, given that it promotes individual dignity, personhood, autonomy, and the like. In some very contentious instances, however, psychology takes exception to one's exercise of this right. Indeed, as some have argued, granting a request for treatment refusal may not be in the best medical interest of the patient. It is at this juncture that chaology, by way of self-organization theory, is relevant and informative. Based on our analysis and critique, we conclude that refusing forced treatment allows natural (self) treatment or healing to occur, and the process of reorganization to unfold. Thus, in a psycholegal sense, chaos theory suggests that exercising a right to refuse treatment is not only *therapeutic* but *just*, especially in relation to the psychiatric citizen.

PART THREE

The Just(ice)

CHAPTER EIGHT

(Un)clear but Convincing Evidence

A Case Study

OVERVIEW. *The purpose of this chapter is to ground the theoretical explorations undertaken in Part II by examining the very real experiences of psychiatric citizens processed through the mental health law system. Part II critically reviewed how several of the more salient principles of chaos theory furthered our understanding of four controversies on the civil side of psycholegal theory and practice. Indeed, we considered how mental illness could best be construed as a fractal, with no one identifiable meaning; how the definition of dangerousness was dependent on an array ecological factors, making its precise prediction elusive if not impossible; how the practice of involuntary civil confinement was informed, not solely on the basis of* parens patriae *and police power justifications but, additionally, on the basis of broader sociopolitical considerations that endorsed shared, commensense meanings for commitment understood as point or fixed attractors; and how the logic of treatment (especially drug therapy) denied an important, life-affirming process that enabled one to self-organize (i.e., healthily adapt) in the face of disorder. What we have yet to describe, however, is how these chaos theory insights explicitly capture and convey the everyday psycholegal realities of persons diagnosed with psychiatric illness.*

This chapter thoroughly examines the process of civil commitment, mindful of how the meaning of mental illness, definitions/predictions of dangerousness, and one's right to refuse treatment directly impact involuntary hospitalization decisions. Given that our focus is on the lived reality of confinement, we canvass, to some extent, research previously mapped by other critical investigators. Our purpose, however, is to describe how chaos theory advances the existing literature by proposing a broader theoretical framework from within which to interpret these studies and the unfolding drama of civil commitment. Thus, we intend to demonstrate how routine determinations to hospitalize persons involuntarily, when subjected to a nonlinear dynamical systems theory analysis, further our understanding of citizen justice in the psycholegal sphere.

In order to explore this process fully, it is necessary to assess actual cases or proceedings in which the medicolegal system constructs the reality of mental illness and determines the fate of persons with psychiatric disorders. In other words, comprehending the lived experience of civil commitment requires that we examine how mental health citizens are judged within the psychiatric courtroom and how the courtroom participants reach these judgments. For purposes of this investigation, the primary data used is the appellate transcript of a homeless woman, living in New York City, who was unwillingly subjected to the dynamics of the mental health law system. The name of this precedent-setting appellate decision is In the Matter of Billie Boggs (1987). In addition, however, we supplement our analysis of Boggs by discussing briefly several, more recent appellate cases. These court rulings demonstrate that the psycholegal positions endorsed in Boggs, regarding mental illness, dangerousness, civil commitment, and treatment refusal, are still operative today in many ways.

We begin the chapter by reviewing several notable studies that critique, although from different perspectives, the dynamics of the psychiatric courtroom. Specifically, these studies include the research of Warren (1982), Holstein (1993), and Arrigo (1993a). Each inquiry tells us something quite profound about the constitution of psycholegal reality and how it manifests itself through courtroom decisions, impacting the everyday lives of citizens such as Billie Boggs. For the most part, none of these investigations employs the insights of chaos theory. Collectively, however, these works reveal something distinctive and compelling about the process of decision making in civil commitment matters. Following our review of this research, we apply the principles of chaos theory to the Boggs case. Again, at issue here is the extent to which nonlinear dynamics contribute meaningfully to our understanding of law, psychology, and justice.

THE CRITICAL BACKDROP

As previously described, several notable studies have been conducted in which the process of civil commitment, including the meaning of mental illness, the prediction of dangerousness and, to a lesser extent, treatment refusal, have been examined. This section establishes the requisite backdrop against which our chaos analysis can be envisioned. Each of the three seminal studies described below portrays certain themes as operative in clinicolegal decision making; these themes critically examine the reality of mental health confinement and the manner in which certain forms of knowledge are incorporated into this cycle of institutional control. In particular, we contend, as articulated by the established research in the field, that societal interpretations of mental illness and dangerousness are shaped by forces beyond the experiences of those for whom such determinations are made. Instead, we argue, consistent with this literature, that psychiatric citizens subjected to involuntary hospitalization are generally defined on the basis of knowledge and meanings derived from commonsense understanding, detached professional constructs, shared languages, and socially constructed presumptions about the reality of psychological being and the lived nature of "normal" identity experienced in the everyday world.

Commonsense in the Courtroom: Warren and the Topos of Mental Illness

The seminal treatise on psycholegal decision making in the civil commitment context was authored by Carol Warren (1982). Relying on the sociology of labeling theory and symbolic interactionism, Warren immersed herself in the fictitiously named "Metropolitan Court," in order to understand how confinement decisions were made and on what epistemological basis. Through detailed participant observation studies, "supplemented by analysis of court documents, visits to other parts of the mental health law system, and interviews with [relevant parties]" (1982, p. 6), Warren obtained a significant pool of ethnographic data from which to investigate the civil commitment process.

What she discovered was that decision making in the psychiatric courtroom took place "at the intersection of legal theories and theories about mental illness" (Warren, 1982, p. 137). Warren found that each judgment was "superseded . . . by commonsense notions [regarding] mental illness" (ibid.). The author explains this phenomenon, suggesting that "in the arena of knowledge, the medical [psychiatric] and legal [juridical] models of human action are in conflict in the mental health courtroom" (ibid., p. 138). Juridical models tend to respect human rationality as the basis of action; psychiatric models tend to attribute behavior to the often hidden dynamics of the psyche (e.g., Wrightsman, 1997). Thus, role conflict ensues between the practitioners of these respective disciplines, emerging from their different interpretive schemes. For example, while the lawyer, through his or her position as advocate, identifies with the protection of one's civil liberties and individual rights, the psychiatrist, through his or her status as healer, treats or helps those who are in need of such intervention, without necessarily hesitating to consider individual rights

(Brooks, 1974; Warren, 1982, p. 138). This conflict, then, must be mediated by some subsequent factor; namely, the topos of mental illness.

Relying upon the insights of Santos (1977), Warren found that certain "topoi" are operative in the context of civil commitment decision making:

> No matter how precisely a norm is written, nor how carefully a legal concept is defined, there is always a background of uncertainty . . . which cannot be removed by any deductive or apodictic method. The only solution is to employ the inventive art . . . of finding points of view or "common places" (*loci communes, topoi*) which being widely accepted, will help to fill the gaps . . . These *topoi* . . . . refer to what is evident . . . , [they] are based on common sense, on the "logic of the reasonable." (Santos, 1977, pp. 15–16; quoted in Warren, 1982, pp. 138–39)

The topos (sing.) of mental illness, then, is a cultural phenomenon. When mental illness becomes defined in psychiatric or legal contexts, these definitions do not replace commonsense notions but, rather, *add* to its already agreed-upon meaning (Scheff, 1966). Thus, when competing accounts materialize (e.g., psychiatric model versus legal model), the topos becomes the basis for a shared understanding that is necessary in civil commitment decision making (Warren, 1982, p. 139).

Warren also indicates that attorneys and others involved in administrative hearings sustaining or extending involuntary hospitalization often refer to the mentally ill as "sick" and "crazy." She offers proof of this, citing interviews with attorneys (both district attorneys and public defenders), judges, psychiatrists, as well as referencing a number of transcripts. According to Warren, what these sources tell us is that the commonsense model of mental illness takes precedence over other interpretive forms. Indeed, when medical and legal paradigms clash, it is the *shared* image of the mentally disabled that "governs the unfolding courtroom process" (Arrigo, 1993, p. 25) and, ultimately, determines civil commitment outcomes. Thus, the notion that the defendant is "crazy" is shared by attorneys, judges, and psychiatrists. This image prevails, despite the disciplinary specific meanings that otherwise *theoretically* anchor law and medicine (Warren, 1982). In sum, then, we note that Warren provides the earliest and most detailed account of how culture, language, and popular image dynamics impact the fate of psychiatric citizens. Indeed, her analysis was to become the impetus for subsequent studies similarly investigating the psychiatric courtroom, including the work of James Holstein.

"Doing Things With Words": Holstein and Interpretive Practice

Holstein's (1993) description of "court-ordered insanity" is, in many ways, a logical extension to Warren's work. Holstein's engagement in his own "Metropolitan Court" is best described as a systematic inquiry into interpretive practice or "how persons involved in . . . [civil] commitment proceedings understand, define, interpret, and use the concept of mental illness or psychiatric disorder . . . to fashion legal decisions" (1993, p. 5). For Holstein, the focus is on "the *process* of invoking and applying definitions, categories, and practical interpretive procedures" (ibid.). In other words, the author considers how categories or labels inform the decision-making process or, rather, how they are employed in courtroom discourse to generate understandings that ultimately impact confinement outcomes.

According to Holstein, "mental illness" is a label or category used to describe behaviors or characteristics of persons in everyday language. Going well beyond conventional labeling theory and symbolic interactionism, he argues that meaning "is not inherent in any particular object, person, or event, but instead is attached through language and interaction" (ibid.). Thus, the meaning assigned to "mental illness" and the "psychiatrically disordered" label affixed to individuals, is understood as a psycholegal process of interaction and discourse through which agreed-upon understandings are generated.

Holstein also attempts to understand how everyday realities such as mental illness are the product of interactive construction or meaning-making. The way people approach psychiatric disorders; that is, the way they describe and interpret them, is what constitutes the lived reality of health and illness. Thus, language is not merely a way of conveying meaning, it is a way of *generating* or *creating* meaning. For example, when two or more persons interact and arrive at some common understanding regarding the subject of their conversation, language is the means by which these persons construct a shared reality. Consistent with Warren (1982), commonsense meaning is important to Holstein's analysis of civil commitment hearings. Indeed, commonsense categories make possible the interpretation of the social world (Holstein, 1993, p. 6; Schutz, 1964). Thus, it follows that if we intend to understand involuntary commitment proceedings, "a focus on [the] participants' use of commonsense knowledge and practical reasoning" is essential (Holstein, 1993, p. 7).

In sum, then, Holstein "analyzes how participants in commitment proceedings use their commonsense knowledge to produce reasoned and reasonable commitment decisions" by appealing to the ways in which they use "descriptive categories, psychiatric constructs, and local knowledge of social roles and institutions to make accountable arguments for and against commitment" (Holstein, 1993, p. 15). Accordingly, "there is no need to determine the 'real' mental status of candidates for commitment because the focus is on what commitment participants *interpret* to be real—mental illness as it is *practically* constituted" (ibid.; emphasis added).

Signifying Craziness: Arrigo and the Semiotics of Illness

Arrigo (1993) also explores the contours of civil commitment decision making. Unlike the research of Warren (1982) and Holstein (1993), Arrigo's assessment is not fundamentally ethnographic nor is it purely sociological. His analysis rightfully falls within the domain of legal semiotics. Similar to the respective projects of Warren and Holstein, however, Arrigo's semiotic inquiry examines the drama of civil commitment. In particular, he critically assesses the way in which language impacts confinement decisions, or, more exactly, how discourse shapes legal decision making at the appellate court level (Morrow, 1998). In this regard, Arrigo's interest lies in decoding what the court "really means when commenting upon the mentally ill or [the process of] involuntary psychiatric hospitalization" (Arrigo, 1993, p. ix).

To facilitate his analysis, two different layers or levels of semiotic analysis provide the methodological basis (i.e., data) from which Arrigo's semiotic inquiry unfolds (Arrigo, 1999). The first level reviews the majority opinions contained in the twenty-eight, precedent-setting appellate court decisions on the civil side of mental health law. Arrigo's intent is to identify the words and/or phrases jurists use to "make sense" of the reality of mental illness and involuntary commitment (Morrow, 1998). Grouping together similar metaphorical terms (i.e., the mentally ill as "magical" thinkers) and referential expressions (i.e., the mentally ill as disordered), Arrigo then identifies a number of themes. He contends that these themes are a constellation of hidden meanings and unstated assumptions, signifying the court's regard for psychiatric citizens and the process of civil commitment. In his second layer of semiotic analysis, Arrigo resituates the metaphorical and referential words/phrases back into their original textual setting. He demonstrates how these expressions cannot be reduced to singular or "exact" meaning, highlighting the profoundly ambiguous character of the words and phrases in question. In other words, despite what appear to be thematic points of convergence located within the first level of semiotic inquiry, the second layer of analysis dramatically reveals how these meanings explode and scatter (Barthes, 1988). This finding has significant implications for civil commitment determinations. As the author asserts:

> . . . we understand that, notwithstanding many of the ambiguities, contradictions, inconsistencies, pluralities, and differences found within the second layer of semiotic inquiry, the Court "selects out," at best unconsciously, certain expressions to convey its regard for the mentally ill and involuntary hospitalization. [It is this selection process] that explain[s] how the psychiatric consumer's identity in discourse is denied, resulting in the legally sanctioned abuse of mental health patients. (Arrigo, 1999, p. 96)

Arrigo (1993) concludes his investigation by drawing attention to the language of "medical model" psychiatry, arguing that it "is the operative discourse" in the appellate cases he examined (p. 133). Indeed, as he indicates, the grammar of psychiatry is overwhelmingly responsible for assigning meaning to phrases like "civil commitment" and "mental illness," and it is these interpretations, with their corresponding hidden assumptions and implicit values, that linguistically (and therefore socially) structure appellate court decisions. In short, the language of psychiatry is *codified* by the courts, invalidating and dismissing competing or alternative discourses and ways of knowing (ibid., p. 134). Thus, civil commitment "is a 'clinical' intervention for persons who are 'suffering,' 'afflicted with disease,' 'in need of treatment,' 'sick,' etc." (ibid.). These terms and expressions, with their privileged psychiatric meanings, eliminate prospects for replacement interpretations regarding the mentally ill, including such words and/or phrases as "consumers," "mental health citizens," "psychiatric survivors," and "the differently abled, etc." (Arrigo, 1993, 1999).

The importance of these linguistic realities is in their inherent relation to knowledge (Arrigo, 1993, 1996). To some significant degree, language shapes and determines what we know, think, and feel. For example, we harbor a certain understanding for what it means to be "sick." When employed in relation to the mentally ill, the term presents us with a certain shared image of disease or disorder, encouraging us to regard this phenomenon as something resembling physical illness. In this process, however, we are denied the possibility of understanding mental illness in alternative ways (e.g., not as an "affliction" or "illness" but as a qualitatively different form of "health"). Thus, rather than talking about "consumers" of "mental health services," we talk about "sick" people "in need" of psychiatric/medical "treatment." Again, as Arrigo (1993) observes, the discourse of medicine informs decision making in the psychiatric courtroom. Consequently, the language invoked to convey circumscribed meaning about mental illness has a profound impact on civil commitment determinations.

Relevance to Present Critique

The critiques developed by Warren, Holstein, and Arrigo are instructive on several levels. Most generally, each embodies a strain of critical thinking about the mentally ill and the process of civil commitment that informs the way we examine psycholegal reality. Indeed, each purports to tell us something significant about how the court system defines mental illness, dangerousness, civil commitment, and the right to refuse treatment. Warren (1982) argues that commonsense understandings of mental illness as images of craziness govern courtroom dynamics; Holstein (1993) describes an interpretive process by which courts come to create and generate meaning in the face of often competing evidence; and Arrigo (1993) explains how psychiatric language, and its limited horizon of medical model meanings, underscore the images jurists rely upon when making confinement decisions. Thus, each study advances our awareness of how, in the face of necessity, psycholegal realities are constructed.

We intend to rely upon the insights of Warren, Holstein, and Arrigo as we assess the manner in which chaos theory might extend their respective observations. To facilitate our inquiry, we present a single case study, *In the Matter of Billie Boggs* (1987). This court decision was carefully selected for several reasons. First, it embodies each of the four psycholegal controversies examined throughout Part II of this book. Thus, it uniquely serves our analytical interests. Second, many appellate decisions in the civil commitment area provide summary findings. The *Boggs* cases, however, is a richly detailed opinion, including dissenting commentary. Thus, it provides ample "data" from which to engage in a chaos theory investigation. Third, the *Boggs* ruling has been examined critically by several scholars, especially given its profound impact on subsequent mental health law decision making (e.g., Arrigo, 1993; Perlin, 1999; Reisner & Slobogin, 1997; Williams, 1998). Thus, there is an established history of evaluating this particular court opinion. Fourth, our purpose with *Boggs* is to draw attention to how chaos theory, as a *theoretical* template for social scientific inquiry, may be serviceable for future psycholegal scholarship. As such, we are not interested in "proving" that nonlinear dynamical systems theory categorically explains important controversies at the crossroads of law and psychology, just that chaos theory can contribute meaningfully to our understanding of justice (or the absence of it) in the clinicolegal sphere. Fifth, although principally focused on the relevance of the *Boggs* decision for purposes of our inquiry, several, more recent appellate cases are also summarily presented. In other words, not only do we include additional mental health law decisions, we comment on a representative number of recent opinions as a way of demonstrating whether or not the conclusions reached in *Boggs* were or were not anomalous.

IN THE MATTER OF BILLIE BOGGS

As previously noted, we chose a single case from which to assess critically the practice of decision making in the psychiatric courtroom. This is the case of Joyce Brown or Billie Boggs. The latter was her self-professed name. The decision in *Boggs* is important because it represents a "classic confrontation between the rights of a citizen against governmental authority trying to confront and remedy a pervasive societal problem" (*In the Matter of Boggs*, 1987, pp. 366–367). The specific problem to which the case alludes is the plight of the "mentally disturbed homeless," as described by Judge Milonas of the Supreme Court of New York in his dissenting opinion.

Ms. Boggs was a noncriminally convicted woman subjected to involuntary civil confinement and forced treatment because she was thought to be mentally ill and dangerous. Thus, we see how this case calls into dispute the four, major controversies examined in Part II of this text. More importantly, however, the decision in *Boggs* makes it possible for us to assess how the principles of chaos theory might apply in the context of real people and actual courtroom practices.

Background

Billie Boggs was a 40-year-old woman living on the public sidewalk in front of a restaurant in the County of New York. The surrounding city streets and alleyways constituted her bedroom, living room, toilet, and generally had served as her home for the past year. Ms. Boggs was civilly committed in late October 1987, after having been identified as a person "in need" of psychiatric care. Mental health professionals affiliated with an organization called "Project HELP" had observed Ms. Boggs on an almost daily basis, over the course of the preceding year. Project HELP was a self-described "emergency psychiatric service for allegedly mentally ill homeless persons, who live[d] on the streets of New York City" (*Boggs*, 1987, p. 343). The staff in question mostly consisted of a clinical team, including psychiatrists, nurses, and social workers. Their responsibilities entailed "travel[ing] around New York City . . . , identifying persons who live[d] in the street and who appear[ed] to be particularly in need of immediate psychiatric hospital treatment" (ibid.). Persons "particularly in need" were equivalent theoretically to persons who "appear[ed] to be in danger of doing serious harm to themselves or others" (ibid.).

Dr. Hess was part of the clinical team of psychiatrists associated with Project HELP. He determined that Ms. Boggs fit the profile of persons "in need" of emergency mental health care (i.e., she was mentally ill and failure to treat her illness immediately would endanger her life and/or the lives of others). Consequently, he arranged for her (involuntary) transportation and subsequent commitment to Bellevue Hospital (a public psychiatric facility in New York City). This initial hospitalization was arranged pursuant to Section 9.39 of the Mental Hygiene Law which authorized a hospital to retain an individual for up to fifteen days if that person was "alleged to have a mental illness for which immediate observation, care, and treatment . . . [wa]s appropriate and which [wa]s likely to result in serious harm to [oneself] or others [if not addressed]" (*Boggs*, 1987, pp. 343–344). The day following her commitment, Ms. Boggs gave notice, challenging her hospitalization and requesting a hearing.

At the initial hearing, the respondents argued for her continued confinement and offered the testimony of four psychiatrists, a psychiatric social worker, the older sister of Ms. Boggs, and an additional witness who photographed the petitioner in the street. In support of her release, the court heard the testimony of three psychiatrists and Ms. Boggs. Given the evidence, the court granted Ms. Boggs' application and directed that she be released from Bellevue. On appeal, however, the appellate court reversed the decision of the lower court and denied Ms. Boggs' petition for release. What follows is a somewhat extensive assessment of the critical issues, various opinions, and assorted statements that played a pivotal role in the appellate court's reversal.

Opinion of the Court: Legal and Psychiatric Analysis

The primary issue before the court was whether the respondents (i.e., the hospital officials) had presented "clear and convincing evidence that [Ms. Boggs was] suffering from a mental illness, which require[d] her immediate involuntary commitment to a hospital for care and treatment since, allegedly, if such an illness [wa]s left untreated, it [would] likely result in serious harm to the petitioner" (*Boggs*, 1987, p. 341). Respondents argued that the state "ha[d] a legitimate interest under its *parens patriae* powers in providing care to its citizens who [we]re unable because of emotional disorders to care for themselves" and, further, "ha[d] authority under its police power to protect the community from the dangerous tendencies of some who [we]re mentally ill" (ibid., p. 342). The primary matter, then, was whether proof existed that Ms. Boggs suffered from "something more serious than [what] is demonstrated by idiosyncratic behavior" (ibid.).

As we have seen, the clear and convincing standard of proof requires that evidence of mental illness and dangerousness be demonstrated at a greater than seventy-five percent degree of confidence. As the court in *Boggs* observed, this level of proof "strikes a fair balance between the rights of the individual and the legitimate concerns of the state" (ibid., p. 343). Thus, justifying the involuntary civil confinement of Ms. Boggs depended on a clear and convincing evidentiary demonstration by the respondents that she was both mentally ill and dangerousness. In reaching its conclusion, the appellate court spoke to this matter:

> . . . we find the clear and convincing evidence indicates that, while living in the streets for the past year, Ms. Boggs' mental condition has deteriorated to the point where she was in danger of doing serious harm to herself when . . . she was involuntarily admitted to respondent Bellevue for treatment; and . . . we further find that clear and convincing evidence supports the continued involuntary confinement of Ms. Boggs to the hospital for treatment. (1987, p. 366)

In defending its reversal of the lower court's conclusion, the appellate court argued that the hearing court derived its evidence from the wrong place. As the court explained:

> the hearing court states, in substance, that the respondents' psychiatrists and the psychiatrists who testified on behalf of Ms.

Boggs "are nearly diametrically opposed in their assessment of mental condition and in their predictions as to whether she is likely to cause herself or others harm. Thus I [the hearing court] derive little psychiatric guidance from them and therefore place great weight on the demeanor, behavior and testimony of [Ms. Boggs] herself.". . . We [the appellate court] find that the hearing court erred in placing "great weight on the demeanor, behavior, and testimony" of Ms. Boggs. . . . 1987, p. 364)

Thus, the hearing court, in the face of competing psychiatric opinions, chose to allow Billie Boggs to speak for herself. Its failure to find evidence of mental disorder and dangerousness, consistent with the appropriate procedural standard and given the conflicting testimony, indicates the lower court's preference to search no further than one's own psychology or psychological comportment when making civil commitment determinations. Interestingly, however, the appellate court found Ms. Boggs' testimony unreliable and elected, instead, to place "great weight" on the opinions of the respondents' psychiatrists as derived from records (e.g., transcripts). Contained within these documents are the competing accounts that the lower court acknowledged, as well as a description of Ms. Boggs' mental illness and dangerousness that was pivotal to the appellate court's reversal. We now examine this evidence. To avoid repetition of case material, we incorporate the critique that chaos theory offers within, rather than apart from, this investigation. What follows, then, is a critical analysis of the way in which the appellate court's conclusions were reached.

CRITICAL ANALYSIS

In this section, we simultaneously rely upon and extend the analyses of civil commitment as articulated by Warren (1982), Holstein (1993), and Arrigo (1993) by turning to chaos theory and its sundry principles. For purposes of clarity and impact, we segment the *Boggs* case in a way consistent with the presentation of our overall project. In other words, we explore the way in which: (a) the meaning of mental illness; (b) the definition and prediction of dangerousness; (c) the practice of civil commitment; and (d) the right to refuse treatment operate within this controversial appellate court decision. Again, our foremost objective is to assess whether it is possible to communicate something more about the everyday drama of confinement, informed by nonlinear dynamical systems theory.

Given this section's general orientation, we employ the same principles of chaos theory examined in Part II of this book and apply them to the appellate decision in *Boggs*. In this context, the proceeding analysis functions to amplify the debates identified and developed in chapters 4 through 7. More specifically, in our assessment of mental illness, dangerousness, and civil commitment, we begin each of these critical reviews by commenting on how Warren (1982), Holstein (1993) and Arrigo (1993) would respond to the these matters, based on their respective conceptual orientations. Our analysis of treatment refusal as contained in the *Boggs* case is structured somewhat differently than the three preceding inquiries. Indeed, Warren, Holstein, and Arrigo offer limited appraisals of this controversy and even less that is relevant to the notion of self-organization as employed in our critique. Thus, commentary found in the subsection on Boggs' right to refuse treatment appears as an integrated reflection. In other words, we do not first provide any critical backdrop, elucidated by chaos theory. Rather, the entire subsection represents an evaluation of coercive intervention (e.g., forced confinement), and Boggs' right to refuse such treatment as seen through the lens of nonlinear dynamical systems theory.

"Tearing Up Money"

The finding of mental illness in the *Boggs* case was informed primarily by the meanings Project HELP staff attached to certain behaviors they witnessed while observing Ms. Boggs in the street. The meanings assigned to these actions were the decisive factors in the construction of Ms. Boggs' reality. Indeed, these interpretations distinguished between conduct arising from normal, appropriate, and healthy motives, and behavior that was the product of underlying abnormality, inappropriateness, and illness. In the *Boggs* case, psycholegal attention was directed squarely at these latter meanings.

We know that Ms. Boggs, on occasion, tore up or burnt paper money that was given to her by strangers. Indeed, Ms. Boggs conceded these behaviors were attributable to her. What is significant from a critical perspective, however, is the way in which the act of tearing up money was linked unquestionably to "commonsense" knowledge, indicating underlying mental illness. In other words, following commonsense notions, what "rational" and "healthy" person would engage in the defacement of money?

Destroying something considered valuable by most standards, is not interpreted as reasonable, logical, or appropriate when it occurs. From a critical perspective, however, we question whether one's motive for such conduct must absolutely be evidence of deep-seated psychiatric disturbance, necessitating civil commitment. Consider the following statement by Dr. Sabatini, a psychiatrist testifying on behalf of the respondents, endorsing the continued involuntary hospitalization of Ms. Boggs, given her behavior.

> It's not a general phenomenon observed and the indications I got were that there was a meaning to the destruction of this money because it represented, when it was given to her, people saying things about her—negative things about her which had a sexual overtone . . . people . . . were . . . trying to control her sexuality through money. And, I think the destruction of money served to dispel that. (1987, p. 353)

From this passage, it appears that Dr. Sabatini ascribes underlying, "private" meaning to Ms. Boggs' action, meaning that is further "tangled up with black males and prostitution" (ibid.). In addition, Dr. Marcos, the fourth psychiatrist to testify for the respondents, also believed that "being given currency was equated with men trying to tell Ms. Boggs that she was a prostitute" and interpreted her "burning of the currency as evidence of her belief that she could gain respect and dispel the idea [that] she [wa]s a prostitute" (*Boggs*, 1987, p. 353).

From the testimony of Sabatini and Marcos, then, the primary signification for Boggs' behavior, defined as unusual or uncustomary, was evidence that her psychological health was, to some extent, diminished. Thus, according to these "forensic experts," the destruction of money was the manifestation of pathological behavior, stemming from a pathological (i.e., noncommensense) belief and, as such, evidence of underlying mental illness.

Contemporary psychology maintains that most behavior is attributable to underlying thought processes that give rise to one's actions. If the conduct in question is indicative of something (e.g., values, beliefs) not customarily understood as meaningful, useful, healthy, etc., within the prevailing sociocultural climate, the behavior is not only defined as "deviant," "diseased," or "dangerous," but the underlying motives for the action are also impugned. Consequently, by way of this psychological perspective, we understand that behaviors designated as irrational by most, must be similarly irrational for those who harbor the thoughts that give rise to the illogical conduct. This is how tearing up money becomes equated with mental illness. What is most important to note, however, is how psychology attributes significance to this behavior; meaning that is understood as pathological without sufficient regard for alternative (and reasonable) motivations that may exist. This very point was addressed by Ms. Boggs and those testifying on her behalf.

One witness for the petitioner was Dr. Gould, an attending psychiatrist at Metropolitan Hospital. Having spoken with Ms. Boggs concerning the tearing of money behavior, he reached a different conclusion than the one articulated by doctors Sabatini and Marcos. As Gould explained, Ms. Boggs "had no delusions about money, rather, . . . when someone threw paper money at Ms. Boggs and she found it insulting or degrading, she would destroy it" (ibid., p. 356). Ms. Boggs confirmed this interpretation when she testified on her own behalf. The petitioner noted that she "destroy[ed] paper money if it [wa]s thrown at her or given to her in an allegedly offensive manner" and that "she ha[d] no delusions about black persons giving her money for sex" (ibid., p. 358).

Critical Backdrop for the Meaning of Mental Illness

A court of law must balance competing stories or accounts when reaching its decision in a given case. The appellate court in *Boggs* was required to determine the emotional state of the petitioner for purposes of sustaining or releasing her from involuntary hospital care and treatment. In this section, we consider how the court derived its ultimate meaning regarding the petitioner's mental condition, given conflicting accounts, informed by the critical analyses of Warren (1982), Holstein (1993), and Arrigo (1993).

Boggs' overt behavior could be regarded as a "commonsense" indicator (Warren, 1982), leading the court to accept certain meanings at the expense of other, less customary understandings. The activity of tearing up money was an important piece of evidence introduced in the psychiatric courtroom. At issue was whether the court interpreted it as an expression of underlying mental illness or as an idiosyncratic response to environmental circumstances. In the face of competing testimony, the appellate court embraced shared and consensual understandings of appropriate thought/ behavior. Notwithstanding the absence of definitive evidence supporting psychiatric illness, the court determined the existence of it on the basis of psychological accounts that merely arose from *behavioral* verification coupled with the attribution of underlying mental dysfunction to this behavior. Why would this conduct be interpreted as a manifestation of illness rather than health?

Holstein (1993, pp. 133–148) suggests that mental illness assumptions are interpretive schemes employed to make (common) sense of an individual's need for hospitalization. The introduction of psychiatric disorder to a given case serves as an organizing scheme within which to interpret all other information regarding that individual. According to Holstein (1993, p. 134), "[a]s court personnel impute mental illness, they implicitly structure their interpretations of patients' behavior more generally. That behavior, viewed as a product of mental illness, then serves to further document the presence of illness itself."

Describing Ms. Boggs as a homeless mentally ill person established a framework from within which to understand her reality. Following Holstein, defining Ms. Boggs as psychiatrically disordered and interpreting her behavior accordingly created a certain dialectic in which mental illness became the basis for understanding her behaviors and her behaviors became the basis or justification for the presence of mental illness. Commencing with an interpretive scheme in which Ms. Boggs was described as mentally ill, homeless, and embodying the characteristic behaviors of such individuals, her mental illness was then interpreted as the deep-seated cause for her actions, including tearing up money. When understood as a manifestation of psychiatric disorder, tearing up money became a justification for the finding of mental illness. The underlying assumption of mental illness, then, provided the "interpretive resources" with which to understand Ms. Boggs' behavior (Holstein, 1993, p. 134).

Similarly, a semiotic critique of *Boggs* would focus on the language employed during the hearing and the subsequent influence that language had on the proceedings. Arrigo (1993, pp. 106–127) drew upon the case of *Boggs* for just such an analysis. He found that a number of words or phrases were employed by various persons throughout the hearing that "communicated deeper meaning about the court's regard for the psychiatrically disordered" (ibid., p. 109). These deeper meanings were more significant than were the superficial meanings conveyed by the words themselves. Arrigo identified ten terms or expressions, including reference to Billie Boggs as "suffering," "engaging in magical thinking," and "speaking in sexual rhymes."

To illustrate Arrigo's point, we examine the word "suffering." It is ambiguous because it communicates at least two distinct psychological states. It may refer to suffering *through* something whose effect is nondisabling. In this context, suffering may convey one's capacity to cope with a psychiatric illness. The term may also refer to a sort of debilitating condition; that is, a particularly agonizing physical or emotional state. In this context, one's suffering is disabling. Thus, we see that the word "suffering" communicates two meanings: coping with mental illness, as well as despairing over it (ibid., p. 112).

With these two different interpretations in mind, it is not difficult to understand how such ambiguity might factor prominently into the appellate court's understanding of Ms. Boggs' psychiatric condition. For example, was she "suffering" in the sense that she was a survivor, an individual who learned to cope with her illness? Alternatively, was she sufficiently debilitated by her illness that she required involuntary hospitalization and treatment? This distinction should have been important in determining the ultimate disposition of the case. However, the meaning conveyed by the appellate court's chosen language served only to further complicate and obfuscate this contrast. Semiotic analyses attempt to uncover or decode the embedded meanings communicated in speech or writing, drawing our attention to the limitless possible significations and degrees of comprehension (e.g., Barthes, 1988). In a similar fashion, chaos theory identifies language as one example of how reality is multidimensional and how the interpretive schemes through which we understand our world are representative of only one perspective, displacing many others (e.g., Arrigo & Schehr, 1998; Arrigo, 1994; Milovanovic, 1997).

Chaos Theory, Fractal Space, and the Meaning of Mental Illness

Recall that our chaos theory critique regarding the meaning of mental illness was premised on the assertion that sense-making must be regarded as incomplete, reflecting no absolute truths about the world. Indeed, meaning is contingent on social constructions with their corresponding and circumscribed (i.e., point attractor) understandings of phenomena. Any signification we attach to a given concept must necessarily be our own cultural, historical, and personal construction, yielding no finite, objective reality, but, instead, a limited point of view. Although we may recognize other perspectives, we employ the one that is uniquely our own when making sense of others. It is in this way that meaning presents itself as something of a paradox: We cannot "see" other perspectives without them necessarily passing through, succumbing to, or otherwise being influenced by our own vantage point.

If mental health is a fractal, it exists as a continuum rather than as a binary opposition (i.e., health/illness) (Arrigo, 1996). As such, "either or" judgments in the psychiatric courtroom regarding particular cases are not only arbitrary but antithetical to a more inclusive conceptualization of justice. As we have argued, employing such inexact and incomplete categories as the basis of truth in decision making, abrogates one's human freedom and liberty. Throughout the appellate court's opinion in the *Boggs* case there are indications that this very reasoning was operative, denying the fractal or multidimensional nature of meaning chaos theory suggests should inform our understanding of psychological being. The example of tearing up money is one case in point.

Because meaning has a fractal nature, behavior can be understood from limitless perspectives. Although some of these vantage points may be more salubrious, depending on the desired effect, no one view is absolutely or universally most desirable. Boggs' destruction of money represented a clash in perspectives. Although, in this instance, her conduct was not necessarily consistent with conventional beliefs concerning appropriate action, her behaviors were open to a variety of interpretations. There are at least two competing perspectives on the meaning of defiling paper currency for Ms. Boggs. The first view was articulated by the psychiatrists endorsing her continued confinement. The second view was described by Ms. Boggs and the psychiatrists testifying on her behalf. In the former instance, the behavior was equated with underlying mental illness; in the latter instance, we redirect our attention to what appear to be idiosyncratic, though justifiable, motives. In this case, the appellate court held that the lower court "erred in placing great weight on the demeanor and testimony of [the petitioner]" (*Boggs*, 1987, p. 364). In contrast to what a perspectival or fractal approach to meaning would suggest, the court declared that the standpoint of Ms. Boggs was irrelevant for purposes of determining her future.

In its finding of mental illness, the court understood the petitioner's thoughts, feelings, and behaviors as adapted from those meanings assigned to them by psychiatry. These significations were operative at the expense of the more personal, though eccentric, meanings described by Boggs herself. Thus, the first critical component of meaning is the denial of subjective experience and the explicit endorsement of "objective" and scientific judgments by the court. In a very real sense, this was the omission of Billie Boggs' subjectivity or humanity from the courtroom in favor of psychiatrically generated knowledge about her identity (Williams, 1998).

Second, although various psychiatrists defined Ms. Boggs based on competing knowledge claims, the appellate court elected to *believe* the testimony of those physicians whose *opinions* were more consistent with the prevailing sociocultural, commonsense understanding of mental illness. This conviction was apparent in the court's refusal to consider seriously how noncommonsense behavior could be indicative of idiosyncratic tendencies as opposed to underlying psychiatric disorder. Conduct consistent with the existing *topoi* was accepted by the court as a more accurate representation of the reality under investigation in the *Boggs* case.

On this matter, chaos theory is instructive. It points out the dangers inherent in accepting one reality as closer to the truth than others. In short, chaos theory describes the *nature* of nonlinear systems as fractals. The fractal of mental health is characterized by an endless number of perspectives, or an endless way of looking at or approaching those phenomena within its confines. The object of investigation inevitably will appear different from the perspective one assumes. The truth or reality of that object is difficult to ascertain, given these limitations. In other words, one cannot approach the truth (of mental health) from any singular perspective. This is not to suggest that a given vantage point cannot present a better view of the reality in question; but, rather, that we cannot approach reality without considering and integrating a variety of perspectives. This integration was lost when the court denied and/or dismissed Ms Boggs' lived experience and, to a lesser extent, the perspective of those psychiatrists testifying on her behalf.

"Self-Destructive Behavior"

The foregoing analysis of Boggs' dangerousness is a continuation of the previous critique on the meaning of mental illness. The definition of dangerousness, similar to explaining psychiatric disorder, is the subject of debate, given its substantial ambiguity and ongoing imprecision. Indeed, a finding that an individual poses a risk of future harm is typically a decision made on the basis of expert forensic testimony (e.g., psychological/psychiatric descriptions and predictions). These expert accounts depend on attributing one's behavior to inherent characteristics endemic to the individual. Consequently, there is a conflation of one's actions with the identity of the psychiatric citizen. Chaos theory tells us that we cannot reduce the two, given specific ecological circumstances occurring outside of the individual over which he/she has limited (or no) control.

Forensic experts and, subsequently, the appellate court, believed that Billie Boggs was a danger to herself on the basis of three justifications. As respondents argued, "the key issue in this case is dangerousness and the record shows three aspects of self-danger. . . . [These included] self-danger from neglect, from actively suicidal conduct, and self-danger from aggressive behavior that [wa]s likely to provoke an attack from others" (*Boggs*, 1987, p. 370). A finding of any one of these would be sufficient to meet New York's statutory standard. Each justification was reflected throughout the court's majority opinion. This notwithstanding, we note that the behaviors exhibited by Ms. Boggs used to interpret her dangerousness were melded to her unique and intrinsic identity. Thus, her context-specific actions were interpreted as the inherent attributes of a violent prone individual, constituting her as a "dangerous" individual.

The appellate court's finding of Boggs' dangerousness was predicated on the testimony of several psychiatrists. The court drew attention to the observations of Dr. Mahon who indicated that the petitioner was not "ready to be an outpatient, since she presently had no capacity to comprehend her need for food, clothing or shelter and, in addition, . . . [could] not comprehend obvious danger" (*Boggs*, 1987, p. 363). In following the decision articulated in the case of *Matter of Carl C.* (1987), the court assimilated Dr. Mahon's opinion into its legal understanding of dangerousness, suggesting that "a threat of serious harm to a mentally ill person 'can result from a refusal or inability to meet essential needs for food, clothing or shelter'" (ibid., p. 364). Boggs' incapacity to comprehend her most basic of needs was a recurring theme in the court opinion and, as such, warrants some further attention.

The notion that one is unable to meet essential life-supporting needs is linked to the "grave disability" dimension of self-danger (Comment, 1983; Schmidt, 1985). In the case of *Boggs*, it appeared most explicitly in the testimony of Dr. Hess. Dr. Hess observed that the petitioner refused food from him and, after eventually accepting it, threw it at him and chased him around the corner (*Boggs*, 1987, p. 345). In addition, Dr. Hess commented on information made available to him by Project HELP staff. The psychiatric outreach team indicated that Ms. Boggs had "throw[n] away warm clothing she had received from personnel representing Project HELP (ibid.). In response, Dr. Hess maintained that the petitioner was a "danger to herself, since she was incapable of accepting food, clothing or shelter" (ibid., p. 346).

There is a key psychiatric assumption embedded in the previous testimony; in short, that Ms. Boggs' unwillingness to accept food and clothing from Project HELP staff was an indication of her inability to comprehend her own needs. But this logic fused the actions of Ms. Boggs with her humanity or intrinsic being. Accordingly, the meaning of the petitioner's refusal of food under specific conditions became synonymous with her "true" psychological identity, absent any reference to those ecological or contextual factors that otherwise influenced her behavior.

Upon closer examination, however, these contextual influences become more apparent and alternative explanations for her actions begin to materialize. For example, there was a recurring tendency for Ms. Boggs to display hostility *only* toward Project HELP staff. This was evidenced by her "twirling an open umbrella to avoid eye contact" (*Boggs*, 1987, p. 344), "curs[ing] and shout[ing] obscenities" (ibid., p. 345), and by being generally "hostile, angry, and us[ing] threatening gestures" (ibid., p. 348). Here, too, we note how the petitioner's behavior was assumed to be a function of her personality. When generalized as they were in the *Boggs* case, anger (affect) and hostility (behavior) were understood as enduring characterological traits, ostensibly stemming from delusions that represented underlying illness. Consequently, Ms. Boggs was regarded as a "dangerous" person.

In addition, we note that evidence of the petitioner's mental illness (i.e., anger/hostility) was also the basis upon which Ms. Boggs met the self-danger criterion such that others were thought likely to injure her. It was believed that the petitioner's anger and hostility was a characteristic that could conceivably encourage others to respond to her in a hostile way, resulting in physical harm. Frankly, as the record indicated, Ms. Boggs had *never been injured nor attacked by another person.* Thus, we are led to reassess the certainty with which the courtroom particpants understood her behavior as linked to persistent personality traits. Again, we note that Ms. Boggs did not exhibit hostile behavior generally but, rather, only in response to specific circumstances, especially the presence of Project HELP staff in her life.

In much the same way that the destruction of money was a response to perceived insult and degradation, Ms. Boggs' feelings and actions toward the mental health outreach team were an expression of pride or a means of maintaining her dignity. The petitioner threw away clothing and food given to her by persons she deemed threatening because of what they represented. Indeed, when testifying on behalf of Ms. Boggs, Dr. Gould explained that her verbal abuse of others was not an indicator of mental illness and a self-destructive personality, but of not wanting to be "disturbed by some individuals who invaded her privacy" (*Boggs*, 1987, p. 356). Again, the expressed purpose of Project HELP was to seek out and provide an emergency psychiatric service to the mentally ill homeless in New York City (ibid., p. 343).

Thus, petitioner's refusal to accept food, clothing, shelter, etc., was an unwillingess to accept what she believed was invasive by those she perceived to be intrusive. Ms. Boggs displayed hostility toward Project HELP staff and not toward the majority of people she encountered on a daily basis. She disposed of food and clothing given to her by the psychiatric team because of the circumstances in which it was offered to her. Indeed, the petitioner stated that she panhandled for money to buy food and had "friends" that provided her clothing when she was in need (Boggs, 1987, p. 351). Thus, rather than an indicator of anger and hostility, Ms. Boggs' demeanor and behavior could just as plausibly represent a deliberate method designed to persuade Project HELP staff to leave her alone. This is not the same as concluding that the petitioner was dangerous and delusional. Indeed, Boggs' refusal of basic life support services may simply have been a desire to have her own agency and subjectivity recognized. In other words, the petitioner arguably saw herself as a *choice-making*, though homeless, citizen. Assistance not requested may have signified a threat to her perceived (and real) capacity in this regard.

We note further the evidence proffered by the respondents as indicative of Boggs' danger to self; namely, her suicidal ideation/behavior. Here, too, attention was drawn to the petitioner's running into traffic to throw away clothing received from Project HELP staff. According to respondent witnesses, this activity suggested an inability to comprehend her basic needs and to care for herself. Further, the manner in which she disposed of the items was suggestive of suicidal ideation. According to the petitioner, however, while she did "run into traffic . . . she had a right to do so. . . . [I]f she got hurt, it was nobody's business but her own" (Boggs, 1987, p. 348). Dr. Mahon interpreted her statement in the following way: ". . . running in front of traffic and saying she ha[d] a right to endanger her life is suicidal and as a psychiatrist, I have to call that suicidal behavior and I have to treat it as a clinician" (ibid., p. 351). Contrastingly, in Dr. Gould's testimony, he noted that the petitioner had never been injured, nor was there any history of severe depression or suicide attempts—historical manifestations usually present in those who are "suicidal" (ibid., p. 357). Again, we see how context-specific behavior is collapsed into one's enduring personality, including the presence of suicidal ideation.

Critical Backdrop for Dangerousness

Warren (1982), Holstein (1993), and Arrigo (1993) offer a valuable back-drop from which to understand the construction of the dangerous individual in commitment proceedings. Similar to the way that mental illness is understood as a process of meaning-making, dangerousness makes sense only from within the context of courtroom constructions of one's reality. Thus, the "meaning" of dangerousness is subject to many of the same criticisms noted in regard to psychiatric disorder. We note further, however, that Warren, Holstein, and Arrigo do not provide a well-crafted assessment on the *prediction* of dangerousness. Thus, the critical template in this subsection directly applies to the problem of defining dangerousness and indirectly to the problem of predicing it.

Warren's (1982) analysis of civil commitment suggests that even in cases where concepts like dangerousness are clearly defined, there nonetheless remains a certain degree of uncertainty. Indeed, courtroom participants confront situations that are plagued by ambiguity, as the significance of the thoughts, feelings, and behaviors that constitute this reality are subject to interpretation. Both psychology and the law have their own interpretations for assessments of dangerousness. In response to the uncertainty promulgated by these differing viewpoints, judgments are made on the basis of socially informed constructions of "objective" reality. Reference to personal experiences tangentially inform these constructions. Thus, we label our lived experiences and the phenomena that comprise them according to preexisting, though learned, conceptions of the world; conceptions that supercede any "professional" understanding in the wake of ambiguity. Among the things we learn is that mental illness is something radically different from mental health. Further, we learn that mental illness "causes" persons to act in irrational ways, with little appreciation for the consequences of their actions. These images are given to us through a number of cultural or institutional outlets (e.g., religion, education, politics, the media), providing the commonsense basis of psychiatic disorder in our society. These shared and accommodating understandings are what Warren (1982) concludes are operative in determinations of dangerousness in specific cases.

Similarly, Holstein (1993) implies that a finding of self-harm or harm to others is a function of an interpretive scheme. In other words, common-sense definitions of mental illness and dangerousness create a backdrop against which the behavior of persons can be measured. Thus, for example, we might turn to the prevailing social conceptions of mental illness and their corresponding assumptions for guidance. The most powerful of these beliefs maintains that persons with psychiatric disorders are more dangerous than their nonmentally ill counterparts. Despite evidence to the contrary, psychiatric citizens are labeled dangerous simply by virtue of their placement in the "ill" or "sick" category. That is to say, having established that an individual (e.g., Ms. Boggs) is mentally ill, the presumption of dangerousness immediately attaches. This presumption, then, becomes the rubric within which the person's actions are judged.

In the case of Billie Boggs, her behaviors (e.g., abusive language toward Project HELP staff) were not evaluated independently; rather, they were assessed *only* with reference to the commonsense and shared interpretive scheme of mental illness. In this regard, mental illness and dangerousness constituted an insidious and invidious tautology: The former was determined with reference to sociocultural understandings of normal human thoughts, feelings, impulses, and actions, and the latter was determined with reference to consensual and accommodating meanings for the behavior of the petitioner. Overall, this interplay of interpretive schemes leaves little room for alternative understandings to emerge; significations that might otherwise reflect the lived experiences of the person in question.

The socially constructed reality of dangerousness wherein interpretive schemes unfold is intimately bound to the domain of semiotics. Arrigo (1993) suggests that to manifest themselves in everyday practice, our social constructions are preliminarily lodged in discourse. In other words, the assembled meanings we attach to the images conveyed always and already occur through language. For example, the words used to describe Ms. Boggs' behavior contain underlying images (i.e., assumptions and values) that are more or less consistent with the "picture" of a dangerous person. Thus, invoking descriptors such as "hostile" and "angry" to communicate her reaction to Project HELP staff establishes a qualitatively different image than when she is described as "defensive," "proudful," "fiercely independent," and the like. Similarly, referring to Ms. Boggs' refusal of food and clothing as an "inability to comprehend" connotes inherently pervasive and extremely negative qualities that arguably impact other facets of her (percieved) identity. By continuously employing courtroom language that evokes adverse images, Boggs' lived reality was reconstituted, consistent with the assumptions conveyed through the prevailing discourse in use. Semiotically speaking, therefore, the images that attached to the language employed, provided a means of "shaping" the way Ms. Boggs was understood by the courtroom participants. These meanings, as originating in discourse, were compatible with the interpretative schemes and common-sense model of decision making in the psychiatric courtroom.

Chaos Theory, Meaning, and Prediction of Dangerousness

We noted at the outset of this section that dangerousness is subject to the same sorts of criticisms that apply to the meaning of mental illness. Indeed, much like psychiatric disorder, defining dangerousness is fraught with complexty, yielding no simple or straightforward solutions. Thus, explaining one's propensity for violence to self and/or others entails some degree of interpretation. In the *Boggs* case, "running into traffic" was described as "suicidal" behavior, but it was also explained as "pride." In addition, throwing away food and clothing was recognized as an "inability" to comprehend basic needs, but also as an effort to maintain some dignity through the act of refusal. In the former instances, the behaviors were identified as enduring characteristics; in the latter instances, they were linked to situational factors or environmental influences that induced the petitioner to behave as she did.

The appellate court ascertained the *meaning* of these events (i.e., indications of illness versus reactions to ecological conditions) primarily from the significance ascribed to them by various forensic specialists. The appellate court concluded that Billie Boggs was unable to care for herself, was suicidal or self-destructive and, therefore, was a danger to herself. These interpretations, however, were premised on assumptions of biological and psychological causation rather than ecological interaction. In the previous section, we suggested that when confronted with uncertainty the clinicolegal court adopted commonsense understandings of mental illness; that is, it endorsed the testimony that most closely resembled prevailing sociocultural notions in order to explain Boggs' behaviors. Similarly, we argue that these shared and accommodating convictions operated in the definition of dangerousness. Indeed, commonsense meanings for harm were informed by causal understandings, linking overt behavior with the petitioner's personality, not with the ecology to which she was connected. Directing attention to the *person* rather than the *behavior* becomes important for assessing both the meaning of dangerousness as well as its prediction (Foucault, 1988).

From the perspective of chaos theory, the court denied the fractal and ecological nature of knowledge, meaning, and the life-world in general, embracing, instead, the logic of mainstream psychiatry. Ms. Boggs' inability to meet her basic needs and her suicidal behavior were cited by the appellate court as manifestations of dangerousness. However, in its review of the case, the court did not acknowledge alternative explanations for these actions. Indeed, as others testified, Ms. Boggs was unwilling to accept assistance from Project HELP staff and, consequently, adopted an angry and hostile posture toward these particular individuals. As chaos theory reminds us, however, interpreting the behavior of a complex nonlinear system cannot occur from a singular perspective. Much like the fractal, it must be understood as a multidimensional reality, possessing manifold configurations and explanations. The respondent *and* petitioner evaluations of Ms. Boggs' reality were decidedly one-dimensional (i.e., clinical). Missing from the appellate court's consideration was the uniquely felt perspective of the petitioner herself. The unidimensionality of reality construction ultimately characterized the court's approach to defining Ms. Boggs, giving way to its particular (and marginalizing) judgment in her case.

Moreover, we note that *predictions* of dangerousness are inexorably linked to the process of defining dangerousness wherein meaning attaches to specific individuals (e.g., Billie Boggs). This association obtains because definitions of one's likely harm are often inseparable from the description of the person in question. In other words, defining dangerousness generally requires a characterization about the individual *as* dangerous, and defining an individual as dangerous suggests that one is likely to engage in self-injurious or other harmful conduct. Thus, describing dangerousness as an inherent attribute of an individual entails a forecasting of future harm (to oneself and/or to others). In a sense, then, classifying a person as dangerous because of an inability to control one's anger, for example, essentially amounts to a prediction that the person will most likely engage in future violent (i.e., hostile) behaviors. Consequently, predictions of dangerousness in the psychiatric courtroom are merely exercises in determining whether an individual meets the criteria typically associated with violent persons.

In the *Boggs* case, we see a displacement of focus from her actions to her underlying psychological state. Several mental health experts understood the petitioner to be dangerous because she had no capacity to "comprehend" her needs; no "capacity" to comprehend danger to herself; and displayed "anger" and "hostility" toward Project HELP staff. Ms. Boggs' reality, then, was constructed by the court based on descriptive signifiers that referred to specific attributes to the exclusion of those ecological circumstances chaos theory would otherwise argue are quite significant. That is to say, comprehension, capacity, anger, and the like were regarded as *part of* Ms.

Boggs' intrinsic humanity, rendering environmental circumstances minimally relevant. As nonlinear dynamical systems theory reminds us, however, psychobiological variables may encourage behaviors to manifest themselves, but they are contributing, not decisive, factors accounting for one's conduct.

Indeed, chaos theory would suggest that we consider the limitless variety of environmental circumstances as more instructive than dispositional states when explaining the actions of complex, adaptive systems. For example, sensitive dependence on initial conditions tells us that the behavior of organisms is ultimately *dependent* on external conditions. The observed phenomenon of bifurcation occurs following a destabilization of the organism that is a reaction to influences from its environment. Indeed, organisms are often predisposed to behave in certain ways. These dispositions do not, however, present themselves as overt conduct unless the circumstances are conducive to such movement.

Thus, Ms. Boggs could be characterized as having a disposition toward hostility. However, did the petitioner's disposition toward hostility manifest itself in all her interactions with others, or only in situations where her dignity was threatened? The testimonial evidence suggested that her hostility was observable only as situation-specific behavior; that is, as a response to the unwanted interventions of persons she knew to be authority figures whose help she did not request. It follows, then, that Ms. Boggs, although *defined* as a hostile person was, instead, a person who exhibited hostility in certain situations. Therefore, following the logic of chaos theory, the question is not whether the petitioner was dangerous; but, rather, whether it is possible to identify the conditions under which she acted hostilely. Again, according to the record, displays of hostility toward others were context-specific, rather than general, occurrences. Given the targeted nature of these exhibitions, it is difficult to conclude that Ms. Boggs was, in fact, dangerous. Instead, we maintain that those conditions that gave rise to her hostility (e.g., self-harm, suicidal ideation) were limited, making a finding of dangerousness more indeterminable and the justification for sustained confinement less apparent.

The Proliferating Population of the "Mentally Disturbed Homeless"

Our analysis of civil commitment in Part II of this text drew attention to the sociopolitical dimensions of involuntarily hospitalizing the mentally ill. At this juncture, it is appropriate to ascertain what role, if any, society and politics played in the decision to commit Billie Boggs. What evidence does exist is not made explicit throughout much of the appellate court opinion. We note, however, that political, economic, and other cultural forces often act in subtle and unrecognized ways. Civil commitment proceedings are but one example. The role of critical social scientific analysis, then, is to discern these subtleties and to develop meaningful insights regarding the impact these forces portend in specific cases and in general social practice.

In the *Boggs* case we are fortunate to have some mention of these sociopolitical influences. Indeed, the dissenting opinion of Judge J. Milonas asks that we consider such possibilities. We do not maintain that the absence of more detailed commentary on those social forces surrounding the *Boggs* decision represent the court's attempt to conceal its (sinister) motives. Instead, the dearth of obvious sociopolitical analysis contained in the opinion suggests how decision making in the psychiaric courtroom is significantly linked to unconscious values and hidden assumptions embedded in the reality jurists construct when selecting out specific words and phrases to convey their meaning (e.g., Arrigo, 1993, 1996). What is evident, however, is that some sociopolitical motivations factored into the appellate court's decision to sustain the civil commitment of Billie Boggs. The extent to which these forces influenced the disposition in this or any other mental health law case remains speculative at best. Accordingly, the following commentary should be read with this caveat in mind.

As noted, the primary place in which political influence is suggested is in the dissenting opinion. Judge Milonas's dissent begins by attending to this consideration:

> This case has attracted considerable attention, since petitioner's involuntary hospitalization represents the first known effort by the city to implement a highly publicized and controversial Mayoral policy directed at dealing with the proliferating population of the mentally disturbed homeless. (*Boggs*, 1987, p. 366)

What is immediately evident, though never mentioned or suggested in the majority opinion, is that Ms. Boggs represented a population of citizens to which New York City had recently directed its considerable attention (i.e., psychiatrically ill street dwellers). Judge Milonas described the case as a "classic confrontation between the rights of a citizen against a governmental authority trying to confront and remedy a pervasive societal problem (ibid., pp. 366–367). Thus, the petitioner found herself in the unlikely position of symbolizing a recent and troubling public policy concern in New York City.

Prior to the actual appellate drama, Ms. Boggs waived her right to confidentiality, giving her consent so that the press could monitor the courtroom dynamics carefully. Consequently, the case received "almost daily news reports" and "prompted a number of television and other media discussions . . . relating to the problem of the homeless" (ibid., p. 367). On a more national or global scale, then, the *Boggs* case stood at the center of a intense public debate, fueled—not simply by the homeless population of New York City—but by a Mayoral directive aimed at remedying this particular social malady.

The controversy surrounding New York's mentally ill homeless population and the policy initiative in response to it posed a unique dilemma for Billie Boggs. In short, there was concern that these forces would thwart prospects for justice in this case. Again, Judge Milonas acknowledged this danger. As he described it, the presence of confounding influences

> . . . [could] obscure the fact that we are not deciding the wisdom and propriety of the Mayor's program and that our ruling will not have a significant impact upon the very real social problem with which that program is attempting to grapple. All that we are authorized to do here . . . is to determine whether respondents may lawfully retain for further hospital observation and treatment one particular individual and, in that respect, our deliberations must be guided exclusively by the statutory and legal mandates as applied to the facts of the instant proceeding. (*Boggs*, 1987, p. 367)

Unfortunately, these two, brief comments are all that was written in the appellate court's opinion specifically addressing the social context within which the *Boggs* case was heard. This notwithstanding, these observations are sufficiently compelling such that a critical assessment of their influence in the case appears discernible and, thus, is warranted. Accordingly, we explore the sociopolitical motivations that, in some way, may have impacted the court's decision in *Boggs*. These motivations go unspoken in the court's majority opinion; however, they are intimately bound to the case, given its extreme publicity. As no social science evidence exists to inform us adequately of the politics of mental illness and homelessness in the petitioner's instance, we cannot arrive at nor can we discuss any implications in a conclusive manner. Further, we are not sufficiently knowledgeable about the Mayoral policy in question such that we could provide a critical analysis of it. Thus, our intention is modest. We intend to offer a speculative chaos theory analysis, yet one based on the possibilities that arise by the mere presence of this Mayoral directive, specifically in relation to Billie Boggs and the civil commitment process to which she was subjected.

Critical Backdrop for the Sociopolitics of Civil Commitment

Warren's (1982) critique of civil commitment and its relevance to the case of Billie Boggs is best understood with reference to labeling theory. Through this frame of reference, we are encouraged to perceive mental illness as a product of social forces or societal reaction to residual deviance rather than psychiatric factors intrinsic to the individual in question. Thus, for example, whether Billie Boggs was identified as "in need of treatment" and subsequently civilly committed is largely determined by nonpsychiatric considerations (e.g., Scheff, 1984). Notwithstanding the appearance of expert psychological testimony and legal procedures, labeling theory would assess whether the determination of mental illness, dangerousness, and the decision to confine Ms. Boggs to a psychiatric hospital was fundamentallly attributable to social forces.

From a labeling perspective, the matter of involuntary civil confinement allows for an examination of the procedures, rules, regulations, etc., that corresponded to societal reactions, and how these reactions subsequently became the basis for formal and specific treatment of residual deviance. In other words, when applying Warren's insights to the *Boggs* case, the petitioner was defined as a social artifact of the civil commitment hearing and process; a procedure that existed and was implemented in New York City as an expressed reaction to political voices that demanded immediate and compelling intervention toward the mentally ill homeless.

In addition, we note that mental illness is a label that serves as a means of categorizing the rule-breaking behavior of persons in situations where other culturally recognized categories are inappropriate (Scheff, 1984). Warren (1982) describes the *topos* of mental illness as a cultural construction or point of categorical reference against which we understand behavior that is inconsistent with prevailing notions of normalcy and decency. These cultural constructions are societal reactions to perceived deviance. They find their way into the psychiatric courtroom, identifying and assessing the persons that are brought before it. Thus, the issue in the *Boggs* case was not whether the petitioner was a mentally ill homeless citizen who was dangerous and in need of treatment; but, rather, whether

her inconsistency with prevailing social constructions of appropriate, normal behavior subjected her to the (deviant) label and, consequently, to New York City's regulations and practices (i.e., civil commitment), which functioned as a means to confine those who were so labeled. The appellate court's decision, and the process by which it was reached, suggests that Ms. Boggs was assigned the deviant status, resulting in her continued confinement.

Holstein's (1993) analysis of civil commitment also addresses the sociocultural dynamics that constitute the meaning of mental illness as deviance, mindful of its attending social reactions. Much like the labeling perspective, constitutive analysis perceives community reaction as the source of one's deviant status (Holstein, 1993, p. 15). Unlike labeling theory, however, this interpretive method of inquiry does not identify the process by which labels are applied or attached to persons. Instead, it concerns itself with the "practice through which deviants are constituted as recognizable entities" (ibid.). Thus, it "refocuses analytic attention on the reality- creating processes" rather than the labels or outcome of the process (ibid.). In this way, Holstein's critique is directed toward the practical constitution of psychiatric disorder as interpreted by the participants in the commitment hearing (e.g., judge, attorneys). Consequently for Holstein (1993), the "real" Billie Boggs is significantly less important than the one constructed over the course of the civil confinement proceeding.

The process of reality construction in commitment proceedings does not depend upon interpretive resources unique to psychology and law. As such, following Holstein (1993), Ms. Boggs' "true" mental state, dangerousness, etc., was not assembled by psychological and legal testimony that defined such matters independent of sociocultural understandings. Indeed, Holstein notes that professional experts refer to the same social constructions for the mentally ill and dangerous labels as does the lay community. Constructing reality (e.g., discerning the mental state of a candidate for civil commitment) is a process that "produces, manages, and sustains meaning" (Holstein, 1993, p. 16). Therefore, determinations in commitment proceedings attempt to control deviance and/or remedy social problems.

We note that the Mayoral directive was a reaction to the problem of the mentally disturbed homeless in New York City. Judge Milonas's dissent referred to it as a "proliferating" problem. (*Boggs*, 1987, p. 366). Further, the dissenting opinion endeavored to sidestep the "managing and sustaining meaning" process to which Holstein (1993) alludes. Indeed, as Milonas opined, ". . . we are not deciding the wisdom and propriety of the Mayor's program . . . [because]our ruling will not have a significant impact upon the very real social problem with which the program is attempting to grapple" (*Boggs*, 1987, p. 367). However, from these two statements it is apparent that the court *was* mindful of its (potential) role to sustain meaning, police deviance, and regulate the behavior of the petitioner through its decision making in the matter of Billie Boggs. Indeed, the New York City policy was "highly publicized and controversial," reflecting the interests of political forces. Consistent with Holstein (1993), this policy was based on interpretive and commonsense (i.e., lay community) notions of disorder (i.e., mental illness and dangerousness) and deviance (i.e., homelessness). We maintain that the combination of the political (i.e., the Mayor's investment in the initiative) and the social (i.e., the public's investment in a remedy for New York City's mentally ill homeless population), underscored how meaning emerged and how the decision was rendered in the *Boggs* case.

Arrigo (1993a, 1996) suggests that the pervading sociopolitics of civil commitment are discernable by decoding the language, whether written or spoken, used to convey meaning. In other words, what one says or what one writes conveys implicit assumptions and hidden values about individuals, situations, and other phenomena. Thus, from a semiotic perspective, civil commitment proceedings represent the interplay of language and the construction of meaning generated by the words and phrases jurists "select out" to communicate their thoughts and ideas.

At issue in the *Boggs* matter, then, was the identification of the court's unconscious intent conveyed through the discourse it chose to employ when describing mental illness and the process of civil commitment (Arrigo, 1993a). Tems or expressions such as " mentally ill," "homeless," "proliferating population," "inability to comprehend," "sick," etc., signified certain meanings. Typically, they conjure up images of a "diseased," "deviant," and "dangerous" person unable to live "normally" in complex, contemporary society. However, from where do these images originate? Arrigo (1993a) contends that their source is language, wherein the various significations for these words and phrases are reduced to prevailing meanings. Indeed, as he has shown, the discourse of medicine, with its deficit model of treatment, saturates the language invoked in the clinicolegal courtroom (Arrigo, 1996). The problem with this reduction in meaning, however, is that alternative interpretations are dismissed; significations that might otherwise embody more fully the lived reality of the person in question are ignored. It is at this juncture that the socio-political nature of Ms. Boggs' confinement becomes psycho-semiotically evident.

The petitioner was identified as part of a proliferating population of mentally disturbed homeless people found in New York City. Even Milonas's dissenting opinion conveyed this sentiment. However, Boggs did not describe herself this way, nor did those who testified on her behalf. Billie Boggs considered herself to be "self-sufficient," "proud," "capable," "justified in her behavior," "resourceful," and "independent." Interestingly, these descriptors were not employed in the construction and articulation of the majority opinion. When comparing the values embedded in these words and/or phrases against the assumptions contained in the previous terms and expressions, we see an obvious difference. These latter expressions are more affirming of the individual's ability to think, act, and live on her own. The former constellation of words and phrases convey just the opposite sentiment. Thus, according to Arrigo (1993a), the appellate court, knowingly or not, selected out specific expressions that marginalized the petitioner first through language and then through effect (i.e., her sustained confinement). Indeed, the court's choice of discourse telegraphed the case's outcome. Thus, as Arrigo (1993a) notes, we see how the force of language in the psychiatric courtroom was politically mobilized to oppress the petitioner, consistent with the Mayor's policy initiative.

Chaos Theory, Society, and Attraction

Recall that we previously described the operation of the point attractor in society. In short, we explained that difference is drawn or "attracted" to a single point (i.e., the point of normalcy or conformity). There is some evidence supporting this behavior in the *Boggs* case. In its majority opinion, the appellate court emphasized Ms. Boggs' courtroom manner. As it stated, "it is hardly surprising" that the hearing court found Ms. Boggs to be "rational, logical, coherent . . . an educated, intelligent person . . . display[ing] a sense of humor, pride, a fierce independence of spirit, [and] quick mental reflexes" (*Boggs*, 1987, p. 365). This was "hardly surprising" to the appellate court because Ms. Boggs "had recently been bathed, was dressed in clean clothes, and had just received approximately a week of hospital treatment" (ibid.).

What is significant about the court's observations is that they convey a conviction that the petitioner had "cleaned herself up" while in the hospital, and that she appeared "normal" as a direct result of receiving a week's worth of psychiatric treatment. Elsewhere, the court in *Boggs* indicated that the petitioner would benefit from hospitalization because it would lead to the establishment of a therapeutic relationship which, in turn, would allow her to "choose a better style of living" (*Boggs*, 1987, p. 363). From these very passages, the court established, in a manner quite explicit, the value of psychiatric treatment for Billie Boggs; treatment that was demonstrably corrective. In other words, the emphasis on the petitioner's presentation *after* hospital intervention and the promotion of therapeutic alliances, offered some evidence of the court's perspective on homelessness in relation to mental well-being. Indeed, nowhere in the majority opinion does the court value Ms. Boggs' *chosen* way of life for its significance to her or for its contribution to society. Consistent with the Mayoral directive on the proliferating problem of the mentally disturbed homeless, the petitioner's life style was regarded as self-injurious and, moreover, deliterious to the social fabric of New York City.

In chapter 6 we argued that the point attractor of chaos theory is representative of certain efforts to normalize the humanity of people; that is, to control difference and diversity (Arrigo & Williams, 1999a). The presence of this regulation is a corollary to the larger interest in controlling and predicting behavior. Normalizing facets of society ensures its smooth flowing linearity. Of course, linearity holds a privileged position in social thought and practice for this very reason: It harnesses uncertainty and change before they even commence. According to nonlinear dynamical systems theory, however, change and uncertainty are to be embraced, not feared. This is because the absolute stability sought by the point attractor does not allow for the necessary degree of robustness that is conducive to positive, healthy social change (Williams & Arrigo, 2000).

It is at this juncture that chaos theory acknowledges the importance of the strange attractor. The strange attractor embodies difference and diversity and encourages an adaptive and ever-changing society, capable of self-organizing in the face of need (Williams & Arrigo, 2000). One representative example of this is found among the homeless population (Arrigo, 1997b). The population of homeless persons who elect to live in the streets represent an element of society that does not (through their difference) propel it toward disorder. Rather, the existence of these street dwellers encourages society to assume the form of order governed by the strange attractor; a form that is healthier for reasons just discussed.

What chaos theory tells us about Billie Boggs, and the sociopolitical conditions in which she found herself, is profound. Mentally disturbed homeless citizens like the petitioner challenged the normalizing point attractor reality, symbolized in the Mayoral policy. Although somewhat speculative, we assume that this directive was thought to embody a more pro-social attitude toward psychiatrically disordered street dwellers. Indeed, involuntary hospitalization could treat and correct their identified mental illnesses, making them functionally well and healthy. However, following chaos theory, we question this logic. We submit that had the appellate court been willing to allow Ms. Boggs and other similarly situated (homeless mentally disordered) persons the opportunity to coexist with the the rest of society, this would have helped to ensure society's overall health because it would have meant an endorsement for diversity and, thus, preparation for adaptation. The nature of the point attractor, in relation to Ms. Boggs, then, could only produce a decision to sustain civil commitment. Similar to our application of Warren, Holstein, and Arrigo, we see how the sociopolitical context of confinement, as critically informed by selected chaos theory principles, explains and advances our understanding of the decision in the *Boggs* case.

"A Fearless, Independent Survival Style"

The right to refuse treatment represents our fourth and final psycholegal controversy. As previously noted, Warren (1982), Holstein (1993), and Arrigo (1993) do not spend sufficient time on treatment issues; thus, a critique similar to what was conducted on mental illness, dangerousness, and civil commitment is not possible. Accordingly, in what follows we assess coercive intervention and Billie Boggs' right to refuse it from the exclusive perspective of nonlinear dynamical systems theory.

In chapter 7 we described how the principle of self-organization functioned in relation to treatment and one's right to refuse it. The general thesis was that a stable individual might be temporarily "knocked off balance" by external and/or internal stimuli and undergo a transitory period in one's life. This transitory period was described as essential to the adaptive organism because it encouraged a reorganization and a newfound sense of order, notwithstanding how different it might appear or feel. Under ideal circumstances, this order takes place through the self-organizing process, following a period of disturbance. In the *Boggs* case, this new, adaptive order (as a homeless mentally ill citizen) was defined as disorder (e.g., suicidal, gravely disabled, a danger to herself), and was a critical factor in the decision to force treatment upon Ms. Boggs, notwithstanding her objection. We note that our discussion in chapter 7 chiefly focused on the consumer's right to reject drug therapy. For purposes of the foregoing critique, however, we examine the right to refuse psychiatric intervention more generally, including civil commitment, which often includes the administration of psychotropic medication.

The conviction that Ms. Boggs harmed herself was premised, in part, on the petitioner's purported inability to care for her own needs. According to Dr. Sabatini, Ms. Boggs needed to be hospitalized for treatment because the hospital environment provided the "protection" of a "structured" setting; one more conducive to mental health than the outside environment (*Boggs*, 1987, p. 352). As he further testified, "[consistent] with some psychiatric patients, [Ms. Boggs possessed the ability] to adapt and to regroup and [to] organize herself . . . in [hospital] settings" (ibid., p. 351). The appellate court relied on this and similar testimony, concluding that the petitioner's interests were best served by confinement to a location that encouraged this type of self-organization.

We take exception to the court's logic. Elsewhere, within the postulates of self-organization, we discused how imposed structure might be defeating. Indeed, we argued that the organizing process that represents the naturally occurring dimension of one's psychological and physical functioning is often fully realized in scenarios where persons are compelled to adapt because of changing internal (individual) and external (environmental) circumstances. A structured ecology does encourage organization. However, it does so at the expense of the adaptive dynamics of the person's unique psychological makeup. In a sense, then, imposed order stifles the natural, fluid, and organic processes that seek realization.

The *Boggs* case provides us with ample evidence of her reorganization. One clear example is found in her adpative capabilities following treatment. This is an illustration of imposed order. Upon closer examination of the case, however, a different sort of organization process is recognizable. This process originated in Billie Boggs' being and, thus, occurred more naturally. Evidence of this particuar self-organization is found through several sources, including the petitioner. We review these sources.

The majority opinion suggested that Ms. Boggs "undisputedly held responsible employment" and was a "productive member of society" until 1984 (*Boggs*, 1987, pp. 363–366). At this time "her mental condition began to deteriorate" (ibid., p. 363). She had a "continuous work history of almost a decade, in which she [was] employed in responsible positions . . . [and] at that time, besides a job, she had a home and a family" (ibid., p. 366). Sometime thereafter, however, she "suffered a 'severe psychosis.'" We are not told explicitly how the petitioner's psychosis led to her separation from her family, nor how Ms. Boggs subsequently established a new home for herself in the streets. What is suggested, however, is that the petitioner made the streets of New York City her home for approximately one year prior to her civil commitment hearing. We question how Ms. Boggs *responded* to her new home. In other words, following those life circumstances that contributed to some loss of her stability, was there evidence that the petitioner was able to *adapt to her new reality?*

Dr. Gould testified on behalf of Ms. Boggs. He commented on her ability to live in the streets. As he noted, "the fact that she ha[d] never been hurt and [that] she . . . [had] never hurt herself strong[ly] indicat[e] that she ha[d] very good survival skills . . . [and that she] provided for herself quite well" (*Boggs*, 1987, pp. 356–357). Indeed, as Dr. Gould concluded, the petitioner was someone who had "worked out a fearless, independent lifestyle and survival style that worked for her, [u]nconventional though it [was]" (ibid., p. 357).

The most compelling testimony was provided by Ms. Boggs to the hearing court. The appellate court summarily included her statements in its review of the case. We note that evidence of adaptation to the changing circumstances of the petitioner's life presented themselves most strikingly in her own words. As the appellate court reported:

> she live[d] next to a restaurant . . . and she stay[ed] at that location. [S]ince there [wa]s a hot air vent . . . she indicated that she had never been cold; she panhandle[d] money for food and, in that fashion, she ma[de] between \$8 and \$10 a day. . . . [S]he claim[ed] that she ha[d] adequate clothes, and that when she needed more she had "friends" who . . . suppl[ied] them to her. . . .
> (*Boggs*, 1987, p. 343)

To the extent that one values Ms. Boggs' own testimony (and that of Dr. Gould), we maintain that she self-organized, creating a sufficiently *orderly* lifestyle, unconventional and unusual though it was.

In his dissenting opinion, Judge Milonas emphasized this process of adaptation, noting that Ms. Boggs fed herself from a local deli with money obtained through panhandling and that, according to the respondent's *own* psychiatrists, she "[wa]s not malnourished and ha[d] no serious physical problems" (*Boggs*, 1987, p. 374). Judge Milonas went on to comment that, "[Ms. Boggs] derive[d] a unique sense of success and accomplishment in her street life . . . [W]hen poignantly describing her ability to endure on the streets, she . . . called herself a 'professional'" (ibid., p. 378).

In a very meaningful sense, Judge Milonas's observations are consistent with those used to describe the results of the self-organizing process. Indeed, following a certain "chaotic" or transformative state, Ms. Boggs adapted to her homeless lifestyle quite thoroughly. She experienced and endured a period of disorder and uncertainty; however, in response, she adapted to her new circumstances (i.e., found an appropriate "home" and secured food and other basic necessities). Without further substantial evidence to the contrary and given the logic of chaos theory, we are led to conclude that Ms. Boggs embodied those natural processes that govern one's intrinsic being and that safeguard one's basic humanity.

Forced treatment, then, in the form of involuntary confinement, only serves to interfere, if not eliminate, this very process. By refusing or challenging involuntary hospitalization, Ms. Boggs demonstrated that she felt confident in and, in fact, proud of her ability to embrace disorder and self-organize in its aftermath. Thus, the petitioner's rejection of mental health treatment was an appeal for the process of self-organization to unfold on its own, without external or forced disturbance. The court's unwillingness to affirm Ms. Boggs' request was a clear indication that adaptation was thought to be "healthy" *only* if its end-state produced normalcy or commonsense understandings of mental health. From the appellate court's perspective, deviation from this shared and accommodating meaning was not regarded as a new, adaptive order, but, rather, as a "deteriorating" disorder. We note further that the healthier, adaptive state that emerged from Ms. Boggs' own disorder was also intimately bound to the court's inquiry into the petitioner's dangerousness. For the appellate court, the absence of order was the manifestation of Boggs' danger to herself (e.g., gravely disabled, homeless). As we have argued, however, the petitioner elected to live as she did, and others, like Dr. Gould, described how well she managed. These facts notwithstanding, the appellate court found that her unorthodox (though self-organized) lifestyle amounted to disorder, necessitating imposed order (i.e., involuntary civil commitment).

POSTSCRIPT: REFLECTIONS ON ADDITIONAL CASES

The controversial case of In the Matter of Billie Boggs (1987) was decided more than a decade ago. Despite this, it remains a landmark decision in the field of mental health law (Perlin, 1999). Indeed, several more recent opinions, addressing the same issues found in the Boggs ruling, are discernible (e.g., In the Matter of the Commitment of D.M. [1995]; In the Matter of the

Commitment of F.J. [1995]; *In the Matter of Lynda Rae Vega* [1997]; *Winnebago County v. Rhonda W.* [1999]). These and other cases indicate that little has changed in the psycholegal arena when questions regarding the meaning of mental illness, the definition of dangerousness, the practice of civil commitment, and one's right to refuse treatment are under consideration. Thus, the outcome in *Boggs* stands as a watershed decision, a paragon for psycholegal thought, reason, and judgement. Having said this, we do not mean to suggest that some courts, in some situations, have not deviated from the logic of the *Boggs* case. Instead, we note that the elements of this controversial ruling (i.e., a civilly committed person thought to be mentally ill and dangerous to self invokes his or her right to refuse treatment) are still prominently featured in the mental health law literature. Moreover, and more importantly, we note that the prevailing modus operandi for the psychiatric courtroom, given these cases, is still largely privileged. Indeed, in varying ways each of the cited cases maintains that mental health systems users are sick and disabled, capable of harming themselves. Thus, treatment (i.e., confinement and drug therapy) is necessary and its refusal is countertherapeutic. However, as we have demonstrated in this chapter, not only does chaos theory critically challenge these assumptions, it provocatively suggests another (organic) way, making prospects for citizen justice not only likely but much more inevitable.

SUMMARY AND CONCLUSIONS

This chapter furthered our conceptual explorations on the meaning of mental illness, the definition and prediction of dangerousness, the process of civil commitment, and the right to refuse treatment by assessing how each corresponds with the lived experiences of real psychiatric citizens. The cornerstone of our analysis was the seminal case of *In the Matter of Billie Boggs*, substantiated, in part, by reference to more recent appellate court opinions. The *Boggs* decision was informative. It contained important aspects of each psycholegal controversy examined in this text. In addition, the *Boggs* ruling offered a fairly detailed description of how these controversies were understood by various participants in the psychiatric courtroom. The supplemental cases, though not exhaustively examined, supported the general thesis as developed in *Boggs* and as critically investigated in our assessment of it.

To situate our chaos theory investigation, we canvassed the related work of Warren (1982), Holstein (1993), and Arrigo (1993). While each of these authors, in his/her own way, provided a compelling critique of the "court of last resort," none of them incorporated the postulates of chaos theory. By relying upon principles contained in nonlinear dynamical systems theory, our intent was to situate the discipline within the critical psycholegal tradition, discerning whether justice was or was not promoted through existing clinicolegal practices.

The title of this chapter ("(Un)clear but Convincing Evidence") indicates the broad thrust of our inquiry. As previously described, civil commitment requires a finding of "clear and convincing" evidence, in relation to one's mental illness and dangerousness, to justify freedom and liberty deprivations. In Part II of this text, we explained why the presence of psychiatric disorder was something that was far from clear and why the definition and prediction of dangerousness was similarly uncertain. This chapter demonstrated how these insights were quite applicable to real cases, affecting the lives of everyday persons experiencing mental illness. In short, the psychiatric courtroom is an arena in which what is *convincing* is premised on that which is *unclear*. Despite the fuzziness, incompleteness, and undecidability of courtroom "evidence," clinicolegal decision brokers often overlook this lack of clarity in favor of commonsense and shared understandings, agreed-upon interpretive practices, and preferred words/phrases with their corresponding meanings. In other words, the court of last resort privileges the imposition of order, dismissing all other variables in the wake of its alienating and oppressive judgements.

To advance this thesis, we showed how reality construction in the psychiatric courtroom was not sufficiently informed by the insights of chaos theory (e.g., the fractal nature of our existences; the ecological perspective on lived-reality; the process of self-organization; and the role of disorder in mapping ongoing, pro-social behavior). Through our critical examination of each psycholegal controversy found in the *Boggs* case, the court's decision making devalued the humanity of the petitioner, and, thus, limited prospects for large-scale social change. As we explain in the next chapter, the denial of these possibilities thwarts opportunities for greater expressions of citizen justice. Indeed, new and different forms of knowledge, integrated with established and familiar ones, is the basis upon which diversity can flourish. We submit that this same logic obtains in the arena of law and psychology. It is to these matters that we now turn.

CHAPTER NINE

Conclusion

Law, Psychology, and Justice

We noted at the outset of this project that our principal interest was with the phenomenon of justice. Thus, through chaos theory and its sundry principles, we sought to establish a better understand of it, as manifested in the psycholegal sphere. Each of the four controversies explored through nonlinear dynamical systems theory was implicitly and indirectly oriented toward our concern for justice. In this chapter, however, we explicitly address this topic as situated at the crossroads of law and psychology. In addition, we reflect upon and review the basic notions discussed throughout this text.

This chapter is presented in much the same manner as was the introduction and the book as a whole. In particular, we revisit the three major divisions of the overall critique—i.e., the theoretical, the controversial, and the just(ice)—mindful of our insights to date. What follows, then, is a brief commentary on the conceptual components of this project, the critical points or conclusions reached regarding the four mental health law controversies, and a more extensive treatment of what justice therefore encompasses and, perhaps, must include in the psycholegal sphere, given our chaos theory perspective.

THE THEORETICAL

Traditional science is based on linearity, homeostasis, equilibrium, order, precision, and predictability. The mathematical representations of the systems measured by conventional or modern science are more or less

accurate; that is, these phenomena are discernible, understandable, predictable, and, therefore, controllable. The discoveries of modern science
were eventually applied to the social level, including, among others, the
domains of politics, law, criminal justice, psychology, and economics.
However, the realm of the social is nonlinear. In other words, it is not
amenable to most classical laws governing the physical sciences. Indeed,
these systems and *all* living organisms are nonlinear, unpredictable, spontaneous, creative, and, ultimately, uncontrollable. Thus, in order to better
comprehend the behavior of these systems on a scientific level, a "new
science" is needed.

Chaos theory represented this new science. Chapter 1 briefly described
the progression of scientific and philosophic thought from modernity to
postmodernity (i.e., from order to disorder), and provided a brief description of chaos and nonlinear dynamical systems theory. Chapter 2 situated
our conceptual analysis within the domain of postmodernism. We argued
that chaos theory is part of a larger tradition within critical theoretical circles. We demonstrated where and how principles of chaos were assimilable
with the postmodern agenda, specifically in relation to several of the latter's
sociological and epistemological assumptions. Given that our psycholegal
investigation eclipsed the justice studies arena, the points of assimilation
emphasized legal and criminological integrations. Chapter 3 furthered our
theoretical assessment of chaology, addressing a number of principles contained in this science of orderly disorder. Though interrelated, we mostly
examined these principles in isolated fashion, regarding them as metaphors
from within which to "see" or "read" the behavior of law and psychology,
society and the individual. As we subsequently discovered, however (chapters 4 through 7) , each metaphor had a basis in reality.

While the principles of chaos theory function as metaphors in the law-
psychology context, these notions describe all sorts of real, living systems.
Indeed, what describes the ecosystem is equally applicable to certain chemical systems; what describes the neurological system is similarly applicable
to the economic system; and what describes the chemical, ecological, neurological, and economic systems, is likewise applicable to the social system,
including the law-psychology divide. As we suggested, then, the potential
value of chaos theory was in its capacity to better inform us about *life*. Thus,
its various principles were not only metaphors, but also descriptive devices
by which we could "see" and interpret that to which they were applied.

Our application of nonlinear dynamical systems theory was limited to
the civil side of mental health law. As we asserted, however, chaos theory's

value to the social sciences should not be regarded as finite. Indeed, its potential utility is boundless. With this in mind, we chose four civil controversies at the crossroads of law and psychology. As exemplars of the pressing debates in mental health law today, we questioned how this "new science" might advance our understanding of them. In the following section, we briefly revisit the critical lessons learned from our rereading of these contemporary controversies.

THE CONTROVERSIAL

Chapters 4 through 7 examined four controversies on the civil side of the law-psychology interface. Each matter represents an important element of justice; that is, a critical component of clinicolegal science's commitment to a more civil society, including the promotion of psychiatric citizens and their unique interests. In a sense, the individual and the larger society to which we are connected are inseparable. Chaos theory suggests that in the "web of life," all components of a system are mutually dependent. In other words, society cannot function without individuals and individuals are, by nature, social beings who must interact with their environment. Thus, in our assessment of selected mental health law controversies we explored the relationship between the psycholegal sphere and the individual. In addition, however, we examined the broader societal implications that emerged from the debates surrounding the meaning of mental illness, the definition and prediction of dangerousness, the process of civil commitment, and the right to refuse treatment. In the following section, we briefly review several significant points relevant to these respective controversies.

Mental Illness

In chapter 4, we offered a critique of the legal, psychological, and clinicolegal construct of mental illness. We suggested, metaphorically at least, that mental illness is a proper subject of geometry (i.e., the configuration of mental illness). However, this geometry is not of the traditional sort. Indeed, psychiatric disorder is not a point; it is not a line; it is not an angle; nor is it anything physically discernable or capable of being quantified as such. It is more rightfully a matter for consideration by *fractal* geometry.

Fractal Space

Mental illness assumes the form of a fractal. A fractal is about space. Space, however, eludes precise measurement because it is everywhere and nowhere at once. For example, the space between two given objects must necessarily vary, depending on the perspective of the observer and the unit of measurement. Although mental illness falls somewhere within this space, and although it assumes a location within this space, the precise position and character of mental illness are impossible to ascertain, given the absence of any clearly definable point from which it emanates. Although we may engage psychiatric disorder from a definable point, our chosen point is merely one possible location from which to proceed. Indeed, mental illness looks different from above rather than from below; from afar rather than from near; and from your vantage point rather than from mine.

Objectivity

Nevertheless, in searching for something identifiable like mental illness, psychology is not especially concerned with the space or the arbitrary point from which its inquiries ensue. Instead, the discipline is interested in reducing the fractal geometry of mental illness and its meaning to a definable (i.e., traditional) geometric structure, so that it can, once and for all, establish the place that psychiatric disorder occupies within this dimensionality. In effect, however, this task requires an illusion; one that allows us to separate white from black, good from evil, healthy from unhealthy, the "correct" point of departure from that which is less correct. This illusion leads us to perceive these realities as binary oppositions (i.e., separate and independent) when, in fact, they arise from the same general space and represent only points along a continuum within a limitless space. The logic of this "either or" sensibility is a fallacy, reflecting the limits of modern science. What psychology seeks to be is a science; what science seeks to be is objective; and what the universe *is*, is relative, existing only in degrees along a continuum of manufactured, artificial contrasts. Psychological science is guilty of wading through the various points within space and determining for itself, for society, and for the law, which ones represent the perspective from which the truth can "really" be ascertained.

Relativity

Similar to the universe, if mental illness is not objective it must be relative. What it is relative *to* are several important factors that influence our perceptions of reality. Historicity argues that our perception of the world is dependent on the time period in which we live. Cultural relativity asserts that our perceptions vary by way of the culture or place in which we live. Thus, attaching absolute values to our reality neglects the important ways in which time and place function as constitutive and contextualizing variables. When we do behave this way, we engage in the process of social construction. In other words, for example, the creation of mental illness typically is constructed as an absolute, objective reality that exists independent of the historical and cultural belief systems and knowledge claims within which it is framed.

With these notions in mind, psychiatric disorder may be less of a "thing" and more of an idea or image, lodged within our social consciousness as a way of differentiating between persons; that is, as a way of categorizing the *value* of persons. In our pseudo-geometric language, our social constructions arise from a given point, to the exclusion of others that have been and continue to be prominent elsewhere.

Perspective

Relatedly, Nietzsche represents one of the leading proponents of the "perspectival" approach to reality. This is a state of awareness in which existence and phenomena in the world are defined through one's own (individual, social, cultural, historical, religious, etc.) perspective and recorded as truth when, in fact, they are no more true than any other awarenesses. Indeed, various perspectives must endure, no one is more accurate than the next, and no one can assume its place atop the mantle of truth. Although in some cases and in some ways we may be able to distinguish between what is right from what is wrong, between what is good from what is bad, between who is sick from who is healthy, the vast majority of human realities are somewhere in between; that is, somewhere amidst all the other perspectives on this never-ending continuum, constituting our existences.

Fractal space is a feature of this continuum. Its reality is such that one-dimensionality, two-dimensionality, three-dimensionality, and the like are not capable of accurately representing the subject matter each seeks to define or explain. Rather, the phenomenon that is perceived varies from perspective to perspective and, consequently, one's unique perception must be understood in that way; namely, as *our* perspective and not *the* perspective; as *our* point of departure and not *the* point of departure.

Knowledge

Given the observations summarized in this section thus far, we note that our knowledge of mental illness is ultimately revealed to us in degrees. In other words, a perspectival approach to meaning is one that acknowledges that truth and sense-making are linked only by shades or traces of understanding. Thus, the meaning of psychiatric disorder is not ascertainable as a singular truth; rather, our knowledge of it is founded upon our perspective, the unique environment of that point of view, and, subsequently, the conceptions that are inherent in that perspective.

For example, psychology begins its inquiry into the meaning of mental illness with certain assumptions about the human condition. These assumptions are an inherent part of its understanding of the world and, especially, the nature of wellness versus pathology, appropriate behavior versus dysfunctional conduct. The psychological sciences offer a certain knowledge about mental illness, yet it is one that is colored by the field's epistemological approach.

Moreover, this same logic applies to culture, to society, to law, and to individuals. All perspectives are unique, deriving value from their uniquenesses. The perspectival approach to knowledge appreciates the values inherent in these differences, and this is what it contributes to our understanding of meaning, knowledge, and, ultimately, justice at the law-psychology divide. Again, it is important that no one perspective be regarded as the ideal viewpoint or truth. No one perspective conveys knowledge inherently more valuable than the others. Each possesses its own *degree* of truth, embedded in the knowledge that it creates. Each perspective contributes something to the overall fabric of our society; a unique piece of knowledge that adds diversity to our understanding of social phenomena, our connection to them, and, by extension, our own psychological being.

Dangerousness

Chapter 5 examined the meaning of dangerousness as the manifestation of isolated behavior rather than as an enduring characteristic of one's humanity. Human actions are of this sort. Although patterns may develop, they are often identifiable only in retrospect. We may find tendencies, patterns, cycles, and the like; however, these are merely expressions of our possibility and are not persistent and/or severe personality traits. The fact that tendencies occasionally manifest themselves is an enduring and continuous characteristic of all things. The particular tendencies that do materialize at a given time, however, are largely dependent upon other factors.

(Inter)Dependent Origination

By definition, possibility depends upon certain things in order for it to actualize. For example, when we say something is possible, we know that it is not inevitable; but, rather, that it might occur given circumstances conducive to its manifestation. There is a foundational principle shared by all schools of Buddhism which states that events cannot come into being on their own. Instead, all events are expressions of intricate, complex, and largely imperceptible relations between an incalculable number of variables, some exerting their influence well before the present moment.

This timeless wisdom is also shared by contemporary physics. In effect, what this means is that we cannot understand any event, any *behavior*, exclusive of and apart from all other variables upon which its manifestation is dependent (i.e., the parts cannot be understood independent of the whole). Any given behavior requires the occurrence of other events for its very possibility to transition into actuality. From this perspective, a behavior is never inevitable and never even possible without inducement from other sources.

Sensitivity

Chaos theory refers to this state of possibility and need for inducement as sensitive dependence on initial conditions. Dynamic organisms are so sensitive to the influence of other forces that their manifest behavior cannot be understood without reference to these sources of encouragement. A slight alteration in conditions can result, over time, in the manifestation of behavior quite different from that which would have occurred without such inducement.

Thus, organisms are both dependent upon external influences *and* sensitive to them. External forces determine, to some extent, what behaviors arise. This is not to imply that chaos theory advances a form of determinism. On the contrary, it differs from traditional "hard" determinism in that it allows room for freedom. The individual does have *some* choice; yet these choices are intimately wedded to the broadly defined environment in which the person behaves. Sensitivity means that changes in ecology can and will have a significant impact on the actions of any given individual. We recall, however, that both psychological and physical environments exert similar influence. Given that individuals are sensitive to perturbations, any number of them might encourage a "jump" to another pattern of thinking, feeling, or acting. For example, losing one's job, if sufficiently traumatic, may increase the likelihood of dangerous behavior. Similarly, attaining a job may decrease this probability. When such circumstances as these encourage "jumps" in thought/feeling/behavior, we refer to them as bifurcations.

Bifurcation

In light of the sensitivity which defines a system, we note that these organisms are particularly affected by environmental stimuli, and the freedom they have within which to act is ultimately bounded to environmental circumstances. When these stimuli are either independently or collectively sufficient, they perturb the balance or stability of the organism, subjecting it to bifurcation. Bifurcation represents a "splitting" process in which behavior becomes more disorderly and more prone to uncharacteristic manifestations. The bifurcation is a "fork in the road" found at each increasing level of disorder. As disorder increases, the behavior of the organism becomes less predictable and, further, becomes increasingly affected by additional environmental stimuli.

Metaphorically speaking, bifurcations represent critical (i.e., positive or negative) events in a person's life. Thus, if an individual is not sufficiently adaptive, his or her sensitivity to displacing circumstances may encourage a bifurcation. In turn, this splitting produces an entirely new dynamic in the thoughts, feelings, and behaviors of that individual. The extent to which we can account for these variables (e.g., level of adaptation, sensitivity, array of environmental stimuli inducing bifurcations), is the extent to which we can accurately envision this new dynamic and predict its consequences.

Prediction

People do not behave entirely from their own free will; rather, circumstances conducive to the manifestation of action, in conjunction with one's attending thoughts, feelings, impulses, etc., give rise to individual behavior. This notion does not deny the potency of self-determined actions. Instead, it merely suggests that even the most adaptive and powerful of wills is subject, at times, to circumstances that jeopardize its freedom.

Accordingly, our prediction of various events can never be put forth with certainty. At best, we can offer predictions of *probability* and not predictions of events. Events display tendencies. Thus, for example, an individual might show a proclivity to behave dangerously, and we might forecast the probability that such behavioral tendencies will occur. However, we cannot predict whether the behaviors themselves will or will not occur.

Quantum physics shows us that, even at the subatomic level, events display only tendencies; that is, they do not occur at specific times and places. We can understand these events as probabilities but not as predictable. The problem with predicting behavior is in the very process we use to understand it. For example, "measuring" something (i.e., the degree to which a person is dangerous) requires that we first isolate the individual so that we might understand his or her characteristics without "noise" from the environment. However, isolating the person removes the "object of inquiry" from the environment of which it is a part. In this way, it is treated as *separate from* rather than as *part of* its larger life-world. As a consequence, whatever is measured is inevitably inaccurate. As we have seen, however, the very characteristics we attempt to measure and the very events we try to predict given these measurements, are *dependent* for their manifestation on that environment from which we isolate these characteristics and events. In other words, our expert assessments of dangerousness are immediately jeopardized when we fail to conceive behavior from an *ecological* perspective with an ecological dynamic.

Ecology

Conceptualizing behavior from an ecological perspective means understanding it as a manifestation of the manifold factors that constitute the internal and external environment of the person in question. As we have suggested, however, too often behavior is attributed to internal character-istics, thought to be intrinsic to the individual's humanity. Indeed, we understand that dangerous behavior signifies the tendency of a dangerous individual (i.e., one with a dangerous personality or an ongoing disposition to engage in harmful acts). This is the interpretation that Foucault (1988) rejected when he asserted that psychiatry's involvement in criminality dis-placed the focus from the crime itself to the individual committing the crime.

Chaos theory does not suggest that individual actions are exclusively determined by one's environment, thus undermining the responsibility of the actor. However, it does maintain that we cannot understand these behaviors solely with reference to some inherently pathologized subject, independent of the interrelated web of life within which the person exists. Indeed, manifestations of one's behavior are, to some meaningful extent, dependent upon context, situation, community, and other environmental factors to which the individual is inexorably connected. If these factors are conducive to the manifestation of, among other things, dangerous behav-ior, then this conduct is more likely to occur. Thus, chaos theory argues that when attempting to curb or eradicate violence-prone conduct specifi-cally from persons diagnosed with mental illness, it is first necessary to assess the contributing factors that give rise to the dangerousness rather than evaluate the psychiatric citizen in question. Indeed, the availability of com-munity-based treatment for the chemically addicted and the psychiatrically disordered, the availability of food and shelter for the hungry and the homeless, and other similar interventions at the level of the *social*, might be significantly more effective than intervention at the level of the *individ-ual*, including civil commitment.

Civil Commitment

To some extent, chapter 6 deviated from the other application chapters in that it considered the broader socio-political implications for civil commit-ment. Mental illness and dangerousness alone are not sufficient conditions for involuntary psychiatric confinement. Rather, there must also be a *demand* for that hospitalization. This demand can be paternalistic (i.e., treatment is warranted because the person needs help) and/or preventative (i.e., treat-ment is warranted in order to protect society from dangerous mentally ill citizens). The significance of the paternalistic or preventative demand is that they stem from institutional forces (i.e. the sociopolitical systems of law and psychology), and not from mentally disordered persons themselves.

Morality

Theoretically, sociopolitical institutions exist and act because of the societal demands of which they are a part. Indeed, social sentiments shape institutions and the institutional practices that define a society. For example, we can imagine how a given society, at a particular historical epoch, is guided by certain moral and epistemological assumptions. Indeed, there is a moral "tradition" which influences, if not governs, the important social and political dimensions of everyday life for that particular culture, at that unique time. This phenomenon is the element of reality construction which subsequently structures society's actions, through its institutional outlets, in accordance with that construction. The worldview of any given culture determines the practices and relations of that culture, including definitions of deviance, conformity, and normalcy. When these definitions become a part of the institutions and institutional practices of that society, they shape the individual realities of the people within it.

Social Control

Societal institutions, then, exist primarily to maintain order in whatever sphere they are assigned or constructed to represent. The discipline of psychology is erected to maintain psychological order; the discipline of law is assembled to maintain legal order. However, the organization they maintain is demanded by the "moral tradition" of that society.

Thus, there is never any real, natural, or organic order in any realm of existence. Instead, there is fabricated, imposed, and artificial order that is often premised on tradition, myth, fear, or, most recently, science. According to chaos theory, the problem is that these definitions of organization are understood to be true, authentic, and real, and sociopolitical practices reflect these interpretations. If something does not fit within these truths, it is defined as abnormal, unreal, deviant, dangerous, and the like. These unhealthy elements of society are then subjected to control and regulation, returning them to a state of institutional order.

In the psycholegal sphere, this form of control includes the process of civil commitment and the application of involuntary treatment. Civil commitment does not exist merely to ensure the safety of the public and the well-being of individuals, it also removes or displaces mental health consumers toward the margins of everyday life. Indeed, fear, discomfort, and uncertainty on the societal level creates an inevitable demand for institutional forces (i.e., the clinicolegal system) to police, discipline, and correct this disorder through institutional practices.

Point Attractors

Remedying a social problem or bringing it back to within the reach of order is akin to "attracting" or pulling something "over there" back to "here." Metaphorically, it is a process of magnetically attracting that which is abnormal to that which maintains normalcy. In our case, this magnet is the psycholegal sphere. Its role is to ensure that nothing ventures too far from its normalizing grasp. When natural attraction alone (e.g., the moral tradition) is not powerful enough to maintain order, coercive attraction (e.g., institutional power) must be exercised to force conformity and unanimity upon the diseased, deviant, and dangerous elements of society.

In this regard, then, both social tradition and social institutions act as point attractors to compel the normal, healthy functioning of society and its citizens. The magnetic core of this attraction is like the center point over which a swinging pendulum continually returns. Although the natural momentum of the pendulum encourages it to explore other territories, the pull is sufficiently strong to keep it safely in place. However, the question is whether the best interests of the pendulum and the larger milieu to which the pendulum belongs are served by this order maintenance. Chaos theory suggests that it may not be.

Strange Attractors

Phenomena in the social life-world—both animate and inanimate—are in some meaningful way part of a nonlinear dynamical process. This process is highly creative and, thus, is largely unpredictable and prone to destabilization, bifurcation, disorder, and the emergence of new forms of organization.

This new order, however, does not reappear as the old. Rather than stable, it appears locally unstable; rather than linear, its processes are nonlinear; rather than pursuing equilibrium, it flourishes in far-from-equilibrium conditions. Systems pursuing equilibrium conditions are best understood as attracted to a state of stability, order, and homogeneity. Conversely, systems pursuing far-from-equilibrium conditions are best understood as attracted to diversity, spontaneity, creativity, adaptation, and growth.

All of these processes are interrelated. Diversity fuels growth; growth necessitates adaptation; and adaptation ensures that life continues to avoid the state of death known as equilibrium. As society is a living system characterized by nonlinear development, its growth is only maintained in a state of diversity, including the diversity that varying forms of mental health contribute. Thus, the point attraction of normalcy, of tradition, of the institutions of psychology and law, to the extent that they promote social homogeneity through institutional control (e.g., civil commitment), are attractors that unknowingly bring society closer to death. A number of conclusions could be drawn from this logic; however, it is important for our purposes that we understand health and psychological functioning as a continuum where every point along its path, no matter the distance from the center, contributes to the necessary diversity of society.

The Right to Refuse Treatment

Chapter 8 explored the matter of psychological treatment in several of its more popular forms. We suggested that mental health treatment is corrective (i.e., intervention designed to bring order to psychological disorder). As we have demonstrated throughout this book, however, chaos theory is not averse to disorder. Indeed, the latter is not a *lack* of the former; rather, it is a different kind of order. Further, not only does chaos theory regard periods of disorder as essential to healthy growth, it recognizes their inevitability given that life processes are dynamic. Although, according to nonlinear dynamical systems theory, life is change, it is not always predictable. Just as the weather may change with very little advance notice, living beings often experience physical, psychological, and/or socioenvironmental changes that necessitate adaptation. Thus, sudden fluctuations or "jumps" that interrupt life's continuity explain why the behavior of living systems must be understood as nonlinear.

Nonlinearity

Suggesting that life is nonlinear draws attention to the "jumps" that characterize the behavior of living systems. Stability is always a temporary phenomenon; continuity maintains itself for only limited periods of time. In between the intervals of stability and continuity are periods of nonlinearity that bring continuity to a temporary halt and encourage the system to become aware of its need for adjustment. In the physical and social lifeworld, these "jumps" vary. They may be the emergence of a thunderstorm after a week of clear skies; the presence of a traffic jam delay after several hours of smooth and continuous traffic flow; or the experience of an unusual amount of personal stress during which time one's customary stability is superceded by anxiety, fear, and uncharacteristic thoughts, feelings, and behaviors. These moments of instability invite the utilization of a capacity inherent in all living things; namely, the capacity to adapt.

Adaptation

Adaptation is a natural process whereby an organism or system adjusts to the changing demands of its environment (i.e., the flux of the internal and external world). The ability to adapt serves not only a psychological purpose but an evolutionary one as well. Adaptation is "fitting in" to the circumstances in which one finds oneself, whether they are the result of processes that are nonlinear, environmental, physical, psychological, or otherwise. If there is one unwavering "truth" about the world that has withstood the entire history of earthbound life, it is the permanency of change. Change is inevitable and, consequently, so too is adaptation. When order moves into periods of disorder, organisms experiencing it are encouraged, by their natural capacity for adaptation, to create a new order from within this disorder. In the discourse of chaos theory, this is the manifestation of self-organization.

Self-Organization

Self-organization theory attends to the process wherein organisms or living systems faced with periods of disorder adapt and form a new, more complex order. Chaos theory refers to this process as order-out-of-disorder or order-from-disorder. As threatening as disorder may seem, it is beneficial. Disorder encourages adaptation to changing circumstances; that is, a transition from an old, antiquated order to a new, more complex, adaptive, and *healthy* order. With the emergence of this new order, the organism is better equipped to live in an intricate world and sustain its health in the midst of elaborate and disorganized circumstances. Disorder is a signal, informing the organism that its present stability and organization are not sufficient to withstand the turbulence of its internal and/or external environment. Disorder, then, is interested in creating a healthier, nonlinear dynamical system.

Health

Informed by chaos theory and the principle of self-organization, we are encouraged to reformulate existing conceptions of health. Medicine presents health as the absence of dis-ease; psychology presents health as the absence of dis-order. When confronted with these conditions, "scientific" intervention emphasizes the cure of one's ailment or the restoration of one's uncoordinated existence.

To be clear, chaos theory does not recommend that we remain diseased or dis-ordered throughout our lives. Rather, it suggests that we reconsider the means employed to prevail over illness. For Nietzsche (1995), health signified one's ability to overcome illness, not the absence of it. Thus, a healthy individual is one who withstands the varying ailments to which one is exposed, becoming more powerful in the face of them. This Nietzschean logic is consistent with self-organization theory wherein the latter affirms our adaptive capacities as instrumental and elemental features of healthy human existence. If intervention disrupts this process, it threatens this very capacity.

As we argued, psychotropic medication "fixes" ailments such as anxiety, depression, and the like. However, it does so at the expense of the individual's natural struggle to overcome dis-order. Drug therapy may alleviate temporarily existing symptoms, but when experiencing similar struggles, the person confronts the same predicament; that is, an inability to effectively "push through" chaos. Notwithstanding possible exceptions in cases of extreme dis-ease or dis-order, nonlinear dynamical systems theory suggests that (disruptive) intervention does not contribute to the overall health of the organism, the system, or the society. The "health" of chaos theory is understood as orderly dis-order.

Orderly Disorder

Disruptive intervention acts as a point attractor in that it tends toward the prevailing conceptions of health as the absence of dis-ease and dis-order. However, chaos theory tells us that health may be, in fact, something quite different. Contrary to the conceptualization of health as a point attractor, it is something more closely resembling the strange attractor. As we explained, the strange attractor indicates an underlying order underneath the appearance of disorder. In this way, it does not appear as order (i.e., health may not *appear* as health but as dis-ease or dis-order). For example, although disturbed on the surface, the schizophrenic may embody an underlying order; that is, a strangely coordinated existence. The strange attractor teaches us to look beyond appearances, beyond our initial observations, to what is inside, underneath, or unseen. It teaches us the difference between that which is truly chaotic and in need of some intervention and that which only seems so (i.e., orderly disorder), requiring no imposed order.

THE JUST(ICE)

This project considered how chaos theory might inform our conception of justice in the psycholegal sphere by examining a number of controversial practices in mental health law. To some extent, this objective can be traced to an existing, though limited, body of scholarship in critical psychology and critical psycholegal studies, committed to the pursuit of a more civil, more humane society (e.g., Fox, 1999; Fox & Prilleltensky, 1997; Haney, 1993; Melton, 1990). In a very real sense, each of these researchers is interested in that which is "just," mindful of how people are socially, politically, economically, and philosophically affected by the clinicolegal system with its *potential* to establish positive, meaningful change in the lives of psychiatric citizens.

What has been conspicuously absent from much of this literature, however, is an adequate theoretical foundation. In other words, a well-developed and critical psycholegal theory, explaining the limits of existing mental health law has yet to be proposed in any explicit, detailed fashion. While the inquiries of those scholars mentioned above are certainly in the interest of promoting a transition to a more just, civil, and humane clinicolegal reality, regrettably, their conclusions are developed with insufficient conceptual alacrity or substance. Admittedly, the insights of Warren (1982),

Holstein (1993), and Arrigo (1993a, 1996), to some extent, provide this sort of theoretical template. Indeed, each in his or her own way helps advance our understanding of the failings of the psycholegal system, specifically in relation to the production of humane decision making within the psychiatric courtroom. Notwithstanding these efforts, there is ample room to integrate and extend these contributions, fashioning a well-crafted, critical, psycholegal theory; one that both identifies the shortcomings of existing practices, while offering a more detailed conceptual understanding of how prospects for justice might be promoted in the clinicolegal arena.

We believe that chaos theory is quite serviceable in this endeavor. Indeed, nonlinear dynamics are at least implicit in one's quest for a more civil and just society. Accordingly, we maintain that chaos theory, and its principles, are the requisite foreground for any critically animated psycholegal scholarship. This is because chaology is about justice. In the following section, we briefly explore how justice might appear from the perspective of chaos.

Justice as an Open, Creative System

As noted in this book's introduction, justice is something intangible; an undefinable and irreducible phenomenon. There are as many definitions of justice as there are contexts to which it may apply. For example, criminal justice is founded upon assumptions different from social justice, environmental justice, and the like (Arrigo, 1999a). More recently, there has been a movement toward victim-oriented justice whose core assumptions differ from offender-oriented justice. In short, then, justice cannot be defined independent of the context to which it is applied, the historical era within which it exists, or the persons or communities engaged in its pursuit. For this reason, we contend that it is best to understand justice as something that is always indeterminate; that is, something "open" to a variety of interpretations as to its "true" meaning. Similarly, chaos theory teaches us that everything is indeterminate and that this indeterminacy is what gives living systems their vitality. Among other things, this indeterminacy provides essential diversity and space for the creative growth of complex, adaptive organisms.

Accordingly, when we speak of justice, we cannot speak of it as an independent reality that either does or does not exist. This logic leads us right back into the prison-house of binary oppositions that quantum physics and chaos theory encourage us to avoid. For example, we cannot therefore suggest that a right to refuse treatment is, in all cases, conducive to justice. Moreover, we cannot suggest that, in all cases, civil commitment is unjust. Rather, chaos theory encourages us to perceive this phenomenon as a complex *web* of interrelated and interdependent types of justices (e.g., an interrelated and interdependent web of the social, political, criminal, civil, individual, psychological) to which it is inexorably connected and from which it takes on lived significance.

With these notions in mind, we might ask, for example, whether the civil commitment of Billie Boggs served the interests of social justice? of criminal or legal justice? of psychological justice? and/or of her own, individualized justice? The answer to each of these queries would be different depending on *who* asked and *how* the question was framed. This is why chaos theory encourages us to perceive justice as an incomplete, undecided, and interpretive phenomenon. Consistent with postmodernism, justice exists as a contingent universality (Butler, 1992); that is, its manifestations are always and already provisional, relational, and positional, absent the embodiment of any absolute Justice.

What this simply means, then, is that all considerations of justice, whether in the mental health law sphere or elsewhere, require the careful consideration of each element that helps constitute this phenomenon in particular instances. For example, in a criminal case, justice might not be served by punishing the offender (i.e., by retribution or, at least, by predefined forms of retribution). Given case-specific circumstances, we might find that victim-offender mediation, community intervention, victim compensation, or some other alternative sentence more closely resembles justice for the system, the person harmed, and/or the offender. Predefined *reactions* to life circumstances (e.g., incarceration, hospitalization, drug treatment) encourage homeostasis or, in the case of living systems, death. Configurations of justice such as these exemplify the work of the point attractor in chaos theory; that is, they attract and normalize the diversity of circumstances, "fitting" them within calculated notions of just resolution. This is antithetical to context-specific or ecologically informed justice. These are best understood, not as reactive processes, but as creative ones. Diversity necessitates inventive problem-solving. Of course, creativity is a product of spontaneity and it only exists when diversity is not forced into preconfigured, reactive approaches to promoting justice.

This creative, multidimensional, and perspectival facet to justice is illustrated, not only in theory, but in mathematics as well. Indeed, when explaining the behavior of nonlinear systems, mathematicians must use nonlinear equations. An interesting aspect of nonlinear equations is that they do not present a closed, identifiable, correct solution. Rather, unlike linear equations, nonlinear equations usually have two or more solutions. They are not attracted to a single right answer or fixed point. Thus, as the degree of nonlinearity increases, the number of solutions increases. Nonlinear "jumps" lead to new states, and new states require new solutions. In significantly nonlinear systems, new states can emerge at any given moment and, consequently, new solutions are continually necessary to describe the system. We can think of systemic "states" as life situations—a new state is like a new situation faced by the system, person, or society. In this way, we see how new solutions are necessary on a continual basis to endure the changing situations that continuously present themselves in the life-world.

Thus, the institutions that seek to promote justice, including the psycholegal sphere, must embody this creativity. Ideally, justice would be advanced by responding to change with creation, to dynamical life with active imaginative, and to nonlinear problems with nonlinear solutions. In short, justice would be advanced by the strange attractor which defines the human drama through open, complex, interdependent, adaptive expressions of humanity, as opposed to the point attractor which defines the drama of life through closed, preconfigured, unrelated, and static manifestations of one's being and becoming.

Justice as Orderly Disorder

The psycholegal sphere interacts within a living, dynamic world. Metaphorically, its molecules are constantly in motion; its people, organizations, communities, etc., are not static elements always at or around equilibrium. Although each of them may seek equilibrium, their reality is often much different. In chaos theory, the concept of *dissipative structures* describes open systems; these are systems that constantly interact with their environment, characterized by periods of instability. These periods are not only where creation occurs, but also where order emerges. Thus, not only is the search for equilibrium and order thwarted by the very nature of living systems, they are averted and precluded by the presence of dis-order and far-from-equilibrium conditions which are themselves constitutive of complex, nonlinear systems.

One of the more interesting characteristics of dissipative structures as related to living systems (e.g., individuals, societies, the psycholegal field), is the emergence of higher states of order, rather than disorder, at bifurcation points. In other words, as a system begins to split, given increasing disorder, a uniform increase in order co-occurs. Thus, "order and disorder are always created simultaneously" (Capra, 1996, p. 189).

The perception of order and disorder generated by chaos theory requires a shift in how we understand the function of equilibrium. In traditional science, order is associated with equilibrium. Contemporary systems such as law and psychology tend to embrace these conventional views, understanding order as the absence of disorder. However, chaos theory suggests a shift in this association. Indeed, through the study of chaos and complexity we learn that the source of order is, in fact, *nonequilibrium* conditions (Capra, 1996, p. 190). The order that emerges at far-from-equilibrium conditions, though, presents itself differently; that is, it is order disguised as chaos. In relation to traditional conceptions of order, this *orderly disorder* tends to be much more complex and, thus, much more healthy.

Embracing orderly disorder rather than traditional order means accepting the unpredictability and spontaneity that was previously described as creative and as constitutive elements of justice. For example, decision making in mainstream law and psychology seeks order, equilibrium, stasis, and predictability. This is the point attractor in operation, appropriate for many linear models of understanding, including those whose foundation is steeped in classical science. Chaos theory, however, maintains that dissipative structures, living organisms, and nonlinear dynamical systems are better understood by employing the notion of the strange attractor. What this means for psychiatric justice is that attraction to a point (e.g., a point of health, predefined resolutions, binary categorizations) is antithetical to the sustenance and growth of the organism as a whole. By extension, it is also antithetical to a civil and humane society that promotes the welfare of its citizens.

There is much to do if the law-psychology divide is to advance the aims of citizen justice and pro-social change. Both theoretically and pragmatically, the discipline must come to accept the logic of chaos theory and it must come to embrace the wisdom of orderly disorder. The discipline has the potential to promote greater manifestations of justice and fuller expressions of humanity. These were the principles upon which the law-psychology domain was founded. This book represents something of a blueprint for how to reconceptualize the psycholegal sphere, making it more consonant with its stated and sorely needed objectives. The question that remains is whether researchers in the field are prepared to advance this agenda. The next step entails the creation of various policies, procedures, programs, management initiatives, and legislative efforts. We did not offer specific recommendations along these and similar lines. This was not our intention. However, we have provided a viable framework from within which these matters might be answered. This is the invitation that awaits. We owe this much to the future of mental health law; we owe this much to the citizens subjected to the system's decision-making practices, we owe this much to the search for justice at the crossroads of law and psychology.

References

Abraham, F., Abraham, R., & Shaw, C. (1990). *A visual introduction to dynamical systems theory for psychology*. Santa Cruz, CA: Aerial.

Adorno, T. (1973). *Negative dialectics*. New York: Continuum.

Al-Issa, I. (1982). Does culture make a difference in psychopathology? In I. Al-Issa (Ed.), *Culture and psychopathology*. Baltimore: University Park Press.

Althusser, L. (1971). *Lenin and philosophy and other essays*. New York: New Left Books.

American Psychiatric Association. (1982). *Statement on the insanity defense*. Reprinted in American Journal of Psychiatry, 140, 681–688.

American Psychiatric Association (1994). *Diagnostic and statistical manual of mental disorders* (4th ed.). Washington, DC: American Psychiatric Association.

Appelbaum, P. (1984). Standards for civil commitment: A critical review of empirical research. *International Journal of Law and Psychiatry, 7*, 133–144.

Appelbaum, P. (1997). Almost a revolution: An international perspective on the law of involuntary confinement. *American Academy of Psychiatry and the Law, 25*(2), 135–147.

Appelbaum, P., & Gutheil, T. (1979). Rotting with their rights on: Constitutional theory and clinical reality in drug refusal by psychiatric patients. *Bulletin of the American Academy of Psychiatry and Law, 7*, 308–317.

Appelbaum, P., & Gutheil, T. (1981). The right to refuse treatment: The real issue is quality of care. *Bulletin of the American Academy of Psychiatry and Law, 9*, 199–202.

245

Aristotle (1985). *Nichomachean ethics* (T. Irwin, Trans.). Indianapolis, IN: Hackett.

Arrigo, B. (1992). Deconstructing jurisprudence: An experiential feminist critique. *Journal of Human Justice* 4(1): 13–30.

Arrigo, B. (1992a). The logic of identity and the politics of justice: Establishing a right to community-based treatment for the institutionalized mentally disabled. *New England Journal on Criminal and Civil Confinement, 18*(1), 1–31.

Arrigo, B. (1993a). *Madness, language, and the law.* Albany, NY: Harrow and Heston.

Arrigo, B. (1993b). Paternalism, civil commitment and illness politics: Assessing the current debate and outlining a future direction. *Journal of Law and Health, 7*(2), 131–168.

Arrigo, B. (1993c). Civil commitment, semiotics and discourse on difference: A historical critique of the sign of paternalism. In R. Kevelson (Ed.), *Flux, complexity, and illusion in law* (pp. 5–32). New York: P. Lang.

Arrigo, B. (1993d). An experientially-informed feminist jurisprudence: Rape and the move toward praxis. *Humanity & Society 17*(1), 28–47.

Arrigo, B. A. (1994). Legal discourse and the disordered criminal defendant: Contributions from psychoanalytic semiotics and chaos theory. *Legal Studies Forum, 18*(1), 93–112.

Arrigo, B. (1995). The peripheral core of law and criminology: On postmodern social theory and conceptual integration. *Justice Quarterly, 12*(3), 447–472.

Arrigo, B. (1995a). Rethinking the language of law and justice: Postmodern feminist jurisprudence. In D. Caudill & S. Gold, (Eds.), *Radical philosophy of law* (pp. 88–107). Atlantic Heights, NJ: Humanities Press.

Arrigo, B. (1995b). Law, crime, and social change: On psychoanalytic semiotics, chaos theory, and postmodern ethics. *Studies in the Social Sciences, 33*, 101–129.

Arrigo, B. (1996). *The contours of psychiatric justice: A postmodern critique of mental illness, criminal insanity, and the law.* New York: Garland.

Arrigo, B. (1996a). Towards a theory of punishment in the psychiatric courtroom: On language, law, and Lacan. *Journal of Crime and Justice, 19*(1), 15–32.

Arrigo, B. (1996b). Rethinking knowledge construction and the guilty but mentally ill verdict. *Criminal Justice and Behavior, 23*(4), 572–592.

Arrigo, B. (1996c). Desire in the psychiatric courtroom: On Lacan and the dialectics of linguistic oppression. *Current Perspectives in Social Theory, 16,* 159–187.

Arrigo, B. (1997). Insanity defense reform and the sign of abolition: Revisiting Montana's experience. *International Journal for the Semiotics of Law, 10*(29), 191–211.

Arrigo, B. (1997a). Transcarceration: Notes on a psychoanalytically-informed theory of social practice in the criminal justice and mental health systems. *Crime, Law, and Social Change, 27*(1), 31–48.

Arrigo, B. (1997b). Dimensions of social justice in a single room occupancy (SRO): Contributions from chaos theory, policy, and practice. In D. Milovanovic (Ed.), *Chaos, criminology, and social justice* (pp. 174–194). New York: Praeger.

Arrigo, B. (1998). Reason and desire in legal education: A psychoanalytic-semiotic critique. *International Journal for the Semiotics of Law, XI*(31), 3–24.

Arrigo, B. (1999). How has the law gone *mad?:* Reflections on semiotics and postmodernism. *International Journal for the Semiotics of Law, 12*(1), 95–101.

Arrigo, B. (Ed.). (1999a). *Social justice/criminal justice: The maturation of critical theory in law, crime, and deviance.* Belmont, CA: West/Wadsworth.

Arrigo, B. (2000a). *Introduction to forensic psychology: Issues and controversies in crime and justice.* San Diego, CA: Academic Press.

Arrigo, B. (2000b). Back to the future: The place of justice in forensic psychological research and practice. *Journal of Forensic Psychology Practice, 1*(1), 1–7.

Arrigo, B. (2000c). Critical criminology and social justice: On integrating knowledge. *Contemporary Justice Review, 3*(1), 7–37.

Arrigo, B. (Ed.). (2000d). Special Issue: Law, Society, and Lacan. *International Journal for the Semiotics of Law, 13*(4), passim.

Arrigo, B., & Bernard, T. (1997). Postmodern criminology in relation to radical and conflict criminology. *Critical Criminology: An International Journal, 8*(2), 39–60.

Arrigo, B., Milovanovic, D., & Schehr, R. (2000). The French connection: Implication for law, crime, and social justice. *Humanity & Society, 24*(2), 161–203.

Arrigo, B., & Schehr, R. (1998). Restoring justice for juveniles: A critical analysis of victim-offender mediation. *Justice Quarterly, 15*(4), 629–666.

Arrigo, B., & Young, T. R. (1997). Chaos, complexity, and crime. In B. MacLean & D. Milovanovic (Eds.), *Thinking critically about crime*. Vancouver: Collective Press.

Arrigo, B., & Young, T. R. (1998) Theories of crime and crimes of theorists: On the topological construction of criminological reality. *Theory and Psychology*, 8(2), 219–252.

Arrigo, B., & Tasca, J. (1999). Right to refuse treatment, competency to be executed, and therapeutic jurisprudence: A systematic analysis. *Law and Psychology Review*, 23, 1–47.

Arrigo, B., & Williams, C. (1999a). Chaos theory and the social control thesis: A post-Foucauldian analysis of involuntary civil confinement. *Social Justice*, 26(1), 177–207.

Arrigo, B., & Williams, C. (1999b). Law, ideology, and critical inquiry: The case of treatment refusal for incompetent prisoners awaiting execution. *New England Journal on Criminal and Civil Confinement*, 25(2), 367–412.

Arrigo, B., & Williams, C. (2000). The ethics of advocacy for the mentally ill: Philosophic and ethnographic considerations. *Seattle University Law Review*, 24, 2, 243–297.

Bacon, F. (1620/1960). *The new organon and other writings*. New York: Library of Liberal Arts.

Baldessarini, R. (1980). Drugs and the treatment of psychiatric disorders. In L. Goodman & A. Gilman, *The pharmacological basis of therapeutics* (6th ed.). New York: Macmillan.

Barak, G. (1988). Newsmaking criminology: Reflections on the media, intellectuals, and crime. *Justice Quarterly*, 5, 565–587.

Barton, S. (1994). Chaos, self-organization, and psychology. *American Psychologist*, 49(1), 5–14.

Beck, A., & Weishaar, M. (1995). Cognitive therapy. In R. Corsini & D. Wedding (Eds.), *Current psychotherapies* (5th ed.). Itasca, IL: F. E. Peacock Publishers.

Beck, J. C., & Golowka, E. A. (1988). A study of enforced treatment in relation to Stone's "thank you" theory. *Behavioral Sciences and the Law*, 6, 559.

Bell, C. (1994). Violent behavior and mental illness: Perspectives on papers in this issue. *Hospital and Community Psychiatry*, 45(7), 711–713.

Benedict, R. (1934). *Patterns of culture*. Boston: Houghton Mifflin.

Benson, R.W. (1989). Semiotics, modernism, and the law. *Semiotica*, 73, 157–175.

Berger, P., & Luckmann, T. (1966). *The social construction of reality*. New York: Doubleday.

Berlin, I. (1956; 1984). *The age of enlightenment*. New York: Penguin

Berry, T. (1996). *Buddhism*. New York: Columbia University Press.

Bertalanffy, L. (1968). *General systems theory: Foundations, developments, applications*. New York: Braziller.

Best. J. (1989). *Images of issues: Typifying contemporary social problems*. New York: Aldine de Gruyter.

Best, S., & Kellner, D. (1997). *The postmodern turn*. New York: Guilford.

Black, D. (1976). *The behavior of law*. New York: Academic Press.

Bohm, D. (1951). *Quantum theory*. London: Constable.

Bohm, D. (1981). *Wholeness and the implicate order*. London: Ark Paperbacks.

Boorse, C. (1975). On the distinction between disease and illness. *Philosophy and Public Affairs, 5*, 49–68.

Borgmann, A. (1992). *Crossing the postmodern divide*. Chicago: University of Chicago Press.

Bottomore, T. (1984). *The Frankfurt school*. London: Tavistock.

Bowes, H. A. (1956).The ataratic drugs: The present position of chlorpromazine, frenquel, pacatal, and reserpine in the psychiatric hospital. *American Journal of Psychiatry, 113*, 530–539.

Bracher, M. (1988). Lacan's theory in the four discourses. *Prose Studies, 11*, 32–49.

Bracher, M. (1993). *Lacan, discourse, and social change: A psychoanalytic cultural criticism*. Ithaca, NY: Cornell University Press.

Braginsky, B., Braginsky, D., & Ring, K. (1969). *Methods of madness: The mental hospital as a last resort*. New York: Holt, Rinehart and Winston.

Breggin, P. (1975). Psychiatry and psychotherapy as political processes. *American Journal of Psychotherapy, 29*, 369.

Briggs, J., & Peat, F. D. (1989). *Turbulent mirror*. New York: Harper and Row.

Brion, D. (1991). The chaotic law of tort: Legal formalism and the problem of indeterminacy. In R. Kevelson (Ed.), *Peirce and Law*. New York: P. Lang.

Brion, D. (1995). The chaotic indeterminacy of tort law: Between formalism and nihilism. In D. Caudill (Ed.)., *Radical Philosophy of Law* (pp. 179–199). Atlantic Heights, NJ: Humanities Press.

Bromberg, W. (1982). *Psychiatry between the wars, 1918–1945: A recollection*. Westport, CT: Greenwood Press.

Brooks, A. (1974). *Law, psychiatry, and the mental health system*. Boston: Little, Brown.

Brooks, A. (1987). The right to refuse antipsychotic medications: Law and policy. *Rutgers Law Review, 39,* 339–376.

Brown, L. & Gilligan, C. (1993). *Meeting at the crossroads*. Cambridge: Harvard University Press.

Butler, J. (1992). Contingent foundations: Feminism and the question of "postmodernism." In J. Butler and J.W. Scott (Eds.), *Feminists theorize the political*. London: Routledge.

Butz, M. (1991). Fractal dimensionality and paradigms. *The Social Dynamicist 2*(4): 4–7.

Butz, M. (1992). The fractal nature of the development of the self. *Psychological Reports, 71,* 1043–1063.

Butz, M. (1993a). Practical applications from chaos theory to the psychotherapeutic process: A basic consideration of dynamics. *Psychological Reports, 73,* 543–554.

Butz, M. (1993b). Family therapy and symbolic chaos. *Humanity & Society, 17,* 199–222.

Butz, M. (1994). Psychopharmacology: Psychology's *Jurassic Park? Psychotherapy, 31*(4), 692–698.

Butz, M. (1997). *Chaos and complexity: Implications for psychological theory and practice*. Bristol, PA: Taylor and Francis.

Cain, M. (1992). Realist philosophy and standpoint epistemologies or feminist criminology as a successor science. In L. Gelsthorpe & A. Morris (Eds.), *Feminist perspectives in criminology* (pp. 124–140). Philadelphia: Open University Press.

Calder, J. D., & Bauer, J. R. (1992). Convenience store robberies: Security measures and store robbery incidents. *Journal of Criminal Justice, 20,* 553–566.

Capra, F. (1996). The web of life. New York: Anchor Books.

Chamberlain, L. L. (1994). Further adventures in psychology's Jurassik Park: The issue of psychopharmacology. *Psychological Bulletin, 29,* 3, 47–50.

Chambers, M. (1972). Alternatives to civil commitment of the mentally ill: Practical guides and constitutional imperatives. *Michigan Law Review, 70,* 1107–1200.

Chodoff, P. (1976). The case for involuntary hospitalization of the mentally ill. *American Journal of Psychiatry, 131,* 1012–1020.

Cichon, D. (1992). The right to "Just say no": A history and analysis of the right to refuse antipsychotic drugs. *LA Law Review, 53,* 283–327.

Cixous, H. (1990). *Reading with Clarice Lispector*. Minneapolis, MN: University of Minnesota Press.

Clark, M. (1990). *Nietzsche on truth and philosophy*. New York: Cambridge University Press.

Clarke, C. (1997). *Oriental enlightenment: The encounter between Asian and Western thought*. New York: Routledge.

Cleveland, S., Mulvey, E., Appelbaum, P., & Lidz, C. (1989). Do dangerousness-oriented commitment laws restrict hospitalization of patients who need treatment? *Hospital and Community Psychiatry, 40,* 266–271.

Cockerham, W. (1992). *Sociology of mental disorder*. Englewood Cliffs, NJ: Prentice Hall.

Cocozza, J., & Steadman, H. (1976). The failure of psychiatric predictions of dangerousness: Clear and convincing evidence. *Rutgers Law Review, 29,* 1084–1101.

Cocozza, J., & Steadman, H. (1978). Prediction in psychiatry: An example of misplaced confidence in experts. *Social Problems, 25,* 265–276.

Cohen, S. (1990). Intellectual skepticism and political commitment: The case of radical criminology. Paper presented at the Inaugural Willem Bonger Memorial Lecture. University of Amsterdam, May 14.

Cohen, S. (1991). Talking about torture in Israel. *Tikkun* 6(6): 23–30, 89–90.

Cohen, S. (1993). Human rights and crimes of the state: The culture of denial. *Australian and New Zealand Journal of Criminology* 26: 97–115.

Cohen, J., & Stewart, I. (1994). *The collapse of chaos: Discovering simplicity in a complex world*. New York: Penguin.

Collins, R. (1975). *Conflict criminology: Toward an explanatory science*. New York: Academic Books.

Comment (1983). Guidelines for legislation on the psychiatric hospitalization of adults. *American Journal of Psychiatry, 140,* 672–679.

Cornell, D. (1991). *Beyond accommodation: Ethical feminism, deconstruction, and the law*. New York: Routledge.

Cornell, D. (1993). *Transformation: Recollective imagination and sexual difference*. New York: Routledge.

Cornesh, D. B., and Clarke, R. V. (1986). *The resasonable criminal*. New York: Springer Verlag.

Corsini, R. (1995). Introduction. In R. Corsini & D. Wedding (Eds.), *Current psychotherapies* (5th ed.). Itasca, IL: F. E. Peacock Publishers.

Couzin, J. (1999, June 14). Nature's blueprints. *U.S. News and World Report, 60.*

Coveney, P., & Highfield, R. (1990). *The arrow of time: A voyage through science to solve time's greatest mystery.* New York: Fawcett Columbine.

Currie, D. (1993). Unhiding the hidden: Race, class, and gender in the construction of knowledge. *Humanity & Society, 17*(1), 3–27.

Daly, K., & Chesney-Lind, M. (1988). Feminism and criminology. *Justice Quarterly, 5*(4), 495–535.

Darwin, C. [1859] (1968). *On the origin of species.* New York: Penguin.

Davies, P. (1989). *The new physics.* New York: Cambridge University Press.

Davis, J. M., & Cole, J. O. (1975). Antipsychotic drugs. In A. Freedman, H. Kaplan, & B. Sadock, *Comprehensive textbook of psychiatry* (2nd ed.). Baltimore: Williams and Wilkins.

de Silva, P. (1995). Theoretical perspectives on emotions in early Buddhism. In J. Marks & R. Ames (Eds.), *Emotions in Asian thought.* Albany, NY: State University of New York Press.

Deleuze, F. (1983). *Nietzsche and philosophy.* New York: Columbia University Press.

Deleuze, G., & Guattari, F. (1977). *Capitalism and schizophrenia: The anti-Oedipus.* New York: Viking.

Deleuze, G., & Guattari, F. (1986). *Kafka: Toward a minor literature.* Minneapolis: University of Minnesota Press.

Deleuze, G.,& Guattari, F. (1987). *A thousand plateaus.* Minneapolis: University of Minnesota Press.

Denber, H. (1967). Tranquilizers in psychiatry. In A. Freedman, H. Kaplan, & B. Sadock, *Comprehensive textbook of psychiatry* (2nd ed.). Baltimore: Williams and Wilkins.

Dershowitz, A. (1974). The origins of preventive confinement in Anglo-American law, Part II: The American experience. *Cincinnati Law Review, 70,* 1107–1200.

Dews, P. 1987. *Logics of disintegration: Post-structuralist thought and the aims of critical theory.* London and New York: Verso.

Dhamma, R. (1997). *The first discourse of the Buddha.* Boston: Wisdom.

Dupre, J. (1993). *The disorder of things: Metaphysical foundations in the disunity of science.* Cambridge: Harvard University Press.

Durham, M. L., & LaFond, J. Q. (1985). The empirical and policy implications for broadening the statutory criteria for civil commitment. *Yale Law and Policy Review, 3,* 395–446.

Durham, M. L., & LaFond, J. Q. (1988). A search for the missing premise of involuntary therapeutic commitment in effective treatment of the mentally ill. *Rutgers Law Review, 40,* 305–368.

Dworkin, R. (1986). *Law's empire.* Cambridge, MA: Belknap Press.

Einstadter, W. J., & Henry, S. (1994). *Criminological theory: An analysis of its underlying assumptions.* Fort Worth, TX: Harcourt, Brace.

Einstein, A. (1956). *The meaning of relativity* (5th ed.). Princeton: Princeton University Press.

Einstein, A. (1961). *Relativity: The special and general theory* (R. Lawson, Trans.). New York: Crown.

Ennis, B. J., & Litwack, T. R. (1974). Psychiatry and the presumption of expertise: Flipping the coins in the courtroom. *California Law Review, 62,* 693–752.

Feigenbaum, M. (1980). Universal behavior in nonlinear systems, *Los Alamos Science 1,* 4–27.

Feinberg, J. (1986). *The moral limits of the criminal law: Harm to self (Vol. III).* New York: Oxford University Press.

Feinberg, J. (1988). *The moral limits of the criminal law: Harmless wrongdoing (Vol. IV).* New York: Oxford University Press.

Foucault, M. (1965). *Madness and civilization.* New York: Vintage Books.

Foucault, M. (1977). *Discipline and punish.* New York: Pantheon.

Foucault, M. (1988). *Politics, philosophy, culture: Interviews and other writings 1977–1984.* New York: Routledge.

Fox, D. (1993). Psychological jurisprudence and radical social change. *American Psychologist, 48,* 234–241.

Fox, D. (1997). Psychology and law: Justice diverted. In D. Fox & I. Prilleltensky (Eds.), *Critical psychology: An introduction.* London: Sage.

Fox, D. (1999). Psycholegal scholarship's contribution to false consciousness about injustice. *Law and Human Behavior, 23,* 9–30.

Fox, D., & Prilleltensky, I. (1997). *Critical psychology: An introduction.* London: Sage.

Frank, J. (1930/1963). *Law and the modern mind.* New York: Doubleday.

Freud, S. (1914). *The psychopathology of everyday life.* New York: Macmillan.

Freud, S. (1927). *The ego and the id.* London: Hogarth Press.

Freud, S. (1949). Three essays on the theory of sexuality. In J. Strachey (Ed.), *The Standard Edition.* London: Hogarth Press.

Gadamer, H. (1975). *Truth and method.* London: Sheed and Ward.

Garfinkel, H. (1956). Conditions of successful degradation ceremonies. *American Journal of Sociology, 61*, 420–424.

Garfinkel, H. (1967). *Studies in ethnomethodology*. Englewood Cliffs, NJ: Prentice-Hall.

Gaw, A. C. (Ed.). (1993). *Culture, ethnicity, and mental illness*. Washington, DC: American Psychiatric Press.

Gelman, S. (1984). Mental hospital drugs, professionalism, and the constitution. *Georgetown Law Review, 72*, 1725.

Gelsthorpe, L., & Morris, A. (Eds.). (1990). *Feminist perspectives in criminology*. Milton Keynes: Open University Press.

Giddens, A. (1984). *The constitution of society*. Oxford: Polity Press.

Giddens, A. (1990). *The consequences of modernity*. Stanford: Stanford University Press.

Gilligan, C. (1982). *In a different voice*. Cambridge: Harvard University Press.

Gilligan, C., Lyons, N.P., & Hanmer, T.J. (1990). *Making connections*. Cambridge: Harvard University Press.

Gleick, J. (1987). *Chaos: Making a new science*. New York: Penguin.

Godel, K. (1962). On formally undecidable propositions, In R. B. Braithewaite (Ed.), *'Principia mathematica' and related systems* (pp. 173–198). New York: Basic Books.

Goerner, S. (1994). *Chaos and the evolving ecological universe*. Langhorne, PA: Gordon and Breach Science Publishers.

Goffman, E. (1959). *The presentation of the self in everyday life*. New York: Doubleday.

Goffman, E. (1961). *Asylums*. New York: Doubleday.

Goffman, E. (1966). *Encounters*. Indianapolis, IN: Bobbs-Merrill.

Goffman, E. (1967). *Interaction ritual: Essays on face-to-face behavior*. New York: Doubleday.

Goldstein, A. (1967). *The insanity defense*. New Haven: Yale University Press.

Goodrich, P. (1990). *Languages of law*. London: Weidenfeld and Nicolson.

Gottfredson, M., & Hirschi, T. (1990). *A general theory of crime*. Stanford: Stanford University Press.

Gove, W. (1975). *The labelling of deviance*. New York: Halstead.

Gramsci, A. (1971). *The prison notebooks*. London: Lawrence and Wishart.

Grisso, T., & Appelbaum, P. (1992). Is it unethical to offer predictions of future violence? *Law and Human Behavior, 16*, 621.

Grob, G. (1994). *The mad among us: A history of the care of America's mentally ill*. Cambridge: Harvard University Press.

Grotstein, J. (1990). Nothingness, meaninglessness, chaos, and the "black hole": I. The importance of nothingness, meaninglessness, and chaos in psychoanalysis. *Contemporary Psychoanalysis, 26,* 257–290.

Guattari, F. (1984). *Molecular revolution: Psychiatry and politics.* New York: Penguin Books.

Groves, W.B., & Sampson, R. (1986). Critical theory and criminology. *Social Problems, 33*(6), 58–80.

Gutheil, T. G. (1980). In search of true freedom: Drug refusal, involuntary medication, and "rotting with your rights on." *American Journal of Psychiatry, 137,* 327–328.

Habermas, J. (1984). *The theory of communicative action. Vol. One: Reason and the rationalization of society* (T. McCarthy, Trans.). Boston: Beacon Press.

Handler, J. (1992). The Presidential Address, 1992, Law and Society: Post-modernism, protest and the new social movement. *Law and Society Review, 26*(4), 697–731.

Haney, C. (1993). Psychology and legal change: The impact of a decade. *Law and Human Behavior, 17,* 371–398.

Hart, H. L. A. (1961). *The concept of law.* Oxford: Clarendon Press.

Harvey, D. (1989). *The condition of postmodernity.* Oxford: Blackwell.

Hayles, N. (1990). *Chaos bound: Order and disorder in contemporary literature and science.* Ithaca, NY: Cornell University Press.

Hayles, N. K. (1991). *Chaos and order: Complex dynamics in literature and science.* Chicago: University of Chicago Press.

Hegel, F. W. [1807] (1977). *Hegel's phenomenology of spirit.* A. V. Miller (Trans.). Oxford: Oxford University Press.

Heidegger, M. (1962). *Being and time.* New York: Harper and Row.

Heisenberg, W. (1958). *Physics and philosophy.* New York: Harper Torchbooks.

Held, D. (1980). *Introduction to critical theory.* Berkeley: University of California Press.

Henry, S., & Milovanovic, D. (1991). Constitutive criminology: The maturation of critical theory. *Criminology, 29*(2), 293–315.

Henry, S., & Milovanovic, D. (1996). *Constitutive criminology: Beyond postmodernism.* London: Sage.

Henry, S., & Milovanovic, D. (2000). *Constitutive criminology at work: Applications in crime and justice.* Albany, NY: State University of New York Press.

256 References

Hermann, D. (1973). Preventive detention: A scientific view of man, and state power. *University of Illinois Law Forum, 1973,* 673–699.

Hermann, D. (1990). Autonomy, self-determination, the right of involuntarily committed persons to refuse treatment, and the use of substituted judgement in medication decisions involving incompetent persons. *International Journal of Law and Psychiatry, 13,* 361–385.

Hiday, V. (1981). Court discretion: Application of the dangerousness standard in civil commitment. *Law and Human Behavior, 5,* 275.

Hiday, V. ,& Smith, L. (1987). Effects of the dangerousness standard in civil commitment. *The Journal of Law and Psychiatry, 10,* 433–454.

Hirschi, T. (1969). *Causes of delinquency.* Berkeley: University of California Press.

Holmes, O. W. (1897). The path of the Law. *Harvard Law Review 10:* 457–478.

Holstein, J. (1988). Court-ordered incompetence: Conversational organization in involuntary commitment hearings. *Social Problems, 35,* 458–473.

Holstein, J. (1993). *Court-ordered insanity: Interpretive practice and involuntary commitment.* New York: Aldine de Gruyter.

Horgan, J. (1996). *The end of science: Facing the limits of knowledge in the twilight of the scientific age.* Menlo Park, CA: Addison-Wesley.

Horkheimer, M., & Adorno, T. (1972). *Dialectic of enlightenment.* New York: Continuum.

Hunt, A. (1990). The big fear: Law confronts postmodernism. *McGill Law Journal, 35,* 507–540.

Hunt, A. (1991). Postmodernism and critical criminology. In B. MacLean & D. Milovanovic (Eds.), *New directions in critical criminology* (pp. 79–85). Vancouver: Collective Press.

Hunt, A. (1993). *A constitutive theory of law.* London: Routledge.

Husserl, E. (1983). *Ideas pertaining to a pure phenomenology and to a phenomenological philosophy* (F. Kersten, Trans.). The Hague: Martinus Nijhoff Publishers.

Irigaray, L. (1985). *This sex which is not one* (C. Porter & C. Burke, Trans.). Ithaca, NY: Cornell University Press.

Irigaray, L. (1990). *The ethics of sexual difference* (C. Burke, Trans.). Oxford: Blackwell.

Isaac, R., & Armat, V. (1990). *Madness in the streets: How psychiatry and law abandoned the mentally ill.* New York: Free Press.

Jantsch, E. (1980). *The self-organizing universe.* New York: Pergamon.

Jessop, B. (1990). *State theory: Putting the capitalist state in its place*. Cambridge, MA: Polity Press.

Kant, I. (1784/1983). An answer to the question: What is enlightenment? In *Perpetual peace and other essays*. Indianapolis, IN: Hackett.

Kauffman, S. (1991). Antichaos and adaptation. *Scientific American, 265*(2), 78–84.

Kellert, S. (1994). *In the wake of chaos*. Chicago: University of Chicago Press.

Kellner, D. (1989). *Critical theory, Marxism, and modernity*. Baltimore: Johns Hopkins University Press.

Kelman, M. (1987). *A guide to critical legal studies*. Cambridge and London: Harvard University Press.

Kerlinger, F. N. (1979). *Behavioral assessment: A conceptual approach*. Chicago: Holt, Rinehart & Winston.

Kessler, R., et al. (1994). Lifetime and 12-month prevalence of DSM-III-R psychiatric disorders in the United States. *Archives of General Psychiatry, 51*, 8–19.

Kevelson, R. (1988). *The law as a system of signs*. New York: Plenum.

Kincheleo, J., & McLaren, P. (1998). Rethinking critical theory and qualitative research. In N. Denzin & Y. Lincoln (Eds.), *The landscape of qualitative research*. Thousand Oaks, CA: Sage.

Kittric, N. A. (1971). *The right to be different: Enforced therapy*. Baltimore: Johns Hopkins University Press.

Kristeva, J. (1977). *Polylogue*. Paris: Editions du Seuil.

Kristeva, J. (1980). *Desire in language*. New York: Columbia University Press.

Kristeva, J. (1984). *Revolution in poetic language*. New York: Columbia University Press

Lacan, J. (1975). *Encore*. Paris: Editions du Seuil.

Lacan, J. (1977). *Ecrits: A selection* (A. Sheridan, Trans.). New York: Norton.

Lacan, J. (1985). *Feminine sexuality*. New York: Norton.

Lacan, J. (1991). *L'envers de la psychanalyse*. Paris: Editions du Seuil.

LaFond, J. Q. (1981). An examination of the purposes of involuntary civil commitment. *Buffalo Law Review, 30*, 499–535.

LaFond, J. Q., & Durham, M. L. (1992). *The future of mental health policy in the United States*. New York: Oxford University Press.

Lahey, K. (1985). Until women themselves have told all that they have to tell..... *Osgoode Hall Law Journal, 23*, 519–541.

Laing, R. (1967). *The politics of experience*. New York: Ballantine.

Laing, R. (1969). *The divided self*. New York: Pantheon.

Laplace, P.-S. (1814/1951). *A philosophical essay on probabilities*. New York: Dover.

Lecercle, J. J. (1985). *Philosophy through the looking glass: Language, nonsense, desire*. London: Hutchinson.

Lee, J. S. (1990). *Jacques Lacan*. Amherst: University of Massachusetts Press.

Levy, R., & Rubenstein, L. (1996). *The rights of people with mental disabilities*. Carbondale, IL: Southern Illinois University Press.

Lidz, C., Mulvey, E., & Gardner, N. (1993). The accuracy of predictions of violence to others. *Journal of the American Medical Association, 269*, 1007–1011.

Lindman, F., & McIntyre, D. (1961). *The mentally disabled and the law*. Chicago: University of Chicago Press.

Litman, C. (1982). A common law remedy for forcible medication of the institutionalized mentally ill. *Columbia Law Review, 82*, 1720.

Livermore, A., Malmquist, R., & Meehl, S. (1968). On the justifications for civil commitment. *University of Pennsylvania Law Review, 75*, 84.

Llewellyn, K. (1930). A realistic jurisprudence—The next step. *Columbia Law Review, 30*, 431–465.

Llewellyn, K. (1931). Some realism about realism. *Harvard Law Review, 44*, 1222–1264.

Llewellyn, K., & Hoebel, A. (1941). *The Cheyenne way: Conflict and case law in primitive jurisprudence*. Norman: University of Oklahoma Press.

Luhmann, N. A. (1985). *A sociological theory of law*. Boston: Routledge & Kegan Paul.

Luhmann, N. A. (1992). Operational closure and structural coupling: The differentiation of the legal system. *Cordozo Law Review, 13*(5), 1419–1441.

Lyotard, J.-F. (1984). *The postmodern condition: A report on knowledge*. Minneapolis: University of Minnesota Press.

MacKinnon, C. (1987). *Feminism unmodified: Discourses on life and law*. Cambridge and London: Harvard University Press.

MacKinnon, C. (1989). *Towards a feminist theory of the state*. Cambridge: Harvard University Press.

Malhorta Bentz, V. (1993). Review of James M. Ostrow's *Social sensitivity*. *Humanity & Society, 17*(1), 121–123.

Mandelbrot, B. (1983). *The fractal geometry of nature*. New York: W. H. Freeman.

Manning, P. (1992). *Organizational communication.* New York: Aldine de Gruyter.

Marcuse, H. (1966). *Eros and civilization.* Boston: Beacon Press.

Margolis, J. (1980). The concept of mental illness: A philosophical examination. In B. Brody & H. Engelhardt, Jr. (Eds.), *Mental illness: Law and public policy.* Boston: D. Reidel.

Marino, G. (1994). Chaos: An overview. *Penn State Liberal Arts Alumni Newsletter, 5*(2), 10–11.

Marks, J. (1995). Dispassion and the ethical life. In J. Marks & R. Ames (Eds.), *Emotions in Asian thought.* Albany, NY: State University of New York Press.

Matson, F. (1966). *The broken image: Man, science and society.* New York: Anchor Books.

McDermott, M. J. (1992). The personal is empirical: Research methods and criminal justice education. *Journal of Criminal Justice Education, 3*(2), 237–249.

Melton, G. (1990). Realism in psychology and humanism in law: Psycholegal studies at Nebraska. *Nebraska Law Review, 69,* 251–277.

Melton, G., Petrila, J., Poythress, N., & Slobogin, C. (1997). *Psychological evaluations for the courts: A handbook for mental health professionals and lawyers* (2nd ed.). New York: Guilford Press.

Merleau-Ponty, M. (1962). *Phenomenology of perception* (Colin Smith, Trans.). New York: Humanities Press.

Milovanovic, D. (1986) Juridico-linguistic communicative markets: Toward a semiotic analysis. *Contemporary Crises, 10,* 281–304.

Milovanovic, D. (1992). *Postmodern law and disorder: Psychoanalytic semiotics, chaos theory, and juridic exegeses.* Liverpool, U.K.: Deborah Charles.

Milovanovic, D. (1993a). Lacan, chaos, and practical discourse in law. In R. Kevelson (Ed.), *Flux, complexity, illusion in law* (pp. 311–337). New York: P. Lang.

Milovanovic, D. (1993b). Lacan's four discourses: Chaos and cultural criticism in law. *Studies in Psychoanalytic Theory, 2*(1), 3–23.

Milovanovic, D. (1994). *A primer in the sociology of law* (2nd ed.). New York: Harrow and Heston.

Milovanovic, D. (1996). "Rebellious lawyering": Lacan, chaos and the development of alternative juridico-semiotic forms. *The Legal Studies Forum, 20*(3), 295–321.

Milovanovic, D. (1997). *Chaos, criminology, and social justice.* Westport, CT: Praeger.

Milovanovic, D. (1997a). *Postmodern criminology.* New York and London: Garland.

Minda, G. (1995). *Postmodern legal movements.* New York: NYU Press.

Monahan, J. (1981). *The clinical prediction of violent behavior.* Washington, DC: U.S. Government Printing Office.

Monahan, J. (1992). Mental disorder and violent behavior. *American Psychologist, 47,* 511–521.

Monahan, J. (1996). Violence prediction: The past twenty years and the next twenty years. *Criminal Justice and Behavior, 23*(1), 107–120.

Monahan, J. (1997). Clinical and actuarial predictions of violence. In D. Faigman et al. (Eds.), *Modern scientific evidence: The law and science of expert testimony.* St. Paul, MN: West.

Monahan, J., & Arnold, J. (1996). Violence by people with mental illness: A consensus statement by advocates and researchers. *Psychiatric Rehabilitation Journal, 19,* 67.

Monahan, J., & Steadman, H. (1994). *Violence and mental disorder: Developments in risk assessment.* Chicago: University of Chicago Press.

Moran, M. (1991). Chaos theory and psychoanalysis: The fluid nature of the mind. *International Review of Psychoanalysis, 18,* 211–221.

Morgan, G. (1997). *Images of organization.* Thousand Oaks, CA: Sage.

Morrison, F. (1991). *The art of modeling dynamic systems.* New York: Wiley.

Morrissey, J., & Goldman, H. H. (1986). Care and treatment of the mentally ill in the United States: Historical developments and reforms. *The Annals of the American Academy of Political and Social Science, 484,* 12–27.

Morrow, J. (1998). The reality is the same: Interpretive implosions. *International Journal for the Semiotics of Law, XI*(33), 329–334.

Morse, S. (1978). Crazy behavior, morals, and science: An analysis of mental health law. *Southern California Law Review, 51,* 527–654.

Morse, S. (1982). A preference for liberty: The case against involuntary commitment of the mentally disordered. *California Law Review, 70,* 54–106.

Mossman, D. (1994a). Assessing predictions of violence: Being accurate about accuracy. *Journal of Consulting and Clinical Psychiatry, 62,* 783.

Mossman, D. (1994b). Further comments on portraying the accuracy of violence prediction. *Law and Human Behavior, 18,* 587.

Mulvey, E. (1994). Assessing the evidence of a link between mental illness and violence. *Hospital and Community Psychiatry, 45*, 663.

Mulvey, E., Blumstein, A, & Cohen, J. (1986). Reframing the research question of mental patient criminality. *International Journal of Law and Psychiatry, 9*, 57–65.

Myers, J. E. (1983). Involuntary civil commitment of the mentally ill: A system in need of change. *Villanova Law Review, 29*, 367–433.

Nehemas, A. (1985). *Nietzsche: Life as literature.* Cambridge: Harvard University Press.

Newman, D. (1995). *Sociology: Exploring the architecture of everyday life.* Thousand Oaks, CA: Sage.

Nietzsche, F. (1887/1967). *The genealogy of morals.* New York: Random House.

Nietzsche, F. (1980). *On the advantage and disadvantage of history for life.* Cambridge, MA: Hackett.

Nietzsche, F. (1995). *Thus spoke Zarathustra* (W. Kaufmann, Trans.). New York: Modern Library.

Note (1974). Developments in the law: Civil commitment of the mentally ill. *Harvard Law Review, 87*, 1190.

Ogloff, J. (1999). Law and human behavior: Reflecting back and looking forward. *Law and Human Behavior, 23*(1), 1–7.

Otto, R. (1992). The prediction of dangerous behavior: A review and analysis of "second generation" research. *Forensic Reports, 5*, 103–133.

Paczak, S. (1989). Pennsylvania standard for involuntary civil commitment of the mentally ill: A clear and present danger? *Duquesne University Law Review, 27*, 325–353.

Palmer, B. D. (1990). *Descent into discourse: The reification of language and the writing of social history.* Philadelphia: Temple University Press.

Pecheux, M. (1982). *Language, semantics and ideology.* New York: St. Martin's Press.

Peller, G. (1985). The metaphysics of American law. *California Law Review, 73*(4), 1151–1290.

Pepinsky, H. (1991). *The geometry of violence.* Bloomington: Indiana University Press.

Perlin, M. (1989). *Mental disability law: Civil and criminal.* Charlottesville, VA: Michie.

Perlin, M. (1994). *The jurisprudence of the insanity defense.* Durham, NC: Carolina Academic Press.

Perlin, M. (1999). *Mental disability law: Cases and materials*. Durham, NC: Carolina Academic Press.

Perlin, M., Gould, K., & Dorfman, D. (1995). Therapeutic jurisprudence and the civil rights of institutionalized mentally disabled persons: Hopeless oxymoron or path to redemption? *Psychology, Public Policy, and the Law, 1*, 80.

Plato (1973). *The Republic* (G. Grube, Trans.). Indianapolis, IN: Hackett.

Plotkin, R. (1977). Limiting the therapeutic orgy: Mental patients' right to refuse treatment. *Northwestern University Law Review, 72*, 461.

Pollock-Byrne, J. (1989). *Ethics in crime and justice: Dilemmas and decisions*. Pacific Grove, CA: Brooks/Cole.

Porter, E., & Gleick, J. (1990). *Nature's chaos*. New York: Viking Penguin.

Posner, R. A. (1986). *Economic analysis of law* (3rd ed.). Boston: Little Brown.

Posner, R. A. (1992). *Sex and reason*. Cambridge: Harvard University Press.

Pound, R. (1908). Mechanical Jurisprudence. *Columbia Law Review, 8*, 605–623.

Poythress, N. (1978). Psychiatric expertise in civil commitment: Training attorneys to cope with expert testimony. *Law and Human Behavior, 2*, 1–23.

Prigogine, I., & Stengers, I. (1984). *Order out of chaos*. New York: Bantam Books.

Quinney, R. (1970). *The social reality of crime*. Boston: Little, Brown.

Rabkin, J. (1979). Criminal behavior of discharged mental patients: A critical appraisal of the research. *Psychological Bulletin, 86*, 1–27.

Ragland-Sullivan, E. (1986). *Jacques Lacan and the philosophy of psychoanalysis*. Chicago: University of Illinois Press.

Rapoport, D., & Parry, J. (1986). *The right to refuse antipsychotic medication*. Washington, DC: American Bar Association.

Reisner, R., & Slobogin, C. (1990). *Law and the mental health system: Civil and criminal aspects*. St. Paul, MN: West.

Reisner, R., & Slobogin, C. (1997). *Law and the mental health system: Civil and criminal aspect* (2nd Ed.). St Paul, MN: West.

Reiss, A., & Roth, J. (1993). *Understanding and preventing violence*. Washington, DC: National Academy Press.

Ritzer, G. (1990). *Frontiers of social theory: The new synthesis*. New York: Columbia University Press.

Rogers, C., & Skinner, B. (1956). Some issues concerning the control of human behavior: A symposium. *Science, 124*, 1057–1066.

Rosenau, P. A. (1992). *Postmodernism and the social sciences: Insights, inroads, and intrusions.* Princeton: Princeton University Press.

Rossi-Landi, F. (1977). *Linguistics and economics.* Netherlands: Mouton.

Roth, L. (1986). The right to refuse treatment: Law and medicine at the interface. *Emory Law Journal, 35,* 139–161.

Roth, L., & Appelbaum, P. (1982). What we do and do not know about treatment refusal in mental institutions. In A. Doudera & J. Swazey (Eds.), *Refusing treatment in mental health institutions—values in conflict.* Ann Arbor, MI: AUPHA Press.

Rothman, D. (1971). *The discovery of the asylum.* Boston: Little, Brown.

Rothman, D. (1980). *Conscience and convenience: The asylum and its alternatives in progressive America.* Boston: Little, Brown.

Ruelle, D. (1991). *Chance and chaos.* Princeton: Princeton University Press.

Ruhl, J., & Ruhl, H. (1997). The arrow of law in modern administrative states: Using complexity theory to reveal the diminishing returns and increasing risks the burgeoning of law poses to society. *University of California-Davis Law Review, 30,* 405–482.

Rumble, W., Jr. (1968). *American legal realism.* Ithaca, NY: Cornell University Press.

Rychlak, J. (1981). *Introduction to personality and psychotherapy: A theory-construction approach* (2nd ed.). Boston: Houghton Mifflin.

Sarbin, T., & Juhasz, J. (1982). The concept of mental illness: A historical perspective. In I. Al-Issa (Ed.), *Culture and psychopathology.* Baltimore: University Park Press.

Sartre, J.-P. (1956). *Being and nothingness.* New York: Pocket Books.

Sarup, M. (1989). *Post-structuralism and postmodernism.* Athens, GA: University of Georgia Press.

Schacht, R. (1983). *Nietzsche.* New York: Routledge.

Scheff, T. (1966). *Being mentally ill.* New York: Aldine.

Scheff, T. (1984). *Being mentally ill* (2nd ed.). New York: Aldine de Gruyter.

Scheff, T. (2000). *Being mentally ill* (3rd ed.). New York: Aldine de Gruyter.

Schmidt, W. C. (1985). Critique of the American Psychiatric Association guidelines for state legislation on civil commitment of the mentally ill. *New England Journal on Criminal and Civil Confinement, 11,* 1–43.

Schopp, R., & Quattrocchi, M. (1995). Predicting the present: Expert testimony in civil commitment. *Behavioral Sciences and the Law, 13,* 159–181.

Schutz, A. (1964). *Studies in social theory*. The Hague: Martinus Nijhoff.

Schwartz, M., & Friedrichs, D. (1994). Postmodern thought and criminological discontent: New metaphors for understanding violence. *Criminology, 32*, 221–246.

Scull, A. (1989). *Social order/Mental disorder: Anglo-American psychiatry in historical perspective*. Berkeley: University of California Press.

Sellers, S. (Ed.). (1991). *Feminist criticism, theory and practice*. London and New York: Routledge.

Serres, M. (1982a). *Hermes: Literature, science and philosophy*. Baltimore: Johns Hopkins University Press.

Serres, M. (1982b). *The parasite*. Baltimore: Johns Hopkins University Press.

Shah, S. (1974). Some interactions of law and mental health in the handling of social deviance. *Catholic University Law Review, 23*(4), 674–719.

Shah, S. (1977). Dangerousness: Some definitional, conceptual, and public policy issues. In B. Sales (Ed.), *Perspectives in law and psychology*. New York: Plenum Press.

Shah, S. (1978). Dangerousness: A paradigm for exploring some issues in law and psychology. *American Psychologist, 33*, 224–239.

Skinner, B. (1953). *Science and human behavior*. New York: Macmillan.

Skinner, B. (1971). *Beyond freedom and dignity*. New York: Bantam.

Smart, C. (1989). *Feminism and the power of law*. London and New York: Routledge.

Smart, C. (1990). Feminist approaches to criminology or postmodern woman meets atavistic man. In L. Gelsthorpe & A. Morris (Eds.), *Feminist perspectives in criminology* (pp. 97–108). Milton Keynes: Open University Press.

Smart, C. (1992). The women of legal discourse. *Social and Legal Studies: An International Journal, 1*, 29–44.

Smith, R. (1995). The inapplicability principle: What chaos means for social science. *Behavioral Sciences, 40*, 22–40.

Solomon, R., & Higgins, K. (1996). *A short history of philosophy*. New York: Oxford University Press.

Srole, L., Langner, T., Michael, S., Opler, M., & Rennie, T. (1962). *Mental health in the metropolis: The midtown Manhattan study*. New York: McGraw-Hill.

Steadman, H. (1981). Critically assessing the accuracy of public perceptions of the dangerousness of the mentally ill. *Journal of Health and Social Behavior, 22*, 310–316.

Stefan, S. (1993). What constitutes departure from professional judgement? *Mental and Physical Disability Law Reporter, 17,* 207.

Stewart, I. (1989). *Does God play dice? The mathematics of chaos.* Cambridge, Eng.: Blackwell.

Stone, A. (1975). *Mental health law: A system in transition.* Washington, DC: U.S. Government Printing.

Swanson, J., Holzer, C., Ganju, V., et al. (1990). Violence and psychiatric disorder in the community: Evidence from the Epidemiological Catchment Area surveys. *Hospital and Community Psychology, 41,* 761–770.

Szasz, T. (1961). *The myth of mental illness.* New York: Dell.

Szasz, T. (1963). *Law, liberty, and psychiatry: An inquiry into the social uses of mental health practices.* New York: Collier Books.

Szasz, T. (1970). *The manufacture of madness.* New York: Harper and Row.

Szasz, T. (1977). *Psychiatric slavery: When confinement and coercion masquerade as cure.* New York: Free Press.

Szasz, T. (1987). *Insanity: The idea and its consequences.* New York: John Wiley and Sons.

Talbott, J. (1978). *The death of the asylum: A critical study of state hospital management, services, and care.* New York: Grune and Stratton.

Tapp, J., & Levine, F. (1977). *Law, justice, and the individual in society.* New York: Holt.

Tarnas, R. (1991). *The passion of the Western mind.* New York: Ballantine.

Teubner, G. (1988). *Autopoetic law: A new approach to law and society.* New York: Walter de Gruyter.

Teubner, G. (1993). *Law as an autopoetic system.* Oxford: Basil Blackwell.

Thiele, L. (1990). *Friedrich Nietzsche and the politics of the soul.* Princeton: Princeton University Press.

Thomas, E. (1927). *The life of Buddha as legend and history.* New York: Alfred A. Knopf.

Torrey, E. (1994). Violent behavior by individuals with serious mental illness. *Hospital and Community Psychiatry, 45* (7), 653–662.

Treffert, D. A. (1971). The practical limits of patients' rights. *Psychiatric Annals, 5,* 91–96.

Treffert, D. A. (1985). The obviously ill patient in need of treatment: A fourth standard for civil commitment. *Hospital and Community Psychiatry, 36,* 259–264.

Van Eenwyk, J. (1991). Archetypes: The strange attractors of the psyche. *Journal of Analytical Psychology, 36,* 1–25.

Wahl, O. (1987). Public vs. professional conceptions of schizophrenia. *Journal of Community Psychology, 15*, 285–291.

Warren, C. (1982). *The court of last resort*. Chicago: University of Chicago Press.

Weber, M. (1978). *Economy and Society*, 2 vols. (G. Roth & C. Wittich, Eds.). Los Angeles: University of California Press.

Weiner, I. (1975). *Principles of psychotherapy*. New York: John Wiley and Sons.

Wexler, D., & Winick, B. (1996). *Law in a therapeutic key*. Washington, DC: American Psychological Association.

Wheelwright, P. (1966). *The preSocratics*. New York: Odyssey Press.

Williams, C. (1998). The abrogation of subjectivity in the psychiatric courtroom: Toward a psychoanalytic semiotic analysis. *International Journal for the Semiotics of Law, XI*(32), 181–192.

Williams, C. (1999). Inside the outside and outside the inside: Negative fusions from the margins of humanity. *Humanity and Society, 23*(1), 49–67.

Williams, C., & Arrigo, B. (2000). Anarchaos and order: On the emergence of social justice. *Theoretical Criminology, 5*(2), 223–252.

Williams, C., & Arrigo, B. (2000a). The philosophy of the gift and the psychology of advocacy: Critical reflections on forensic mental health intervention. *International Journal for the Semiotics of Law, 13*(2), 215–242.

Winick, B. (1995). Ambiguities in the legal meaning and significance of mental illness. *Psychology, Law, and Public Policy, 1*(3), 534–611.

Winick, B. (1997a). *Therapeutic jurisprudence: Applied essays on mental health law*. Washington, DC: American Psychological Association.

Winick, B. (1997b). *The right to refuse mental health treatment*. Washington, DC: American Psychological Association.

Wittgenstein, L. (1953). *Philosophical investigations*. Oxford: Basil Blackwell.

Wolf, F. A. (1981). *Taking the quantum leap: The new physics for nonscientists*. New York: Harper and Row.

Wolf, F. A. (1984). *Star wave: Mind, consciousness, and quantum physics*. New York: Macmillan.

Wolinsky, S. H. (1991). *Trances people live with: Healing approaches to quantum psychology*. Norfolk, CT: Bramble.

Wolinsky, S. H. (1993). *Quantum consciousness: The guide to experiencing quantum psychology*. Norfolk, CT: Bramble.

Wrightsman, L. (1997). *Psychology and the legal system* (3rd ed.). Pacific Grove, CA: Brooks/Cole.

Young, T. (1991). Chaos and social change: Metaphysics of the postmodern. *The Social Science Journal, 28*(3), 289–305.

Young, T. R. (1992). Chaos theory and human agency. *Humanity and Society, 16*(4), 441–460.

Young, T. R., & Arrigo, B. (1999). *The dictionary of critical social sciences.* New York: Westview.

CASES CITED

Addington v. Texas, 441 U.S. 418 (1979).

Barefoot v. Estelle, 103 S. Ct. 3383 (1983).

Bell v. Wolfish, 441 U.S. 520 (1979).

Davis v. Hubbard, 506 F. Supp. 915 (N.D. Ohio W.D. 1980).

Dusky v. United States, 363 U.S. 402 (1960).

Ingraham v. Wright, 430 U.S. 651 (1977).

In the Matter of Lynda Rae Vega. (1997). Unpublished opinion from the State of Minnesota Court of Appeals. Available online at: http://www.courts.state.mn.us/library/archive/ctapun/9712/1549.htm

In the Matter of Billie Boggs. 132 AD2d 340 (1987).

In the Matter of the Commitment of D. M. 285 N.J. Super.481. (1995).

In the Matter of the Commitment of F. J. 285 N.J. Super.481. (1995).

In the Matter of the Mental Commitment of Rhonda S. W. (1999). Available online at: http://www.wisbar.org.

Jackson v. Indiana, 406 U.S. 715 (1972).

Knecht v. Gillman, 488 F.2d 1136 (8th Cir. 1973).

Lake v. Cameron, 364 F. 2d 657 (D.C. Cir.), cert denied, 382 U.S. 863 (1966).

Lessard v. Schmidt, 421 U.S. 957 (1975).

Mackey v. Procunier, 477 F.2d 877 (9th Cir. 1973).

Matter of Carl C. 126 AD2d 640 (1987).

O'Connor v. Donaldson, 422 U.S. 291 (1975).

Rennie v. Klein, 462 F. Supp. 1131 (D.N.J. 1978).

Rogers v. Okin, 634 F.2d 650 (1st Cir. 1980).

Rouse v. Cameron, 373 F. 2d 451 (D.C. Cir. 1966).

Scott v. Plante, 532 F.2d 939 (3rd Cir. 1976).

Smith v. Goguen, 415 U.S. 566 (1974).
Washington v. Harper, 494 U.S. 210 (1990).
Wyatt v. Stickney, 344 F. Supp. 373 (M.D. Ala., 1972).
Youngberg v. Romeo, 457 U.S. 307 (1982).

About the Authors

CHRISTOPHER R. WILLIAMS is an assistant professor of sociology and criminology at State University of West Georgia. He received his Ph.D. from the Institute of Psychology, Law, and Public Policy at the California School of Professional Psychology-Fresno. His previous scholarship has appeared in such journals as *Social Justice*, *Theoretical Criminology*, *American Journal of Criminal Justice*, *New England Journal on Criminal and Civil Confinement*, and *Humanity & Society*. He is presently completing, with Bruce A. Arrigo, a monograph tentatively titled, *Reading Prisons: A Humanistic Perspective* (Praeger, forthcoming).

BRUCE A. ARRIGO is Professor of Crime, Law, and Society and Chair of the Criminal Justice Department at the University of North Carolina–Charlotte. Formerly the Director of the Institute of Psychology, Law and Public Policy at the California School of Professional Psychology–Fresno, Dr. Arrigo began his professional career as a community organizer and social activist for the homeless, the mentally ill, the working poor, the frail elderly, the decarcerated, and the chemically addicted. Dr. Arrigo received his Ph.D. from Pennsylvania State University, and he holds a master's degree in psychology and sociology. He is the author of more than 100 journal articles, academic book chapters, and scholarly essays exploring theoretical and applied topics in critical criminology, criminal justice and mental health, and socio-legal studies. His recent scholarship has appeared in such periodicals as *Criminal Justice and Behavior*, *Crime, Law, and Social Change*, *Justice Quarterly*, *International Journal of Law and Psychiatry*, *Social Justice*, *Law and Psychology Review*, *Theoretical Criminology*, *Deviant Behavior*, *Contemporary Justice Review*, *International Journal of Offender Therapy and Comparative Criminology*, and the *International Journal for the*

Semiotics of Law. He is the author, coauthor, or editor of five books. These books include *Madness, Language, and the Law* (1993), *The Contours of Psychiatric Justice* (1996), *Social Justice/Criminal Justice* (1998), with T. R. Young, *The Dictionary of Critical Social Sciences* (1999), and *Introduction to Forensic Psychology* (2000). Dr. Arrigo is the founding and acting Editor of the peer-reviewed quarterly, *Journal of Forensic Psychology Practice*. He was recently named the Critical Criminologist of the Year (1999–2000), sponsored by the Critical Criminology Division of the American Society of Criminology.

INDEX

271